Pirate of the Adriatic

The Untold Story of
Captain Thomas G. Fuller DSC, RCNVR

Sean E. Livingston

Library and Archives Canada Cataloguing in Publication
Livingston, Sean E., author
Pirate of the Adriatic/Sean E. Livingston

Issued in print and electronic formats.

ISBN: 978-1-998501-46-5 (paperback)
ISBN: 978-1-998501-47-2 (ebook)

Cover Design: Axel Peralta
Cover Illustration: Matthew Therrien
Interior Design: Richa Bargotra

Double Dagger Books
Toronto, Ontario, Canada
www.doubledagger.ca

For my son, Liam.

Table of Contents

Forward

In a quarter century of travel to and from battlefields of the Second World War, through nearly fifty years of interviewing thousands of veterans at home and abroad, and virtually every day documenting the stories of those men and women who served Canada in the armed forces in the 20th century, I have never stopped discovering. And among the steepest learning curves in my study of Canadian army, navy and air force engagements proved to be my research and writing about the Battle of the Atlantic. Indeed, I conducted my first interview with RCNVR sailors of the Second World War in 1976, and my most recent just prior to the publication of my book *Battle of the Atlantic: Gauntlet to Victory* in 2022.

Over the course of my wanderings and gatherings on the subject, I had the good fortune to meet and befriend Sean Livingston, a schoolteacher and reserve officer. I devoured his insightful 2014 book *Oakville's Flower: The History of HMCS Oakville* and picked his brains to expand and sharpen my own working knowledge of RCN process, protocol and precise terminology. Repeatedly, despite rigorous demands on his teaching and service schedule, Sean donated hours of his time to help me avoid common mistakes in naval parlance and to broaden my understanding of Canadian wartime naval history.

During one of our lively exchanges of navy lore, he suddenly said, "Have I ever told you about Thomas Fuller … the pirate of the Adriatic?"

It sounded as if Livingston was about to regale me with swashbuckling tales along the lines of British privateer Francis Drake or Spanish pirate Benito de Soto or maybe Confederate blockade runner Raphael Semmes. But no. First of all, Fuller was no fable. Second, he was a distinguished Canadian commander. And most important, Sean was elated to have sought out and captured the essence of his Second World War story in a full-length book. Fuller had fought his way – through military inertia, ingrained agism and bureaucratic red tape – to serve in the Royal Navy's Coastal Forces, commanding motor torpedo boat flotillas in European waters, escaping capture in the Mediterranean, and acquiring, quite rightly, the moniker "Pirate of the Adriatic." That alone made writing his story imperative.

But more than just write the narrative of Fuller's extraordinary rise to prominence wreaking havoc among enemy formations in the Aegean, Mediterranean and Adriatic in 1943, author Livingston felt compelled to scope out the nature of this unconventional MTB commander – a man whom he calls paradoxical for being "a stickler for tradition and rules, notably his own, while other times he freely tossed both over the side"; not to mention stomaching great risk in the heat of battle because he was chronically prone to seasickness in the process; all the while employing a sly sense of humour to combat the tension of more than five years of front-line military leadership. By war's end, Fuller had collected three Distinguished Service Crosses, unique in the services, as well as shrapnel in his right leg and foot, and was invalided home to Canada suffering from what was described then as an "anxiety state."

All of this made Captain Thomas G. Fuller a war hero. But why was he so little known and given such sparce recognition back home in Canada? Indeed, what happened to the man's stellar legacy? And where did he end up? That's the part of the yarn nobody but Sean Livingston has plumbed deeply enough to reveal, and one I'll not attempt to paraphrase here. Read the extraordinary chapters that follow, to discover for yourself. Livingston has recounted Fuller's story the way nobody else before him has – based on original research, assembly of correspondence and interview material gathered first-hand, and most important, written cinematographically to place every reader there aboard Fuller's MTB in the heat of battle, but not exactly sure how the hell he'll pilot you or his crew through each deadly tangle with the enemy.

This is creative nonfiction at its best. Swashbuckling, yes, but as accurate a telling as any contemporary military history. And who better to navigate you through these wartime channels than a navy man such as Sean Livingston?

---- Ted Barris, author of *Battle of the Atlantic: Gauntlet to Victory*

Acknowledgements

Nearly a decade ago, a relative of Captain Thomas G. Fuller DSC**, MiD, set me on a journey that led to the creation of this book. I'm thankful to Rhea Lautens, not only for bringing my attention to the story of a truly unique RCN legend but also connecting me with her cousin, Tony Fuller. I'm also grateful to Simon Fuller for his guidance, revelations, and suggestions. He graciously gave his time to an overly keen and enthusiastic naval officer, and I appreciate his patience and kindness. Little did I know what lay ahead – years of research, travel, connections, and remarkable revelations.

I was fortunate to be assisted by numerous people along the way. My good friend Roger Litwiller, himself a naval author and a trove of naval knowledge, has always been a trusted sounding board and generously agreed to review my manuscript. He also introduced me to Dean Boettger, Assistant RCN Heritage Officer working for Department of National Defence, who not only linked me with Lauren Buttler at the Directorate of History and Heritage, but also helped me access files on site. There I learned of Dean's own connection to Captain Fuller, and he was kind enough to allow me to share that story for the epilogue of this book.

HCapt(N) (Ret'd) Gordon Laco, Senior Communications Advisor, RCN, and naval advisor on a multitude of films and shows, notably the movies *Greyhound* and *Master and Commander*, both adaptations of famous works of naval fiction, has been a tremendous help on various projects, including this one. Despite a demanding schedule, Gord still manages to find time to answer my questions and I appreciate him vetting this work. His technical understanding helped flesh out things referenced by Fuller, as well as clarify parts that lacked proper descriptions. I even quote him in some footnotes – his explanations are fantastic.

It's nearly impossible to mention busy timetables and not think of renown author and historian Ted Barris CM who wrote the forward to this book. He has been a steadfast supporter of mine and anyone with the good fortune to have met Ted will agree that he is a gem of a person. His suggestions, feedback, and mentorship have been critical in my development as an author. After reading an early draft, he challenged me to rework my prose and utilize a creative, non-fiction approach to the narrative, which I believe will help you, the reader, connect with Fuller and his wartime experience. I am also thankful he introduced me to Patrick Crean CM, a titan of Canadian publishing, who also backed my work.

Fuller's service during the Second World War was primarily overseas and on loan to the RN. As such, records in Canadian archives were incomplete – parts have remained in the UK and were held by the Ministry of Defence. Thankfully, a good friend and fellow Knight of the Order of St. Joachim, James "Dicky" Dickaty KCJ, offered his assistance. Dicky served many years in RN submarines and, by a happy coincidence, was keen on Coastal Forces history. His efforts helped me to secure vital information that shed light on some missing elements of this story. I also appreciate the aid of the Coastal Forces Heritage Trust who provided key interviews of individuals who served alongside Fuller during the war.

I'd especially like to thank the Naval Association of Canada for providing access to original transcripts of Mak Lynch's interview as well as the Library Archives of Canada for allowing me to study primary sources, notably Fuller's service file and recordings. These, combined with slews of personal anecdotes people have shared with me over the years, were all key in painting a picture of who Fuller was.

While most authors obligatorily acknowledge their publisher, working with Double Dagger Books has been a breath of fresh air. I have thoroughly enjoyed working with like-minded individuals who are keen to promote our nation's military history. Phil Halton and his staff are filling a void in the Canadian publishing industry and providing readers stories that deserve to be celebrated and remembered. Thank-you for your trust, patience, and belief in this work. On that note, I would be remiss if I didn't also acknowledge my editor James M. Leslie, Publicity Manager for Double Dagger, for all his help in preparing this book for print, as well as answering a plethora of questions from yours truly.

It deserves noting that none of this would be possible without the loving support of my family, who on so many occasions have put-up with me spending hours locked away in front of a screen.

Captain Fuller is one of the most courageous, gritty, and larger-than-life personalities ever to serve in any of the Commonwealth's navies. He was a man who held himself and others to a high standard, and I hope this work not only reaches that bar, but more importantly, honours the memory of a naval hero... the Pirate of the Adriatic.

Sean E. Livingston MStJ, CD

Note Regarding Sources, Dialogue, and Fuller's Post-Nominals

Various primary and secondary sources have been utilized in the creation of this book. In-text citations are provided for all resources, save those taken from Fuller's interviews with the Naval Officers Association of Canada (now the Naval Association of Canada) and various other news agencies (e.g. RCN news audio recordings). Much of the dialogue which appears in the narrative, most of which is Fuller's, has been comprised from these interviews to ensure authenticity and accuracy. To avoid being unduly repetitive and visibly distracting, these parts are only referenced in the bibliography. Aside from the stories related by Dean Boettger in the epilogue, in-text citations are provided for all other sources where appropriate.

At times, bits of dialogue have been tweaked or created to assist with the overall flow of the narrative. Care was taken to ensure these additions remained both realistic and in-character, utilizing the perspective and views of those with first-hand knowledge of the related incidents and people. The events that transpire in the book are historically accurate.

Lastly, the author is aware that use of "DSC**, MiD" is an inappropriate way of displaying post-nominals. However, as that was the way Fuller preferred to write it (it even appears as such on his grave) and this is a book dedicated to honouring his memory, it will be used in the text. If Fuller wanted to let people know that he was the recipient of not one but three distinguished services crosses, as well as being Mentioned in Dispatches, who is the author to object?

Glossary of Abbreviations and Terms

Note: The abbreviations used in this book reflect those that were generally used at the time and, in some cases, differ from contemporary versions.

1st Lt – First Lieutenant. In contrast to the army, this is an appointment in the RN and RCN.

2nd Lt – Second Lieutenant, also an appointment in the RN and RCN.

AB – Able Seaman

AMC – Armed Merchant Cruiser

Asdic – Ship-based sonar, often thought to be named after the Anti-Submarine Detection Investigation Committee. The basis of the acronym is hotly debated in naval circles.

BR – Books of Reference

BGen – Brigadier-General

Cdr – Commander

CO – Commanding Officer

Cox'n – Coxswain

C-in-C – Commander in Chief

Cpl – Corporal

CPO – Chief Petty Officer

Capt – Captain*

Dog Boat – Specific nickname for the Fairmile D

DSC – Distinguished Service Cross

DSM – Distinguished Service Medal

DSO – Distinguished Service Order

ERA – Engine Room Artificer

E-Boat – Short for 'enemy boat', it was the Allied designation for the German Schnellboot (fast boat), or S-Boot. It was a general term that referenced a variety of Nazi coastal vessels and could range from a small patrol craft to a large armed gunboat or torpedo boat.

Flt Lt – Flight Lieutenant

Gash – naval slang generally meaning rubbish, broken, of poor quality, or superfluous.

Gp Capt – Group Captain

GM – George Medal

HMCS – His Majesty's Canadian Ship

HMS – His Majesty's Ship

HQ – Headquarters

Kriegsmarine – Literally meaning 'war navy' it was the name given to Nazi Germany's naval forces from 1935 to 1945. It replaced the interwar 'Realm Navy' (Reichsmarine), which superseded the Imperial German Navy (1871–1918).

* The abbreviation is only used when referring to the rank, and not the appointment/ position of captain.

Kye – A late night treat consisting of warm, sweetened, hot chocolate, typically made by blending bits of shaved chocolate into hot water.

L/Cpl – Lance Corporal

LCol – Lieutenant-Colonel

LCT – Landing Craft, Tank

LGen – Lieutenant-General

Limey – Derogatory term for RN sailors, possibly originating from 'lime-juicer' in the mid 1800s, in reference to the practice of adding lemon/lime juice to the daily rum ration. Vitamin C helps to prevent scurvy.

LS – Leading Seaman

LST – Landing Ship, Tank

Lt – Lieutenant (Navy)

Lt Cdr – Lieutenant-Commander

MA/SB – Motor Anti-Submarine Boat

Maj – Major

MC – Military Cross

MFP – Marinefahrprahm, also known as Naval Ferry Barge.

MGB – Motor Gun Boat

MGen – Major General

MiD – Mention in Dispatches

ML – Motor Launch

MM – Motor Mechanic

MO – Medical Officer

MP – Military Police

MTB – Motor Torpedo Boat

NAAFI – "Navy, Army and Air Force Institutes." Created by the British Government in 1921 when the Expeditionary Force Canteens (EFC) and the Navy and Army Canteen Board (NACB) were combined for the purposes of providing personnel recreational outlets that would sell goods.

NCO – Non-Commissioned Officer

NDHQ – National Defence Headquarters

NOIC – Naval Officier in Charge

NSHQ – Naval Service Headquarters

OBE – Order of the British Empire

OS – Ordinary Seaman

OOW – Officer of the Watch

PMC – President Mess Committee

PO – Petty Officer. Currently, the rank is broken into: Petty Officer 2nd class (PO2) and Petty Officer 1st Class (PO1).

QO – Qualified Officer

RAdm – Rear Admiral

R-Boat – Small German Minesweepers. The "R" stood for "Räumboote" (clearing boats).

RCAF – Royal Canadian Air Force

RCMP – Royal Canadian Mounted Police

RCN – Royal Canadian Navy

RCNR – Royal Canadian Naval Reserve

RCNVR – Royal Canadian Naval Volunteer Reserve

RM – Royal Marines

RN – Royal Navy

RNVR – Royal Navy Volunteer Reserve

RT – Radio Telephony

SBS – Special Boat Section, renamed the Special Boat Service in 1987.

Sg Lt – Surgeon Lieutenant

Sgt – Sergeant

SLt – Sub-Lieutenant

SO – Senior Officer

SOE – Special Operations Executive

SOP – Standard Operating Procedure

Sparks – nickname for a telegraphist

TBS – Talk Between Ships

Torps – nickname for a torpedo officer

USN – United States Navy

USS – United States Ship

WRCNS – Women's Royal Canadian Naval Service

Wren – Member of the Woman's Royal Canadian Naval Service and/or Women's Royal Naval Service, collectively referred to as 'Wrens'.

WRNS – Women's Royal Naval Service

WT – Wireless Telegraphy

XO – Executive Officer

PROLOGUE

—◇◇◉◇◇—

"The Pirate"

Just before midnight on April 4, 1944, two schooners crept into the open sea beyond the shelter of Murter Island. The full moon silhouetted the black shapes a few miles off the Croatian shoreline, the 90-ton *Ennesta* and 50-ton *Dante*. Both vessels were heavily laden with supplies – wheat, firewood, ammunition, and 20mm cannons – destined for Nazi troops battling resistance fighters along the Adriatic coast.

Nestled close to shore and, unseen by the Kriegsmarine sailors, two Allied navy warships stalked the schooners using the coastline as camouflage. One a Royal Navy motor torpedo boat, the other an RN motor gun boat were painted to blend into the surrounding rock, their freeboards lay low, just over a meter above the waterline. Lighter, faster and more agile than the German schooners, the MTB and MGB needed only idling speed to keep pace, so the sounds of their engines never reached the enemy's lookouts. For all intents and purposes, the Allied boats and crews were unheard and invisible. All part of the plan of the seasoned Allied commander in charge of this hunt.

The flotilla's senior officer, a Royal Canadian Naval Volunteer Reserve Lt Cdr, raised a cup to his lips. Usually, he'd be nursing his remedy for seasickness, tea with a splash of scotch, but rum was the only thing available this evening. It would have to do. He was standing in the open bridge, just behind the boat's commanding officer. From here he could easily keep tabs on his vessels, issue orders and, if necessary, take direct control. He reached for his binoculars and peered once again at the distant shapes. Making out details was a challenge in the dark, but he confirmed that the schooners were without escort. Easy pickings.

"Got ya," he said, a smile poking out from behind his thick, dark beard. His eyes were fixed on the prize, eager and determined.

"All ahead full," he ordered.

The signal was dutifully given; engines roared to life, filling the air with high-octane petrol as coastal vessels sprang from their cover. Bows lifted like rearing horses, motors biting into the water and propelling them towards the enemy. White plumes streaked behind each boat as they closed on their targets.

The SO watched as the Partisan soldiers on the bow of his boat steadied themselves and readied their equipment. Each vessel had a compliment of commandos, equipped with sub-machine guns, ladders, and grappling hooks. His tactic was unorthodox – the SO doubted many of his superiors would approve, but he'd made a career of going against established procedures, especially when he found them ineffective. And thus far, it had earned him two DSCs.

Tonight, he was again trying something different.

"Yarr!" he bellowed over the roar of the engines, surprising the Lt at his side. The younger man managed a nervous smile, which only made the SO laugh.

Both boats parted. The SO chose the smaller of the two vessels, his MTB approaching at speed on the schooner's starboard – the side facing land. Details quickly emerged – a wood painted hull lined by portholes, two masts and a multitude of rigging. The sails were yet unfurled, and more importantly, none of the crew appeared to be keeping watch from this vector. Not that it would matter much. At this speed and with the cover of night, by the time any of the enemy heard or spotted the MTB, it would already be too late.

It took a skilled hand and nerves of steel to bear down at full throttle on a slow-moving vessel in the dark. For his tactic to work, the SO would have to cut engines only meters from the schooner. The timing had to be just right: too early and they'd lose the element of surprise. Too late, and they'd crash right into it.

The SO wasn't concerned – he'd mentored each skipper and crew, putting them through drill after drill until each maneuver was perfected. They'd all grown accustomed to his tough, no-nonsense style of command, and had already seen their fair share of action. The tactic was already routine, the steps well-choreographed.

They bore down on the schooner – 100 meters..., 75 meters..., 50 meters...., 25 meters...

"All stop," he ordered.

The bow dropped as the vessel settled into the water mere feet away from the schooner's hull. Then, once the wake struck the stern of their boat, giving them a second jolt of speed, he ordered full reverse and a two second burst of thrust given to the engines. The result slowed them enough so that the MTB's bow struck the schooner with enough force to jostle the larger vessel but not damage either craft. The impact threw the enemy off balance – sailors tumbled to the deck, hit bulkheads, and were thrown into each other's arms. They traded confused glances and wondered the same thing: had they just run aground?

"Board!" the SO barked.

The Partisan's sprang into action, tossing their grappling hooks over the schooner's rails, lashing the two vessels together, and extending ladders to act as bridges. The commandos let loose a battle cry as they climbed onto the enemy vessel, weapons pointed at stunned crewmembers – a mix of Italian and German sailors – who only now understood the gravity of the situation. They'd been taken completely unawares – the schooner had been captured without firing a single shot. It was a similar story for the larger vessel the MGB had overtaken as well. As expected, the SO's plan had been executed to perfection.

Both ships and crew were now under his control. The vessels, along with their cargo, would be put to good use helping the Partisan resistance. He ordered that towing lines be affixed to the schooners so that they could be hauled back to base.

While heading back to his MTB, he heard one of the captured sailors whisper the word 'pirate' to another. He stopped, staring daggers at the man he suspected had made the remark, his steely blue eyes cutting any chatter amongst the prisoners. He didn't say anything – he didn't need to. Boarding his vessel, he purposefully stroked his black, unkempt beard, supposing he did resemble more a pirate than a naval officer. It didn't bother him.

Let the enemy fear the Pirate of the Adriatic.

CHAPTER 1

———◇◇◉◇◇———

Works and Bricks

It was mid-September 1939 and only days ago the country declared war. The military mobilized as fast as it could – in cities and towns across Canada, recruitment offices popped-up like weeds in response to the throngs of citizens rushing to enlist. Line-ups formed on streets, people, anxious about the future, impatiently waiting their turn to join the fight against Nazi Germany. One of these offices opened their doors at the corner of 38 Rideau Street in Ottawa, a stone's throw from the Chateau Laurier. Unlike the latter building, this one wasn't anything spectacular; red brick, corporate, and functional in appearance. Nor did anything really stand out about the second floor RCAF recruitment office within. The set-up was predictable. A trio of flags – Canadian Red Ensign, Union Jack, and RCAF flag – grouped near a varnished wood desk with pencils, paper, bible, and necessary recruitment forms methodically placed on its surface. There was a seat for the recruiter behind it and few more for the applicants in front, the set-up sandwiched between wood-paneled walls covered with a generous smattering of obligatory Air Force propaganda posters, each neatly centred, and all seemingly leading to the portrait of the King hanging on the back wall. The space felt bureaucratic and temporary, as if assembled using a standard war recruitment office box kit.

The man who just walked in, determined to join the war as a pilot, wasn't the average applicant. He was feeling confident and came prepared, presenting an arsenal of qualifications, recommendations, and impressive experiences to the RCAF officer sitting across the table: a pilot's license, flying logbook, membership with the Trenton Air Base, prior military service, and a letter of endorsement from none other than the Chief of Air Staff, Air-Vice Marshal George Mitchell Coril. A founding member of the RCAF and the officer responsible for securing the Air Force's independence from the Canadian Army, Coril wrote in his letter that the man was a capable pilot and "a good fellow". It was a golden ticket, meant to guarantee the man's acceptance; he'd be flying in no time.

"We can't touch you," the officer said. "You're in a reserved occupation."[1]

It was blunt and not what the would-be pilot expected to hear.

The government had deemed certain jobs as essential to the war effort and he just happened to be co-owner of a construction company, a role that restricted him from enlisting. But the man who'd entered the room wasn't the type to shy away from a challenge.

Thomas George Fuller had already spent a portion of his adult life overcoming obstacles. He was confident, experienced, and shrewd in a way that could only be gained by years of work and army reserve service. He'd carved-out his own living, worked tough jobs, and built his own company. Unlike other enlistees, war wasn't an opportunity for him to secure employment and escape the decade-long depression; he didn't have to join to further his career or help support a family. Fuller was in that office because it was the right thing to do, and he wasn't about to let others fight on his behalf. And he'd be damned if he'd let some bureaucratic red tape stop him from joining the war. That simply wasn't Fuller's style.

He was a doer.

And so Fuller gathered his things, went back down the stairs, and walked into the morning with a plan. He'd go to his office at 215 Sussex

Street, the headquarters of *Fuller Construction*, and get his business partner, George Rich, to draft him a letter. If being in a reserved occupation prevented him from flying, then the solution was simple.

In short order, he was on his way back to 38 Rideau Street, new letter in hand. He entered the building, charged up the stairs, and returned to the office, cutting in front of some other applicants. The same recruiter was still at his desk and probably surprised to see Fuller return. A letter landed before him; Fuller's trump card. It read that Rich had bought Fuller's share of the business for a dollar and had "duly fired him". He was free to enlist.

"You're too old," the officer stated, sliding the letter back.

Fuller bristled at the mention of his age. At thirty-one he was older than the average recruit, but far from being physically unfit.

"What do you mean, too old?" he demanded.

"You're above the age we recruit pilots," he replied. "We can't put you on a flight list."

He reached for another paper, a smile forming.

"But I can bring you in as Works and Bricks."

Air Force slang for the department responsible for construction and infrastructure maintenance, typically the building and upkeep of airfields. Fuller wanted nothing to do with it.

"No dice."

Fuller exited the building, passing a line of men awaiting their turn with the recruiter. They looked inexperienced and barely of age. Undoubtedly, they would be accepted as pilots. Fuller sighed, feeling deflated.

"I'm the oldest man that ever lived," he thought.

He watched the busy downtown traffic pass by – streetcars, taxis, and finally a man wearing a uniform, which only added salt to his wounded ego.

Why couldn't he fight? He was in good health and didn't have any restrictive medical conditions. Granted, he was older than the young men lining-up outside the building, but why should that matter if he was already a pilot and in shape? Wasn't there a war going on – didn't the country need pilots?

Seeing as his hopes of flying against the Nazi's were grounded, Fuller headed back to his office. He needed to find a way around this roadblock.

Again, quitting wasn't his style.

The next two days were uneventful. Fuller busied himself with construction projects and trying to brainstorm a way out of his predicament, but he'd yet to stumble upon a solution. The phone on his desk rang and he snatched it up.

"Hello?"

"Mr. Fuller?"

He recognized the voice on the other end – the RCAF recruiting officer.

"Speaking."

"I've got wonderful news for you, wonderful news," the man said. "They'll take you straight in as a Flight-Lieutenant."

His eyebrows rose. A Flt Lt was the equivalent of a Cpt in the army or a Lt in the navy; the most senior of the junior commissioned ranks and a few promotions up from the typical Pilot Officer rank RCAF officers started at. Recruitment did this sort of thing when trying to rapidly build a wartime fighting force – could it be they finally realized they had a star candidate? It seemed a little too good to be true; Fuller wanted to see the fine print.

"Does that mean flying?" he questioned, putting extra emphasis on the last word.

The recruiter hesitated before replying, "No, Works and Bricks."

Fuller sighed heavily. He couldn't stand being misled.

"Don't annoy me like that," he snapped. "I can do Works and Bricks. I'm building airports now and getting goddamn well paid for it, far more so than if I join the service."

He would either serve as a pilot or not at all, a point he made clear before slamming the phone on the receiver.

A few more days passed before the same recruiter, anxious to fill billets, tried his luck yet again, this time sweetening the previous offer with a higher rank – Squadron Leader.

"I'm still not interested," Fuller stated.

That evening, before heading home, he decided to visit a familiar haunt – the Britannia Yacht Club. It was a large monolithic building with a maroon, sloped roof, nestled against the eastern part of Lac Deschene on the Ottawa River. The land was well manicured, replete with colourful gardens, trees, and open space for picnics and games. It's where he kept his boat – a forty-foot auxiliary schooner. Sailing had always been one of his favourite past-times.

Fuller drove down to the building and parked in the members' lot. He needed a drink and distraction from his problems and the club's bar was an excellent place for it. And from the sounds of muffled chatter and music coming from the main entrance, he'd chosen the right night to pay a visit.

The social room was bustling – patrons huddled around tables and a crowd swarming the bar. It was standing room only tonight. He moved through the masses, luckily catching the bartender's eye who promptly produced his usual drink. Fuller was grateful to bypass the line, ignoring the glares of those in que and moving to a free space along the wall by a railing and cabinet of polished silver sailing trophies. There he savoured his first sip, feeling the burn as the alcohol made its way down his throat. He scanned the crowd and immediately noticed a man in a blue uniform – an Air Force Gp Capt.

"So much for forgetting my troubles," he thought, taking another drink.

Then again, perhaps this was an opportunity. With renewed determination, he closed on the officer and introduced himself to J. E. Hunter. They struck up a conversation. Fuller asked about the man's service and learned the Gp Capt had a "purple" career, having spent time in all three elements, first as a naval medical officer before transferring to the army and eventually winding up in the Air Force as a Chief Medical Officer. It didn't take long for Fuller to address the real reason he decided to speak to him: his issue with the RCAF's recruitment.

"What in hell does the Air Force want with all these schoolboys as pilots?" he asked.

Hunter didn't have a good answer but did suggest another approach.

"Have you given thought to joining the navy?"

An interesting proposition – Fuller was a qualified yachtsman and even worked as a Sea Scoutmaster in Ottawa and Toronto.[2] Maybe this was something he should have already considered. He set his drink on the table and leaned in.

"You think they'd take me?" he asked. "I'm not 'too old'?"

"Tell you what I'll do," Hunter replied, "I'll contact the Naval Secretary and Paymaster, Captain Cossette, and set up an appointment for you myself."

Fuller grinned.

"Let me get you another drink."

————

Fuller felt a renewed sense of hope as he walked down Queen Street on a late September morning. Things were finally turning around – he might even be sworn-in before the end of the day. True to his word, Hunter called Cossette who in turn arranged for Fuller to meet with an RCN recruiter. Now, just over a week after meeting the Gp Capt, he was again on track to joining the war. Perhaps the navy would appreciate what Fuller had to offer his country. It may not be flying but the sea ran through his veins and he felt confident that his seamanship skills alone would impress. He could imagine himself in naval uniform.

He walked into the office and noted that it looked pretty much the same as the one on Rideau Street – swap-out the RCAF flag for the White

Ensign, change the posters, and put the King into naval uniform and the layout was identical. However, this time the recruiter was expecting him.

"Mr. Fuller, please have a seat," the man said with a smile. He waited for his visitor to get comfortable before continuing, "I've got an offer for you."

Fuller beamed – this was it, his ticket into the war.

"We can offer you a Warrant Officer's job in Works and Bricks."

Fuller froze. He must have misheard the man.

"Come again?"

"We're prepared to offer you a Warrant's billet in Works and Bricks," the man confirmed.

Fuller glared at the recruiter who seemed unfazed by his client's disappointment. A Warrant Officer wasn't even a commissioned rank.

"A Warrant Officer's job?" he questioned. "I just turned down a Squadron Leader position because it was in Works and Bricks."

The officer blinked, the smile fading from his face.

"I'm sorry Mr. Fuller but that's all I have to offer at the moment."

"Well when you can offer me a commission on a ship, give me a call."

And with that Fuller stood up and left the office.

He felt thoroughly deflated and sauntered back down the street, his dream now further away than ever.

"Christ," he thought, "I'm going downhill!"

———

Months passed without any progress. Fuller kept trying both RCAF and RCN recruiters but the answers were always the same, either outright denying him or steering him clear from combat roles. It didn't add up: the country needed pilots to fly planes and sailors for warships, and yet they rejected him – a pilot and seasoned sailor – at every turn, all the while accepting younger, inexperienced men. The only thing they ever offered was Works and Bricks but Fuller wouldn't budge – he wanted to fight.

Adding to his enlistment woes, the gadflies at the yacht club ribbed him relentlessly about his failed attempts. It became a run-on joke.

"Any luck this time Tom?"

"How's that uniform coming along?"

"You flying yet?"

Fuller played along but resented their mockery.

The final blow came that summer. On August 6, 1940, he received a letter from Capt J.O. Cossette, thanking him for his desire to serve but making it clear the RCN could not offer him "immediate entry". Cossette acknowledged Fuller's multiple attempts to join and clarified that "It will not be necessary to repeat your application as your name will not be over-looked when an opportunity of using your services arises".[3] Fuller understood the subtext: don't call us – we'll call you. His prospects with the navy had run aground. Two out of three elements had denied him and he wasn't particularly interested in re-joining the army. After nearly a year of repeated attempts, he was no closer to his goal.

His fortunes finally turned later that month when he received an unexpected call at his office.

"Good day Mr. Fuller," a booming, unfamiliar voice said. "I'm Lieutenant-Commander Robertson."

"What can I do for you?" Fuller replied, his tone suspicious.

"Your name has been given to me as a person who might be interested in joining the navy," Robertson explained.

Something in Fuller snapped. After months of rejections, weeks of taking flak from the gentlemen at the yacht club, he was convinced this was nothing more than an ill-conceived prank. And he wasn't in the mood.

"Who in the hell are you kidding? Look, I'm a busy man and don't have time for jokes."

"No, no, I'm serious," Robertson reassured him. "Can you come around and see me?"

Something in the man's voice stopped Fuller from hanging-up the phone.

"This had better not be for Works and Bricks," he warned.

Robertson chuckled. "I can assure you, it's not for Works and Bricks Mr. Fuller. Like I said, this is about joining the navy," he said, stressing the last word. "Are you still interested?"

Fuller felt a surge of excitement run through his body but kept his cool.

"When do you want me to come down?"

———

Lt Cdr Owen Robertson of the RCNR, commonly known as 'Big' or 'Long Robbie' because of his height, was exactly the sort of person Fuller needed – a serious, no-nonsense individual who recognized an opportunity when he saw one. Robertson had come to Ottawa around March of that year to assist in filling billets for a growing RCNVR, and most of the ratings and officers joining were quite young and inexperienced. Unlike previous recruiters, Robertson saw promise in Fuller. He knew that a man accustomed to managing men and running large-scale operations, not to mention being a skilled sailor, would make a fine officer. Fuller was exactly the sort of person he wanted.

Big Robbie's office was located at NSHQ at 72 Queen Street, between Metcalfe and Elgin. It was an odd spot, occupying the third and fourth floors of an aging, six-storey building which also served as the headquarters for the department of Agriculture and Public Service.[4] It didn't impress, especially since it was located beside a deli market. But such was the nature of Canada's hasty mobilization program.

Things weren't any better inside. It was tight quarters with little hallway space, close cubicles and shoulder-to-shoulder workspaces. Only the Chief of Naval Staff, Rear-Admiral Nelles, had his own office. At least it wasn't hard for Fuller to spot Robertson – even sitting, his head stood out from the crowd like a ship's mast. His moniker was well earned.

Despite the limited space, Robertson managed to squeeze Fuller into a corner to interview him. In short order, he found his initial gut-feelings were correct – he liked Fuller's candid and direct demeanour and was overall impressed by his strength of character and impressive curriculum vitae. By the end of their conversation, Robertson shook Fuller's hand and promised that he'd receive word about his enrolment soon. And this time Fuller felt he wasn't being misled.

On August 21, another letter from Cossette arrived at Fuller's office. This time, it was good news. It instructed him to head to the Ottawa RCNVR Division and report to the CO to be medically examined. If found fit for duty, Cossette explained that Fuller would be "attested as Acting Lieutenant RCNVR (temporary) and drafted to arrive to Halifax, September 10."

This was the moment Fuller had waited nearly a year for – it was finally happening.

The letter went on to explain transportation details and noted that Fuller would be paid at the Canadian rate once he disembarked. He'd receive more details regarding his passage to England once he reported to the CO in Halifax. The only remaining matter was his uniform – as an officer, he'd have to arrange to get one made. An allowance of $150 would be paid to him by the accounting officer at the RCN barracks in Halifax to cover the tailoring fees.[5]

But before he could do that, he needed to pass his physical.

The next day, Fuller went again to Queen Street, this time heading into the local RCNVR division's HQ, which was in eyesight of the NSHQ building on the opposite side of the street. After a quick meeting with the CO, he was sent to the MO to be examined. For nearly a year, Fuller couldn't even get to this stage of the enrolment process.

Geoffrey W. B. York, the attending physician, welcomed Fuller into his office. Once the door was closed, he had him strip down to his underwear and began his survey: **weight**: 167 pounds; **height**: 5ft 8 ¾; **eyes**: blue; **vision**: 6/6; **hair**: dark; **complexion**: medium; **build**: slim. It was clear to Fuller that this wasn't the MO's first examination – he was quick and methodical, pausing only to jot down information on a notepad. York went on to note visible marks on Fuller's body, listing a hernia scar on his left, a scar on the back of the head, and another scar on the bridge of his nose. He then proceeded to check Fuller's hearing, use of lower extremities, flexibility, and medical history. About twenty minutes later, York concluded that the applicant was in good health and "fit to serve."[6]

Fuller left feeling upbeat and wasted little time informing his business partner and family about the news: he was finally entering the navy. He also made certain to visit the yacht club that evening – this was cause for a celebratory drink and he particularly wanted to share the information with the busybodies who'd been teasing him the last few months. Soon to be Lt Fuller RCNVR would have the last laugh.

On August 24, Fuller was finally sworn in. He signed his attestation form and "Offer of Service For Hostilities (Naval)".[7] He immediately set about getting his affairs in order in preparation for his departure to Halifax. A little over a week later he returned to Ottawa Division on September 2 and signed his engagement form with the RCNVR.[8] After so much time, Fuller was finally in the war as an Acting Lt.[9] He had a uniform made by Gedeon Gauthier, the same tailor used by many military greats, such as Air Marshal "Billy" Bishop*, and then proceeded

---

* Gauthier worked at George E. Preston and Sons Ltd in Ottawa, famed for creating suits for likes of Prime Ministers Laurier, Borden, Meighen, Bennet, and King. Unfortunately, he didn't have a spare set of the appropriate rank insignia for Fuller's uniform. RCNVR stripes were different from those worn by RCN officers – rather than being straight, the gold braid had a distinct, zigzag, pattern (hence the RCNVR's nickname, "wavy navy"). The one on hand was reserved for John Villiers Farrow, the award-winning screenwriter, film director, and producer who had been recruited to head the RCN's information section. Gauthier received permission from Farrow's wife, actress Maureen O'Sullivan, to use it for Fuller's uniform on the condition that she personally sew it to the sleeves.

to gather his kit and take a train to Halifax. There he'd board a troop ship and begin the long journey across the North Atlantic to Liverpool, England.

Unforeseen circumstances had delayed Fuller's entrance into the war, but they no longer mattered. His mind was focused on what lay ahead, the beginning of a new chapter and the opportunity to do what he could to help counter the fascist war machine. And while nothing about Fuller particularly made him stand out in the eyes of those around him – he was but another naval officer heading overseas – fate had something special planned for him. When all was said and done, Fuller would not only be one of the most highly decorated and battle-hardened men in the RCN, but return from the war a naval legend.

CHAPTER 2

King Alfred

Thomas 'Tom' George Fuller IV was born in Ottawa, Ontario on December 13, 1908. His parents, Thomas William Fuller III and Ethel Jane Fuller, had two children; his sister, Caroline Belford Fuller, was older than him by two years. They lived a comfortable life in the nation's capital, a family reputed for their architectural achievements. His grandfather, Thomas Fuller II, built part of the country's Parliament buildings, specifically the Langevin Block, and his father served as Dominion Architect in 1927, helping to design the Confederation Building in Ottawa as well as constructing a slew of notable structures across the country.[10] Building and designing were in the family's blood, and young Tom took an early interest.

By his own admission, Fuller was a "terrible student". It wasn't that he found the curriculum difficult to grasp – he was intelligent and possessed a wickedly sharp wit – but his natural, hands-on talents were at odds with the one-way, lecture-based academic structure of education in the 1920s. Frankly, he found it dull and couldn't motivate himself to study and complete assignments. In fact, he never even completed high school. He was in third form (the equivalent to Grade 11) at Lisgar Collegiate Institute in Ottawa when he was called out of class to meet the Principal, Dr. A.H. McDougall, in his office.

"Do you know why I've asked you in here?"

Fuller had just taken a seat across the man's desk and shook his head. He hadn't a clue.

"It's because there's nothing more we can do for you."[11]

Fuller straightened in his chair, "I'm being kicked out?"

"I think school isn't for you," McDougall answered, his expression softening, "and, if you're honest with yourself, I think you know that as well."

Few occasions left Fuller at a loss for words, but this was one of them. Deep down, he knew the man was right. He didn't care about grades or attending university – what good would staying do him? So, rather than object, he simply shook the man's hand, gathered his things, and walked out into the real world.

It was time to work, and Fuller was ready to begin his career. What he lacked in the classroom he made-up with street smarts, grit, and raw business knowhow. He also wasn't without experience, having already joined the 3rd Divisional Signals, Royal Canadian Corps of Signals. From 1923-1927 Fuller learned the ins-and-outs of being a militia soldier: uniform upkeep, drill, range, and the use of his rifle and bayonet. His equipment was from the First World War, as were the tactics and experiences from his senior instructors. He spent some weekends drilling and days in the summer training at camps, understanding field-craft, sleeping in bell tents, defending trenches, as well as laying communication wire and operating signals equipment. The meals were passable, but the pay was underwhelming. After becoming a L/Cpl, Fuller decided it was time to move-on from the army and pursue a career in construction.[12] His father gave him some advice.

"Whatever you do, don't be an architect," he cautioned. "Remember that the contractor is the only one who makes the money."[13]

Fuller became a sandhog, the nickname given to underground labourers digging sewers around the city core. He learned to work in dark, pressurized tunnels, where staying safe required constant vigilance.

The careless use of machinery could result in horrific injuries or even lead to dreaded cave-ins, and few survived being buried under tons of earth.[14] If one wasn't crushed to death, they'd most likely succumb to asphyxiation before rescuers could reach them.

After two-years of tunneling, Fuller figured he'd best find a safer job and became a forest engineer for the Canadian International Paper Company in Ottawa. The new position put him in charge of managing the company's survey operations, requiring him to direct workers on various sites. He was good at it but the $60 a month didn't quite meet his expectations.[15] A year later he accepted a position as a supervising engineer for Campbell and Shepherd Ltd.[16] Now he managed up to five-hundred construction workers and routinely travelled between major Canadian cities to oversee various large-scale projects. Some of the buildings he worked on included the Confederation Building and the Canadian Heating Plant in Ottawa*. It was an immense amount of responsibility for a young man, especially as these contracts involved millions of dollars, but Fuller shouldered it confidently. He was finally being noticed and by the time he celebrated his twenty-first birthday, represented two construction engineering firms and managed a contract totaling $3.5 million.[17]

Solving problems and creating innovative solutions were a hallmark of Fuller's management style. An example would be the time he investigated and resolved an issue related to a delay in a critical shipment of granite from Stanhope, Quebec. He received a message from the buyer who was panicking because their supply of granite had inexplicably stopped.[18] Fuller hadn't been notified of any shortages or problems in transport, so he picked-up his phone and called the site's office.

"Hey, what's going on with the granite?" he asked. "I've just been told that one of my clients isn't getting his stuff."

---

* Fuller noted the budget for this project was $3,497,000 in an Officer Qualification Questionnaire (CNS Form 2324) that he completed in 1951.

"The supplier skipped and the quarrymen haven't been paid," the man replied. "They've all stopped working."

"We need to get these guys back on the job," Fuller insisted.

"I get that Tom, but they won't budge until they're paid what they're already owed."

"So, why not just pay them?" Fuller countered.

"Because we don't have any pay statements or records," came the reply. "If there were any, they're all gone."

Now things were making sense to Fuller. Still, they couldn't afford to remain unproductive. Time was money and a business depended on their reputation to thrive in this industry. So, Fuller proposed a solution.

"Go and ask the workers what they're owed and send me the information."

The man hesitated. "But we have no way of knowing if what they say is true. What if they exaggerated their wages?"

"Of course, they'll exaggerate it," Fuller acknowledged, "but we've got to do something."

The man hung up and immediately began surveying the workers for the necessary information. It didn't take long for Fuller to get the report. While he already expected that the claim would be inflated – anyone would be tempted to boost their earnings – he still hoped it would be within reason. Unfortunately, the workers decided to seize the opportunity and strongarm their employer, submitting a number that, to Fuller's eyes, felt like ransom. He couldn't believe it. Either the quarrymen were delusional or just plain stupid. Either way, if they believed he'd approve such an outlandish claim, they had another thing coming. Tom Fuller was the wrong guy to cheat – the only thing he would be paying would be a visit to Stanhope.

The trip to the quarry was direct and took little time thanks to Fuller's personal aircraft. He'd equipped the plane with skis, which allowed him to take-off and land virtually anywhere, so long as the terrain was decently level, spacious, and snow-covered. Fuller used the solitude of flight to strategize. How was he going to persuade the workers to be forthcoming about their wages? If he accused them outright of lying, they'd simply dig their heels in, and he seriously doubted any attempt to appeal to their moral sensibility would yield anything better.

"Wait a minute," he thought. An idea began to form in his mind. "I might not be able to get them to tell the truth, but there is someone who could."

And that's why Fuller stopped by the local Catholic church before proceeding to the site. When he did arrive at the quarry's office, he wasn't alone.

"I want the men to come in one at a time," Fuller instructed.

Dutifully, the workers formed a line outside of the office and, one by one, entered to see not only Fuller sitting at the desk, but their local parish priest standing behind him. From there it was simple: each man was instructed to swear on the Bible, before their priest no less, that what they were owed was accurate. By the time the last worker had made his declaration, the payroll had been cut in half.[19] The men were paid and back to work the following day.

That's how Fuller operated – outside the box.

He'd discovered his passion and read everything he could get his hands on relating to construction and engineering. Fuller subscribed to multiple magazines and amassed quite a library of related books and manuals.[20] And as his knowledge base grew, so too did his reputation in the industry. Eventually, he set out on his own, convincing a wealthy man to give him a $1 million credit line to start Fuller Construction*. By the time Fuller decided to join the war, he was already a successful, self-made business owner. He owned his own home, had a boat and plane, and even a membership at the Britannia Yacht club. Compared to the average Canadian living through the Depression, Fuller managed

---

* Despite his comfortable upbringing, his father couldn't financially support his son's venture. "My grandfather lived to the limit," Fuller would explain. "He had to wait for payday every month to pay the bills."

to successfully overcome the crippling economic situation and make a name for himself.

Fuller didn't need to go overseas. He could have easily stayed home and profited from the war – the government was offering various construction contracts as part of its mobilization program. But above anything else, Fuller valued honour. He'd sooner risk his life than have anyone label him coward. Besides, sitting back felt foolishly near-sighted. Hitler's ambitions were plain, and anyone who hadn't buried their head in the sand could deduce what the world would look like if the Axis were victorious. How could he just sit back and let it happen?

He'd made his decision while sailing the Ottawa river. It had been one of those idyllic days. The sun hung high in a nearly cloudless sky, a slight breeze providing some respite from the hot, weather – surprisingly high, even for the first day of September. The forty-foot boat made only a few knots, but that bothered no one aboard. It was a pleasure sail after all, and that meant relaxed clothing, radio, sunglasses, and drinks. Fuller manned the wheel, his eyes attentive to the sails and river beyond. Wake from the schooner's low-profile hull rolled gently ashore and soft orchestral music played, blending with the light banter and surrounding calm sounds of river life. He uttered a command and observed one of the passengers pull at a sheet, eliminating the slight ripple he'd caught on the main sail. Taking a sip of his drink, Fuller took it all in with a smile.

"Now this is the life," he thought.

That's when a special news bulleting interrupted the radio show. The chatter dwindled and someone raised the volume. A voice announced that Germany had invaded Poland and while the information didn't come as a great surprise, especially after the Nazis' repeated violations of the Treaty of Versailles, it still soured the mood. Even with the writing on the wall people still hoped that war could somehow be avoided. Now the final straw had broken.

As the broadcast continued, a portion of an address by Hitler was inserted into the program. It needed no introduction – everyone recognized the voice. Two of Fuller's guests happened to be visiting from Germany and began translating the Fuhrer's words. After the speech was done, the women continued speaking in private, their mannerisms jarringly juxtaposed to everyone around them. They appeared excited and even started laughing.[21]

"You both need to shut up," someone said.

The women snapped-out of it, finally noticing the glares around them. Fuller figured it was time to head back to port before someone threw them overboard. His guests disembarked and the two German women were well on their way back to the Fatherland by the time Canada declared war on Nazi Germany on September 10, 1939.

That was over a year ago. Now, Fuller found himself crossing a very different body of water aboard *SS Duchess of Richmond*, a 601-foot passenger liner serving as a troopship. Rather than the gentle waters of the Ottawa River, Fuller beheld the grey rolling mass that was the barrier between home and his destination – the North Atlantic. These were frigid and dangerous waters, and everyone aboard was aware of the threat of U-boats. Nowhere was that more true than the very centre of the North Atlantic, an area where aircraft couldn't provide cover for Allied shipping. Although formally referred to as the 'air gap', sailors gave it a different name: the Black Pit. Here, more than anywhere else, the wolf pack waited to pounce on convoys.

Naturally, Fuller was aware of the risks, but he was also feeling optimistic. He'd wanted this after all and while he didn't quite know what to expect at least he already had some training and military experience. The stakes were certainly clear. This war was a different beast. On the surface it might appear to have similarities with the Great War – unchecked military growth and mobilization, nationalist rhetoric, and age-old disagreements between competing European nations – but at its core was something different and sinister.

Fascism.

Duchess of Richmond's passage to Britain was thankfully uneventful and Fuller arrived at Liverpool by late September. From there he travelled south to HMS *King Alfred**, a shore establishment in Hove, near Brighton, Sussex, where he was added on loan to the RN. It was what sailors commonly called a stone-frigate, a bricks and mortar naval building given the designation of a ship. Fuller's initial take was that it had been repurposed – it didn't look like something built for the RN. In fact, the building was originally designed as a leisure centre but, due to its proximity to the RNVR divisional base and facilities, the Admiralty quickly appropriated it for the navy's use. The structure was a large, evenly proportioned red brick rectangle peppered with standard windows, broken-up at regular intervals by large, chequered glass panels that hinted at the gymnasiums and exercise facilities within. The whole building was sandwiched between two generous fields and a parade square. It had underground parking, and a RNVR gun battery was located behind it.

Fuller had been taken by taxi to the front entrance, which was nestled closely against the Kingsway, the southernmost artery running along the waterfront of Hove and Brighton. Three sets of double doors were before him, along with two ratings standing guard, wearing gaiters, and holding Lee Enfield rifles. Here the bricks were painted white and above the doors, in dark, clear letters, the name of the ship was inscribed. This was the birthing ground of all RNVR officers. Fuller walked forward, returned the salute given by the guards, and entered the building. In short order he found himself in the Commandant's office.[22]

Capt John Pelly retired from the RN in 1934 but, like many seasoned officers, was recalled to duty in 1939. He was a veteran of the First World War and went on to command his own ship before serving as staff to the C-in-C. Now back in uniform, he'd been charged with overseeing

---

* The stone-frigate was in fact the second ship to take on the name: the first was a Drake-Class armoured cruiser launched in 1900 and served during the First World War (she was torpedoed by a German U-boat but managed to survive the attack)

the training of new officers, such as the thirty-one-year-old Lt standing at attention across his desk.

"At ease," he commanded, his voice clear but soft. Pelly was an old-schooled naval officer and exhibited the self-assured countenance of a gentleman. Since retiring his hair had turned white and he'd added several inches to his waistline. "I trust your travel across the pond was uneventful?"

"Yes sir," Fuller replied, relaxing his stance.

"I make it a point to greet all candidates," Pelly explained.[23] He folded his hands across his stomach and leaned back in his chair. Fuller noted the four, straight gold bars and executive curl that adorned the sleeves of his tunic*. "Centuries of service experience have shown that certain qualities are necessary if a naval officer is to carry out his normal duties: alertness, enthusiasm, broadmindedness, a sense of responsibility, conscience and good humour, as well as a basic knowledge of technical subjects."[24]

He leaned forward, resting his forearms on the table.

"My aim is to instil that in every man that comes here."

Fuller nodded – he'd expected as much.

"Tell me a bit about yourself Lieutenant," Pelly encouraged, gesturing to a chair across his desk. "Always a pleasure to welcome aboard a Canadian."

Fuller took a seat and the two spoke for a while. He quickly grew to appreciate Pelly's sincerity. The Capt came across as genuinely interested and approachable. Fuller respected an officer who could navigate maintaining the presence of command while avoiding coming across as toxic and dictatorial. At the conclusion of the conversation, Pelly stood, rounded the desk, and extended Fuller his hand.

"Happy to have you with us, Lieutenant," he said with a hardy shake. "Good luck."

---

* The rank of a Captain in the RN. Unlike Fuller's 'wavy' patterned gold bars, regular force officers wore thicker, straight bars to donate their status and differentiate them from reservists.

Fuller exited the office and headed back to the orderly room for messing. His training started promptly the next day with a weeklong New Entry Training Course that would take him to the end of the month. It wasn't anything exciting – drill classes, uniform upkeep, and lectures on basic military knowledge. Most of it he already knew from his time with the militia, so he figured it would be an easy week.

––––––––

Fuller stood on *King Alfred*'s parade square, taking instruction from a senior NCO. His class was doing drill movements – right turns on the march.

"Let's try that again, sirs," the instructor barked, careful to add the appropriate courtesy – some, like Fuller, were already commissioned officers. "Smartly this time, if you please."

He readied himself to resume marching when he noticed a messenger appear at the edge of the square, hurrying across the deck towards the instructor. Clearly, he had something to relay, so the NCO commanded "Stand easy – take a few minutes," before turning his attention to the newcomer. Happy for the break, Fuller stretched his back and felt a slight breeze come from the nearby water. *King Alfred* was situated on the shores of the English Channel, less than 240 kilometres away from land now occupied by the Nazis. Yet, on a calm afternoon such as this, it felt hard to believe they were so close to the enemy.

That's when something in the distant sky caught his attention – a grouping of tiny black dots. Fuller had trained as a pilot and knew they were aircraft, but before he could say anything the sound of sirens filled the air. The dots grew larger and soon a squadron of German bombers was visible to the naked eye. It was a raid.

The aircraft dove from the clouds and appeared to be heading their way. Shouts emerged over the klaxons: "take cover!" Fuller was already half-way across the deck, bolting towards a dugout along the concrete perimeter of the square. He leaped over a parapet and landed feet first on the soft earth, bringing his hands over his ears in anticipation of the coming explosions. He stole a glance over the sandbags by his head, searching the sky for the aircraft. The whistles of bombs screamed from somewhere above, and then several plumes of dirt and debris erupted in the distance, followed by the delayed sounds of the explosions. The ground shook ever so slightly and even at this distance, he could feel some of the kinetic energy of the blast. Anti-aircraft fire shot into the sky from various locations around them, but Fuller didn't notice if the gunners scored any hits. From what he could gather, the bombs had missed their mark. The aircraft didn't wait around to make another pass, banking and gaining altitude as they made for the clouds. RAF fighters were already inbound to intercept but as quickly as it all happened, any trace of aircraft had vanished from sight.

Fuller emerged from the bunker and patted the dirt off his trousers. To his surprise, their NCO was already back on deck, gesturing for the candidates to reform in division. In fact, everyone seemed to have a nonchalant response to the attack and were resuming as if nothing had transpired.

"There's that English stiff upper lip," Fuller thought.

He later learned the bombs hadn't done much damage, most landing in fields and outright missing *King Alfred*, although he couldn't be certain if the school was even a target. It wouldn't be the only time the enemy attacked during his induction week. In fact, raids routinely interrupted instruction, sometimes more than once a day, and often during one of Fuller's outdoor drill sessions. As reported by *Townsville Daily Bulletin*, the school was at times "exposed to the hourly menace of air attacks"[25] and it became clear that *King Alfred* was indeed the focus of some of these strikes. By the end of the week, Fuller and his course mates learned to eye the aircraft first, wait for the bay doors on the underside of the aircraft's fuselage to open, and then judge where to run based on the angle of the bombs' descent.

Welcome to the war Tom.

Before Fuller's journey across the Atlantic, Operation Sea Lion had already transitioned into what Churchill had coined the Battle of Britain. Now he and his course mates were witness to some of that aerial conflict, although, thankfully, the enemy wasn't as interested in Hove in comparison to larger targets, such as Portsmouth and Liverpool. Still, Pelly ordered the entire school re-located to *King Alfred's* underground carpark. It was sizable, originally designed to house 480 cars, and quickly retrofitted to train candidates. Hastily constructed dividers on wheels, some equipped with chalk and corkboard, were rolled in as temporary walls, surrounding groups of chairs and desks to form makeshift classrooms. Training equipment also found new homes in the cool and damp space, even cumbersome and heavy gear, such as those used for gunnery practice. Part of the underground became a mess, complete with sleeping accommodations made up of "dormitories with rows of double-decker bunks."[26]

Fuller completed his new-entry induction by October and moved onto the next phase of his training, a two-week course in gunnery, navigation, seamanship, and minelaying. Now, this was more to Fuller's liking, or at least it would have been had it not been mostly theory and conducted underground. He'd rather be on the water, learning through application and practice, but tried to make the best of it. At least many of his instructors, based on ribbons adorning the upper left of their tunics, were experienced veterans. A well-placed question could lead to an off script dit*, which everyone enjoyed.

However, Fuller drew the line at the underground quarters. The cheap bedding, along with the damp concrete floor, made it hard for him to sleep. His back was rigid every morning and was sore most of the day. Denis O'Hagen, a fellow officer on his course, suffered similar problems and, together, they secured permission from Pelly to arrange for alternate accommodations – at their own expense – in town. Pooling their wages,

---

* Refers to any story about a sailor's experience while in the service. They could be shared verbally or in writing.

they set off the next evening and came upon a vacant apartment on Preston Street, a narrow strip that linked to the Kingsway. It was a typical urban looking street for the area – a long line of connected buildings stretching the length of the block on either side of the road. Those on the west side of Preston formed a wall of four to three-storey condos, the vents of their red-bricked chimneys jutting upwards like small-tubed fingers from outstretched block hands. The first floors mostly consisted of various shops, restaurants, and services, while the upper levels were reserved as living accommodations. Across the street was a similar set-up, although featuring single and two-storey structures. The location was perfect – less than a ten-minute drive from the base.

The apartment they found was a fourth-floor flat belonging to a "big-game hunter in Kenya". The landlord owned the entire building and furnished each room with various taxidermized animals he'd hunted over the years, as well as various trinkets and souvenirs from his many travels. Their rental came fully furnished and boasted a common room, kitchen, and separate bedrooms for Fuller and O'Hagen. The windows offered a generous view of the water to the south, although blackout curtains had to be drawn for nighttime. Of all the items, a large hurdy-gurdy particularly drew their attention. It lay propped against the wall by the main entrance and every time one of them left, they'd give the instrument a crank. It's distinctive droning "ta-da-dum" sound could be heard even in the elevator down the hall.

Fuller fondly remembered having "a damn good time in that place". They'd invite some of the other officers over for drinks after a day's worth of lessons and hosted evening socials during their downtime. Parties were a good way to deal with their present situation and the stress of regular performance checks. But in his spare time, Fuller preferred heading down to the Kit Kat Club at 9 North Street, which was only a few blocks away from his rental. The outside of the building betrayed little of the joyful celebrations that occurred within; it was the sight of great dancing and live music. A woman by the name of Josey – a Floradora girl[27] in her youth – operated the establishment and Fuller found the place suited him. He became a regular and visited whenever he was in the area. When the Canadian Army came to Brighton, downtime was usually had at the club and it became the go-to spot for service personnel to loosen-up and have a good time. For Fuller, it was one of the great highlights of being overseas.

"If only those back home knew what they were missing," he thought.

CHAPTER 3

—◇◇◉◇◇—

Gramps

On November 5, 1940, Fuller completed his initial naval officer training and was promoted to a fully substantive Lt in the RCNVR, with seniority dating back to September 4, 1940. He left *King Alfred* and boarded HMS *Chitral*, a single-stacked AMC running almost 550 feet from stem to stern. The repurposed transport ship now sported a faded grey coat of paint and guns had been mounted to her deck for escorting convoys in the frigid waters of the Northern Patrol. Fuller's training would now continue at sea, after which he'd be fully qualified for his first, true posting.

The AMC didn't impress. *Chitral* clearly wasn't designed as a warship and struck Fuller as a cheap, band-aid solution to not having enough proper escorts. How effective would the ship truly be in a fight? Moreso, *Chitral* launched nearly two decades ago and was showing her age. It just wasn't the sort of ship any officer or sailor wanted to serve in, but he didn't have a choice. So, accompanied by a steward carrying his gear, Fuller proceeded up her gangplank and was quickly shown to his quarters. If there was one perk of being a former ocean liner, it was spacious cabins and privacy. There were plenty of berths aboard and no need to share with another officer. By the time he finished unpacking and reported to the bridge, *Chitral** was well on her way out to sea. There was a lot of work to be done and naval ships could afford little time being idle.

Some trainees were already being put through their paces, moving about their tasks with a seasoned officer in tow. They stood out despite wearing the same uniform, awkward and lacking the self-assured swiftness of their trainers. A few looked stressed – they probably preferred being in a classroom – but this type of learning suited Fuller just fine.

The navigation officer spotted him and waved him forward.

"Here we go," Fuller thought.

He moved up to the chart table and began what would be weeks of learning at various stations, all designed to build him into a functioning bridge officer. Fuller's seamanship background allowed him to adapt quickly and soon he was performing duties without supervision. It wasn't much cause for celebration – he was growing bored with the slow pace and repetitiveness of these patrols. It was almost like the war was happening somewhere else.

By February, Fuller began working on the final part of his training: practical navigation. He learned to operate using various tools, including regular and bubble sextants**, how to calculate and plot a course, issue helm commands, and direct the ship to and from an anchorage, which was by far the most challenging part. It was an immense amount of responsibility – the safe passage of the ship rested squarely on their shoulders. The role also required direct communication with the CO, who at times could be a stern task master. Course alterations and changes meant having to recalculate plots on the fly, and captains demanded

---

* Fuller stated that he spent about four and a half months in the Arctic in two AMCs: *Letitia* and *Chitral*. The latter ship was the primary vessel Fuller was assigned to for his training, as per his service file

** Night made traditional navigation a challenge. A regular sextant required the horizon to be used as a reference point, but it was often impossible to see at night. Bubble sextants resolved the problem by providing the user with an artificial horizon.

quick and accurate answers. The stress and burnout were high – this part of their training was make or break.

After months at sea, Fuller successfully completed the final phase of his training and travelled back to *King Alfred*. He was giving serious thought regarding his future as a naval officer. He never wanted to set foot in another AMC and even the prospect of serving in a proper surface warship, such as a destroyer, no longer compelled him. Most postings involved convoy escort, which didn't interest him. There was a reason he initially tried to become a fighter pilot – he needed something a little more stimulating. That's why, when he received his orders after graduating, he threw a fit.

It was an AMC.

Fuller was done playing. He made a b-line to Pelly's office, bypassing his secretary.

"Sir, I need to speak with you about my posting."

The Cpt didn't appreciate Fuller barging in but could see that the man was upset. He decided to hear him out.

"What's the matter Lieutenant?" he asked.

"I didn't come all across the Atlantic to serve on an AMC," Fuller replied. "I'm hoping you'll consider giving me another posting.

The Capt reached for his tea, blew on it, and asked "such as?"

"I've given it some thought, and I want to go into submarines."

Pelly paused, the brim of his cup inches from his lips.

"I'm sorry, but did you say submarines?"

"Yes," Fuller confirmed.

He lowered the drink and rested the cup back onto the matching saucer. "You can't be serious."

"Why not?"

"God, we're retiring COs at thirty-two because they're too old!" Pelly explained, shaking his head. Fuller felt his temperature rise – there was his age again. The fact that he was also thirty-two added salt to the wound.

"I'm sorry, but it's not possible," he said, again picking up the cup and taking a sip. "I appreciate your spirit Lieutenant, but there's only so much I can do.

Fuller frowned and dug-in his heels. He wasn't going to back down.

"Well, what about MTBs or something?

"Coastal forces?" The look on Pelly's face was incredulous. "No."

"Because of my age?" Fuller questioned.

"Yes, your age!" Pelly snapped. "Look, you're too old – you can't do anything like that."

The Canadian leaned forward, clenching his fists and resting his knuckles on top of the Capt's oak desk. Pelly instinctually pulled back.

"What is it you want?" he challenged, "physical strength or guts?"

Pelly looked surprised and raised an eyebrow. "What do you mean?"

"Let me put it to you this way," Fuller began, his business instincts kicking in. "On this building there's parapet wall around the top, correct?"

The Capt nodded.

"And you've got, what, a thousand officers here, most of them limeys?"

"Around that number," he replied, beginning to sound impatient. "What are you driving at man?"

"Let's ask for volunteers and head-on up to the roof. We'll have everyone tie one leg up behind their back and hop around the parapet wall to see who quits. If they want to have a free-for-all, I'll take them on one at a time."

His blue eyes were frosty and determined. "I won't lose because I have what most of these boys don't – guts."

Pelly met Fuller's stare and rubbed his chin thoughtfully. The man was bold, determined, and a little too insubordinate for his taste, but those qualities were an asset in the world of Coastal Forces. Unlike escorts, who took a more defensive approach, chasing away U-boats much like sheepdogs protecting a herd, coastal defence craft actively hunted the enemy. They were the predators, tasked with disrupting shipping, sinking enemy merchant vessels, laying mines, conducting raids, and executing guerrilla style attacks on warships. Grit and tenacity were the hallmarks of some of their best captains and Pelly figured Fuller might be a good fit. At the very least, if things didn't work out the Canadian would be their problem, not his.

"Oh, hell," he finally said, giving in. "I'll make some calls and arrange it."

Fuller stood back up and allowed himself a smile. "Thank you sir."

Pelly nodded and dismissed him.

———

True to his word, Pelly made the arrangements. Fuller's new orders arrived shortly afterwards – he was to head north to start training at yet another shore establishment: HMS *St. Christopher*, the RN's Coastal Forces training base.

The drive was long and took Fuller deep into the Scottish Highlands. It might have been a picturesque commute, especially as his driver took him along the length of Loch Linnhe*, if not for the gloomy weather. The skies were overcast, and sporadic showers detracted from the raw beauty surrounding him. Pressure was starting to form in his sinuses, the early onset of a headache. He refrained from asking "are we there yet?"

They entered Fort William, a well-established and populated town, as far as highland urban centres went – it would be considered tiny in relation to Brighton and Hove. Then, the car began moving west as the motorway wrapped around the northern end of Upper Loch Linnhe. Snow-capped mountains dominated the skyline, especially to the east

---

* Loch Linnhe is about 15kms long and 150 meters deep, although the depth ranges greatly depending on the location. It is one of the largest lochs along the country's west coast and the upper portion of the Loch is shallow-silled.

where Ben Nevis*, the tallest mountain in the British Isles, loomed over the town.

"Just about there," the driver indicated.

The car exited onto a smaller road that led to the village of Corpach, about 4.5 miles from the main town. Here, along the northernmost banks of Upper Loch Linnhe, connected by canal to the outward-bound Loch Eli, *St. Christopher* was situated. Fuller looked around, noting various brick buildings, sheds, slips, and rounded nissen huts. The driver brought him up to the front of the administration building and Fuller exited the vehicle to stretch his legs.

As he feared, there was a chill in the air, accompanied by what he'd later describe as a persistent "scotch-mist" which quickly began to bead on the outside of his dark, great coat. It was March 8, 1941, and spring was still a few weeks away, although he suspected that would come even later in this part of the world. He didn't even try to hide his displeasure as he glanced around, pulling down on the visor of his headdress.

"What a God-forsaken country," he thought. "Now I know why we have so many Scotsmen living in Canada."**

Several anti-aircraft guns and searchlights scattered the area, and he noted what appeared to be MGBs docked along the shore. The sight lifted his spirits, and he took a moment to appreciate their long and sleek designs. The vessels weren't heavily fortified, the mahogany painted hulls lacked any plating, but they weren't built to take hits – they were made to be doing the hitting. Fast and low-profiled, speed and maneuverability was their primary defence, while an impressive array of guns made them fierce combatants (MTBs were also equipped with torpedo tubes on the port and starboard sides). Although tempted to take a closer look, it would have to wait. His first responsibility was to report to the CO and commence the in-routine process. Paying the driver, he grabbed his bag and entered the building.

---

* 1,345 meters above sea level.

** Despite the visible splendor of the highlands, the climate tainted Fuller's perception.

Cdr Arthur Eric Pole Welman wasn't anything like Pelly. Although only five years apart in age, Welman looked substantially younger. He was slim, in excellent physical shape, and lacked Pelly's easy-going nature; a demanding, by the book, sort of officer. There was no room for insubordinate behaviour under his command and Fuller noted, among his many decorations, two DSOs, two DSCs, and the French Legion of Honour.[28] Welman was a distinguished Coastal Forces veteran, having taken part in some of the heaviest fighting during the previous war. He was a man that had nothing to prove.

Unfortunately, the two would mix as well as water and oil.

Fuller entered the CO's office, came to attention, and saluted.

"Ah yes, Lieutenant Fuller," Welman noted in a sharp tone. "Captain Pelly spoke to me about you."

He stood up and circled the desk, eyeing Fuller with hawk-like eyes. "You were quite 'insistent' on joining us."

"Yes sir," Fuller replied, deciding to keep his answer short. Something in the man's tone was making him feel unwelcomed.

"Most of our candidates are in their early twenties."

Fuller's eye twitched, but he kept silent.

"My standards are high," Welman continued, "and I don't make exceptions." He reached for Fuller's file, which lay centred on his desk. All his stationary was meticulously placed and orderly.

"Hmmm, I see you have some experience operating small boats," he observed. His fingers flipped through the pages, fastened by a pair of metal clips to the back of the folder. "Also, a trained pilot... Interesting."

Welman appeared to consider something in his mind before closing the folder and returning to his chair.

"You'll be billeted in one of the local hotels, likely the Highland*. My secretary will give you the details. Be ready Monday morning, 0600 sharp in clothes for PT. Dismissed."

---

* Officers were billeted in the nearby Highland, Waverly, and Grand Hotels.

Fuller saluted, did an about-turn, and left the office. He collected his documents from the CO's aid, a typical Wren – young with short-kept hair, clean uniform, and meticulous administration skills. Before leaving, he gestured to Welman's office and asked, "is he serious about doing exercise in the morning?"

"Afraid so," she replied, a hint of pity in her voice. "He leads all the officers on a run up the Ben and back."

"The Ben?"

"Ben Nevis," she clarified, and seeing that he wasn't catching on, added, "that great big mountain you passed on the way in."

Fuller gasped. "You can't be serious."

The Wren slid his billeting and messing information into a folder and handed it to him, a sorry look on her face.

"Welcome to *St. Christopher*, sir."

————

Fuller tugged at his clothes, joining the division of men formed up outside the old, stone hotel. He felt ridiculous. They were naval officers, not schoolboys waiting for a gym teacher. Exterior lights shone down on the group with yellow light, and he could see the men's breath in the morning cold.

"It's too damn early," he thought, taking note of the long, winding road leading down the hill upon which the building was located. If it wasn't so dark outside, they'd at least enjoy a view of Fort William's waterfront. He could hear the lapping ebb and flow of tides, nudging boat fenders against docks, and the coos of red-throated loons echoing into the distance. No other sounds could be heard, not even the engine of a single passing vehicle. It was five minutes before 0600 and his calf muscles were already aching. The whole town was built on hills and his body was already protesting the coming ordeal.

He glanced at those around him. From what he could see, he was easily the oldest person, the man to his right looking no more than twenty years old.

"Anyone else wanting to go back to bed?" Fuller voiced, just loud enough for those around him to hear. Several chuckled but before anyone could respond, the front doors of the Highland Hotel opened and Welman exited, looking perfectly rested and energized. The man's physique was that of a marathoner, the sort that relished running long distances. Fuller already disliked him.

"All accounted for?" he asked the officer in front. The man nodded and without even giving the group a second glance, Welman turned down the driveway and ordered: "Right, on me. Smartly lads."

And so, it began with a warm-up march through the streets of Fort William. Plenty of local shops lined their route. They were small and featured basic wares and goods – nothing too exciting. It was the sort of place Fuller imagined one came to retire. The morning sun began to poke from behind the colossal mountain in the distance. It would have been a breath-taking sight, the sort artists strove to replicate on canvas, but the fact that he had to run up it spoiled the scene.

About halfway to Ben Nevis, Welman started a jog trot. He led from the front, pressing on to the waiting giant. Fuller was in decent shape for his age, but regular exercise, especially running, was never one of his top priorities. This would be unlike anything he'd done before – it seemed foolish to take something on like this without proper training. Still, he wouldn't give anyone the satisfaction of seeing him struggle, especially Welman who was just shy of his forty-eighth birthday.

More aches emerged as the graduating incline began to push his limbs and lungs. Sweat beaded on his forehead, and if it was still cold outside, he could no longer feel it. The mountain's summit was still far off and looked no nearer than it had before – and they still had to run back once they conquered the climb. Later, Fuller would calculate that the run was nearly twelve kilometres one way, the first half almost entirely uphill. At least gravity provided some relief on the way down, and Welman insisted on them jogging all the way back to the hotel's entrance. Then, it was a mad dash to the showers, after which they dressed in uniform and proceeded to *St. Christopher* for a full day of training. Fuller managed to keep up, but when he finally arrived at the hotel, his muscles were aching. Pain throbbed in areas he never realized could hurt.

"Well done, gramps," an officer praised, patting Fuller on the shoulder as he passed him in the hallway. Some laughed, but the young men respected his performance. Fuller's age had been the elephant in the room, and he figured some doubted his ability to keep up. Still, he didn't like being called 'Gramps' and would have fired a snappy comeback if he wasn't so tired and in pain. What he didn't realize was that the nickname would stick. "It was the title they afterwards dubbed me," he later explained. "I was known in the service as 'Gramps' all the time."

As it would turn-out, Gramps was a particularly gifted coastal vessel officer. The younger candidates sought to emulate Fuller, and the moniker quickly became a badge of respect, something he used to emphasize his authority. "Respect you elder," he often would say, and the other candidates would acquiesce.

There was still the problem of Ben Nevis. Despite his seamanship skills, his prospects of commanding his own vessel would be dashed if he sustained an injury while exercising. He needed a way to survive those insufferable runs. The following day, Fuller's muscles were in full protest – his legs were stiff, and his muscles felt like they'd been torn in numerous places. It hurt to walk, and it took effort to hide his discomfort from the others. He did his best to stretch out his limbs before heading to the rally point.

"What's with Welman, anyways?" he spat after taking his place in division. They were all shivering, standing outside the hotel in the dark. "We're coastal forces, not commandos for Christ's sakes."

Tired laughs and nods began what quickly became a heated, although whispered, conversation. Fuller noticed that even the most athletic among them questioned the logic in Welman's daily practice. All discussion ceased once the CO appeared. He bounded lightly down the steps, checked their numbers, and day two of their ordeal commenced.

This run proved more gruelling than the first. It was the same route, but Fuller's body objected with every step. Everything hurt – his feet, legs, back, and even his neck. He was tough, and if need be, he would force himself to complete the run, even at the risk of breaking his body, but he couldn't abide doing something he found pointless.

At that moment, something warm and pleasant caught his nose. The scent made him momentarily forget about his discomfort.

Fresh-baked bread.

The others noticed too, a collective 'Mmmmmm' emanating from the running party. Way up ahead, Welman didn't even flinch, mind set to the task. Fuller scowled and glanced around for the source of the smell. They were in the main part of town, and he spotted what looked like a café through a gate leading to an adjacent street. Instantly, a plan formed. He pushed through the run, making it a second time up and down the mountain, but secretly vowed it would be the last. When they finally returned to the hotel, Fuller was through behaving himself.

"That tears it!" he announced, as he headed down the hall to his room. He could hardly appreciate the beauty of the hotel's décor, which was quite resplendent. "Welman's a physical fitness fiend!"

"Hear hear," someone replied.

"What for it?" another asked, "it's his ship, his rules."

"I can't imagine how you're dealing with this Gramps," said an officer passing Fuller and opening the door to his room. "I'm easily ten years younger than you and feel broken."

"I've got news for you," Fuller started, opening his own door, "I'm through playing this game. I came to drive boats, not run-up mountains."

Those in the hall stopped and looked at him. Fuller flashed a mischievous smile.

"I've got an idea. Just do me a favour and don't say anything to Welman."

———

As expected, Wednesday morning began with yet another run. Welman set the pace, the candidates falling-in behind the agile Cdr. Part of Fuller admired him for leading by example, but he also couldn't help noting that Welman never bothered to keep tabs on his men. Once their PT started, the CO paid little to no attention to anything besides his own exercise.

And that was exactly what he intended to exploit.

When they approached the place where Fuller had noticed the cafe, he made his move. Bolting from the group, he dashed towards the closed gate that led into a narrow stone passageway. He stopped, pressed his shoulder against the archway, and carefully poked part of his head around the building to see if anyone had noticed him leave. A few of the men that were closest to him were glancing in his direction, but the majority – especially Welman – proceeded unfazed. Bringing a finger to his mouth, Fuller mouthed "Shhhh" and gave a wink before opening the rod-iron door and slipping into the alley.

The aroma of fresh baked goods was enchanting and grew stronger as he passed between the buildings and approached the café. He emerged onto another street which looked much like the one he'd just been on, minus the eatery across from him. Crossing the road, he entered the building and beheld a counter showcasing fresh baked buns, hot out of the oven. There was an older man at a seat, enjoying some of the bread along with several slices of white cheddar and cold milk. Fuller stepped up to place an order and dug a hand into his pocket, pulling out some money – he came prepared.

Once his order was ready, he took the food and drink to a seat by the main window. Tearing into the bun, steam rose into the air and released a sweet burst of yeast. He checked his watch before taking a bite – for his plan to work, he would have to rejoin the group upon their return. Thankfully, Welman always used the same route, which meant Fuller could decently estimate when the party would return. Most of the officers weren't anywhere near the COs shape, and large gaps inevitably formed between runners. This worked to Fuller's advantage – he would wait for a gap somewhere in the middle of the group and sneak back in for the final leg to the hotel. Not only did it allow him to rejoin unnoticed, but he could also return to the Highland in time to enjoy a hot shower before the tanks were depleted.

It became his new morning routine. While the others ran up and down the mountain, Fuller enjoyed a nice breakfast with cold milk, skimming a newspaper while he waited for the right time to regroup. Welman never caught on and nobody bothered to tip-off the CO to the scheme. A good thing too, because if he ever discovered that Fuller had been playing him for a fool, he might have broken a few rules himself and keel-hauled the Canadian!

Fuller was paradoxical. Sometimes he was a stickler for tradition and rules (notably his own), while other times he freely tossed both over the side. Basically, if he didn't see the value in something, or he figured he knew a better way, then he didn't hesitate to do things differently. His practical business sense, and ability to see and work angles, made him unique in a dogmatic world of discipline and uniformity. Perhaps those qualities were the reason he would distinguish himself above so many during the war, leading the way in adapting daring and innovative tactics in the presence of the enemy. His wasn't the mindset of a prim and proper naval officer, and while he likely didn't realize it at the time…

… at heart, he was a pirate.

CHAPTER 4

—◇◇◉◇◇—

The Little Ships

For the next three weeks, Fuller and his course mates dove headlong into the world of the 'little ships' of the RN. The style of instruction suited Gramps; mostly out on the water, ripping up and down Loch Linnhe, primarily aboard MGBs and MLs*. It was all about the fundamentals, what they would need to successfully lead their vessels against the enemy: plotting, combat tactics, gunnery, signals, the various approaches to conducting raids during the day and night, and the use flags, smoke, and flares. When ashore, the lessons were also practical, such as aircraft recognition, manoeuvres to evade sky-based attacks, and always followed by exercises in their boats. Experienced officers, usually a Lt in rank, guided each of them aboard their respective craft. Many were recovering from wounds sustained in combat and shared valuable first-hand knowledge.

Fuller learned such strategies as the 'circling movement', a technique to escape being shot and/or bombed by multiple aircraft. It required a steady flow of instructions to the helmsman, while coordinating

---

* MLs were small anti-submarine vessels and minelayers, intended for harbour defence and air-to-sea rescue. Depending on the type, they could range from 63-112 feet in length. Numerous were built during the Second World War – for instance, by 1945 over 1000 Fairmile B MLs were commissioned.

suppressing machine-gun fire concentrated in various directions.[29] He also practiced how to engage and disengage from the enemy, something that might have seemed intuitive but required a lot more than simply charging at the target, firing, and turning about, especially at night when one could unexpectedly encounter a superior force. Fuller took charge of his boat through simulated attacks, ordering the vessel to zigzag while guiding the helm through alterations in speed, which would hopefully cause enemy fire to either fall short or overshoot them. The training may have been compressed, but certainly proved thorough. Fuller's quick application of techniques and boat handling skills impressed his instructors. He was a natural. What's more, commanding an MGB at speed was an unmatched adrenaline rush. The chill of bow spray against his face, the roar of the engines as they vibrated to life, and even the smell of petrol, were deeply satisfying to Fuller. Unlike serving aboard AMCs, this felt right – he was meant to do this. Moreover, he would likely get his chance to face the enemy head-on.

Although crew compliments varied depending on the type (MGB, MTB, ML, etc.) and design of boat, certain positions were common aboard all vessels. There were only two to three officers, command typically going to an RNVR or RCNVR Lt. The skipper's experience usually dictated the vessel they received. For example, the iconic Fairmile D MTBs, commonly referred to as 'Dog Boats', often went to an experienced officer with a proven record in the presence of the enemy. COs were older than the rest of the crew, usually in their early to mid-twenties (hence Fuller's first moniker). In larger vessels, a 1st Lt, possibly commissioned from the ranks, acted as XO, while a third officer, commonly referred to as pilots since they were principally tasked with navigating the boat, were freshly minted midshipmen or newly made SLts.[30] Smaller craft, because of their size, required the CO to make do with only one officer, a subaltern who took on all the aforementioned duties.

A career navy PO acted as cox'n and took charge of the boat when the officers were ashore. Their experience in seamanship and managing sailors proved essential in dealing with a green crew. A second cox'n might be appointed to assist the boat's senior rating, typically a LS in rank with a few years' experience in coastal vessels.[31] A fortunate CO would also be granted two to three able seamen who had some sea-time; the rest of his upper deck crew would be made-up of newly trained ordinary seamen, who would operate the various weapons and perform onboard husbandry duties (i.e. ship maintenance).[32] Additionally, he would be assigned a telegraphist, usually nicknamed 'Sparks', and a radar operator. However, coastal vessels were not provided a signalman; the pilot and 1st Lts would deal with all light and hoisted signals from the small open bridge, where a locker, afore the mast, contained a complete set of flags and pennants. Despite having a galley, and the expectation of patrolling for multiple days, cooks weren't assigned, forcing the cox'n to persuade one of the sailors to take on the duties. Naturally, finding just the right person could have a big impact on the crew's morale.[33] Finally, no boat could operate without the ever-essential motor mechanic (also a PO, possibly a CPO), assisted by a leading MM and some stokers, one who might have previous experience. Therefore, a CO might have a handful of experienced hands aboard.[34] At sea they lived in close proximity and ate the same food. As such, despite the separate messes, there was little segregation. Smaller boats might have as little as a dozen sailors aboard, whereas the total crew capacity on a 115-foot Dog Boat could include up to three officers (possibly four if the SO was aboard) and thirty-four crew members.[35]

Above deck layouts and armaments varied on both MGBs and MTBs; the larger the vessel, the more it carried. MGBs typically had a variety of anti-aircraft and boat weapons, including twin Vickers 0.5-inch machine gun turrets, 20mm Oerlikon cannons, 2-pounder 40mm pom-pom guns, and even a 6 pound gun on the larger vessels. A couple of depth charges might also be added on deck. MTBs were similarly armed, with the addition of long torpedo tubes on the port and starboard sides of the vessel, making it a significant threat to larger ships.[36] One of the great things about these vessels was their versatility. For example, if the mission required it, torpedo tubes could be removed from a boat and be replaced with depth charges, only to have the tubes reinstalled upon return. And compared to larger surface vessels, these alterations could be accomplished quickly by shore-based crews.

Although their speed also varied, they were generally designed to be fast. The ability to move quicker than other surface vessels was an essential part of their design. They were meant to perform speedy, guerrilla-style attacks, and evade enemy fire. The Fairmile D, for instance, powered by up to four supercharged engines, could achieve top speeds of just under 40 knots (class depending). However, their speed meant they lacked any real defensive armour – unlike battleships, their hulls weren't meant to take a beating. Apart from some armour around their gun turrets, bullets would easily penetrate the vessel. Their best defence was to keep moving. If their engines broke down or were damaged, a coastal vessel's only remaining protection would be their relatively small size, which made them harder to see in the dark. However, if caught under the light of a full moon or, worse yet, a rising sun, skilled gunners could make short work of an immobile coastal vessel.

Overall, their speed and firepower made them a vital asset, one often underestimated by naval historians. Perhaps no other vessel performed as admirably in disrupting enemy supply lines, conducting and supporting coastal raids (e.g. transporting and supporting commandos or gathering intelligence from spies), and, naturally, defending home waters from enemy vessels. A flotilla of MTBs, if operating under favourable conditions (i.e. a cloudy night), could easily sink a larger warship and wreak havoc on a convoy. Their limited range – they weren't designed to operate mid-ocean – was perhaps their principal drawback, but they could also operate in areas larger ships couldn't maneuver. Even submarines were prey for these little ships.

Of little surprise, the main threat to a coastal vessel, besides enemy aircraft, was another coastal vessel.* The Kriegsmarine constructed the formidable Schnellboot, or S-Boot, which proved more than a match for little ships of the RN. These 'fast boats' were well constructed and slightly quicker (top speed of 40 knots) than anything the Allies had. Although the appropriate designation would have been S-boat, they were often simply referred to as 'Enemy' boats, hence the use of the letter 'E' (see list of abbreviations and terms for more information).

Despite lengthy training days, often continuing after supper and moving into the late evening to take advantage of the dark – coastal vessels were primarily nocturnal – Fuller's time at *St. Christopher* wasn't void of entertainment. He did befriend some interesting people, such as fellow-Canadian James Ralph Hilborn Kirkpatrick. Called 'Kirk' by his friends, Kirkpatrick graduated from RMC and trained aboard Canadian destroyers *Skeena* and *Saguenay*. When war broke out, he was studying law at Osgoode Hall and was transferred to HMCS *York* in Toronto, so that he could continue his studies.[37] From 1939-1940 he served briefly in an examination vessel, operating out of Saint John, New Brunswick, before putting the remainder of his studies on hold and going overseas to *King Alfred*. He completed his course prior to Fuller's arrival and then apprenticed aboard AMCs, serving in HMS *Patroclus* when it was torpedoed by U99. After his rescue, Kirkpatrick transferred to coastal forces, no longer wishing to be on the receiving end of that variety of enemy attacks.

Another friend was Alan Villiers, a famed yachtsman who Fuller admired for his seamanship skills. Surprisingly, Villiers was a year or two older than Fuller, although there is no mention of his being teased about his age.[38] His reputation proceeded him – he'd had quite the adventurous life prior to joining the RNVR in 1940. An Australian-born author, sailor, and photographer, he was a bit of a lone wolf and, like

---

* Coastal forces were less likely to encounter aircraft during night operations.

Fuller, tended to follow his own instincts. In 1940 Villiers also accepted a commission as a full Lt and chose to do his part in the war fighting with coastal forces.

Fuller, Kirkpatrick, and Villiers made an interesting trio and from time to time wound up in trouble for their shenanigans. One such incident involved a Lady Donald[39] who, upon hearing that some Canadians were based at *St. Christopher*, invited the officers to attend a party at her dwelling in Glencoe, a short drive south of Fort William. Fuller happily accepted the invitation – this would be a real party, not afternoon tea – although he didn't appreciate that stuffy "old Welman" would be acting as a chaperon. He felt certain their CO wasn't the sort of naval officer to let loose and have a good time, even at a mess dinner. Regardless, the three, along with the other officers, dressed up in full uniform and commuted across the Ballachulish-Onich ferry to attend the social. They'd try to have a good time despite their CO's presence. At least they weren't compelled to travel with him.

Kirkpatrick decided to head to the party on his own, telling Fuller and Villiers that he would meet them there. When pressed for a reason, he insisted on staying quiet. "You'll see," was all he said.

Lady Donald's home looked much like Fuller expected – darkened stone, weathered steps, and dark, polished wood furnishings that hinted of bygone generations. The space emanated a sort of regalness, and the food and drinks were abundant. It felt of old money.

Their host, clearly poised and trained to entertain, like a person groomed since childhood for a role of importance, also had a sort of youthful energy. She was outgoing and even a little cheeky with the men, insisting on doing away with formalities. This was meant to be a party and she wanted everyone to let loose and enjoy themselves. Fuller was beginning to like her, especially after accepting his second drink. She didn't skimp on the good stuff.

He was a bit surprised that Welman had yet to arrive. Their CO was punctual and Fuller half expected him to arrive before anyone else, even if only to chide his students for being late. Several of their instructors were present, enjoying the food and company and he wondered if it would be too much to hope that Welman had been called away at the last minute. Just knowing that their CO could arrive at any moment dampened his mood. It didn't feel safe to let loose yet. Lady Donald seemed to sense his unease, because she came over straight way and struck up a conversation with him and Villiers.

It was also around this time that Fuller realized Kirkpatrick hadn't arrived. "What could that man be up to?" He wondered. As if on queue, a woman entered the main entrance, followed by Kirk, who extended an arm, a satisfied look plastered on his face.

Fuller stopped chewing his food and signaled Villiers to look behind him with a nod of his head. It seemed everyone took notice at the same time, the room suddenly growing quiet. It wasn't so much that Kirk brought a date – it was the woman herself that silenced the chatter. From her overly revealing clothes and general demeanour – she hadn't even registered the change in mood and instead appraised the room with a smug "nice place" look – it was clear what her profession was. When Villiers turned back, his thoughts were plastered all over his face: "Did Kirk really just bring a prostitute to the party?"

There were so many questions. Neither man could even guess where Kirk found her. Fort William wasn't big enough for a red-light district, and a couple of weeks was more than enough time to become familiar with the area. Yet, at no time did Fuller or Villiers notice a prostitute working the streets (not that they were seeking out their services). Apparently, Kirk had done a more thorough search of the area than they had.

Fuller returned his attention to Lady Donald, anticipating the mere sight of the escort would offend the host. Instead, the woman remained calm, taking it in stride, and put on such a convincing display of hospitality that Fuller couldn't tell if she was genuinely indifferent or acting.

"Welcome," she said as the two approached, "and thank you for attending."

"Our pleasure," Kirk replied, reaching out and snatching a couple of drinks off the platter of a passing waitstaff. He handed one to the woman.

Fuller still couldn't find his voice. Manners clearly weren't the woman's strong suit – she chewed loudly on a piece of garnish that had lined the beverage, her mouth open and smacking with an air of impudence. She playfully swirled the liquid in her glass, eyeing a silver serving tray with vulture eyes. He figured the staff were already keeping a close tab on her.

"And what's your name?" Villiers asked, unable to help himself.

She glanced at the Australian, eyeing him up and down with a bemused smile.

"Does it matter?"

Fuller raised his eyebrows and turned to hand off his drink, grateful to receive a fresh one. He was going to need quite a few more before the night was through. Thankfully, Kirk took the woman to the back of the room where a food table lined one of the walls. Fuller leaned towards Villiers and whispered, "classy lady."

"I guess somewhere between the hotel and MacBrayne's Bus Line he found his date," Villiers added with a chuckle. He brought his drink to his lips and took a sip, but something over Fuller's shoulder caused him to choke.

"Light weight," Fuller teased while Villiers, doing his best to suppress the onset of a coughing fit, gestured towards the main entrance.

There was Welman, in his uniform, and looking particularly unhappy. His eyes were staring across the room at Kirk and his date and unlike Lady Donald, he wasn't going to let it slide.

"Lieutenant!" he growled, snapping his fingers and pointing to the floor in front of him. Everyone knew that meant "here, now!" Thankfully, Kirk knew better than to bring his date with him, who seemed unfazed by his sudden absence. One would have to be blind not to see that the CO was livid.

"Sir?" he replied, instinctively coming to attention. Welman, kept his tone quiet, but his words were hard as steel. Fuller could just manage to make out what he was saying.

"You dare bring a prostitute into Lady Donald's house!"

Kirk started to respond, but the CO cut him off. "This is not the behaviour of an officer in His Majesty's service. I have half a mind to drag you out of here for such a faux pas, but making a scene might upset our host." His eyes narrowed. "We'll chat after the party."

Again, Kirk tried to speak, but this time Welman pushed right past him, greeting their host with a pleasant smile, like he hadn't just quietly rebuked a subordinate. Fuller and Villiers went to their friend, who looked as if the blood had drained from his face.

"I'm a dead man," he muttered.

Fuller patted his shoulder and handed him his drink, which Kirk eagerly downed. He would have said something to comfort the man, but what could he really say? Kirk was right – he was about to find himself in a world of pain.

————

Welman wasted no time enacting his punishment the moment the social was done.

"You hear what's happening to Kirk?" Villiers asked.

"Yeah, Welman's banishing him to *Abercrombie*."

The base depot ship, an old hulk and the destination of many defaulters. The officers at *St. Christopher* jokingly referred to the ship as *Altmark*, after the German oil tanker and supply ship used to house Allied prisoners of war. Fuller and Villiers put their heads together during breakfast, trying to develop a scheme to help their friend, but they couldn't come up with anything decent. Welman was on the warpath, and even saying something to defend Kirk would likely land them both in trouble. Fortunately, a guardian angel appeared to help Kirk.

The next morning, a car pulled up in front of *St. Christopher's* administration building. Fuller was still ashore, prepping for another day on the water, and just happened to notice the vehicle pull in. Curious, he decided to observe what was happening.

A well-dressed chauffeur exited the driver's seat and circled the vehicle to open the rear passenger door. Fuller could just make out Lady Donald's head over the roof of the car. She turned, taking in the base, and noticed Fuller in the distance. She smiled and beckoned him over.

"I heard that one of your officers was reprimanded for bringing his date to my party," she said.

"Yes ma'am," Fuller confirmed. "Poor Kirk is in a heap of trouble, although I must say that I'm surprised you've already heard about it."

"News travels fast in these parts," she replied, a smile creeping onto her face. "Well, I suppose I'll have to address the matter with Commander Welman."

She proceeded into the building with the air of a flag officer doing an impromptu facility audit. Being a civilian didn't appear to faze the woman in the least, and she walked past both door sentry and the CO's secretary without either protesting. Despite himself, Fuller stopped what he was doing and followed, close enough to eavesdrop but careful to stay out of sight. Welman glanced up, momentarily confused by the sudden intrusion and sight of Lady Donald.

"Good morning, ma'am," he said, clumsily standing from his desk. "To what do I owe this… unexpected visit?"

"I came to say that I've never enjoyed myself so much," she replied, gracefully lowering herself into a seat across the desk. "The company of your officers was fantastic – a marvellous evening."

Welman slowly sat back down, clearly confused.

"The pleasure was all ours," he replied, choosing his words carefully. "We're ever grateful for your Lady's hospitality." He paused, considering something in his head, before saying "I'm delighted, although surprised, that you came down to tell me this in person."

"Oh, that's not why I'm here," she clarified, a slight edge to her tone. "I understand that you've punished one of your officers for his behaviour last night?"

He sighed, looking embarrassed. "Yes, and I sincerely apologize for what transpired. Rest assured; the matter is being dealt with seriously."

"I'm glad you do take this seriously," she said, "because I want it distinctly understood that there is to be no disciplinary action taken against this officer."

Welman blinked. "I beg your pardon?"

"You will not punish this officer," she clarified, locking eyes. "If you do, there will be an international incident, because it was my hospitality that caused it."

For a moment, the CO stared at her and then began tripping on his words. "Well, you see, it's really, I don't–"

"Commander," she interrupted, leaning towards him, "I'll make this plain: I would be very disappointed if you embarrassed me by insisting on punishing this officer for something that occurred at my home."

Again, Welman appeared at a loss. He searched for an argument, but eventually gave up and agreed: "of course ma'am, that would be the last thing I would want."

"Good," she said, hopping back to her feet. "I have your assurance?"

The CO also stood. "While it does go against my own judgment – those entrusted with the King's commission must be held to a higher standard – I'll see to it straight away, if only as a courtesy to you."

Lady Donald smiled and extended a gloved hand.

"Thank you, Commander. A pleasure."

"All mine," he replied, gently accepting her hand, and giving a courteous nod. "May I see you back to your car?"

Fuller was impressed with how quickly Welman recovered. The CO walked Lady Donald back out of the building, not even noticing Fuller standing beside his secretary.

"Good to have friends in high places," he noted, and the Wren nodded.

Moments later Kirk was free and, as Fuller would later summarize, "that was the end of the incident."

On March 28, Fuller finished his training at *St. Christopher*. At the completion of the course, officers were given the option to request appointments. Surprisingly, a few decided to leave coastal forces, putting in for corvette or larger ship postings. For Fuller, he'd found his place and, like many of his peers, waited for word of any "assignments at sea, preferably within range of the enemy."[40]

Unfortunately, his billeting was lackluster: Welman posted him as a 2nd Lt aboard a ML in Belfast. Not only was he not given a command, Northern Ireland was as far away from combat as one could get this side of the Atlantic. Fuller refused to accept it, and like he'd done back at *King Alfred*, he marched right into the CO's office to protest.

"Fuller," Welman acknowledged, his eyes noting the paper. "A question about your billet?"

"You're damn right," Fuller snapped, roughly closing the door behind him. "I gave up a job that was paying me fifty thousand dollars a year to come over here to fight a war, not to sit on any goddamn harbour defence motor craft in Belfast."

Welman stiffened. "You forget yourself, Lieutenant."

"Well, I have news for you, sir," Fuller pushed, meeting his CO's glare. He was through playing nice. "If the navy has no better use for me than that, I want to put in an official request to be relieved of my position on loan to the Royal Navy."

Welman hadn't expected that. All he could say was "Oh?"

Fuller tossed the paper onto his desk. "I'd sooner return to Canada and tender my resignation from the service than sit around doing nothing – I came over to get into a scrap."

The Cdr's face turned a bright red. "Oh, you want a scrap?" he snapped, staring back at the audacious Canadian. He wasn't about to have any of Fuller's attitude. "Sit down, Lieutenant," he ordered, "you're about to get exactly what you want."

Picking up his phone, Welman spoke to the operator and requested a connection to the Second Sea Lord's office. After a brief overlay, a voice answered and the CO asked, "Is that Miss Dalrymple?"

Across the desk, Fuller noted the name and tucked it away in the back of his mind. An old sales trick he'd picked up during his twenties.

"I've got an officer here who wants to fight," Welman continued. "Have you any openings?"

The man nodded his head a few times, saying "yes, yes, yes" to various things Fuller couldn't make out, before finally saying "*49* you say – yes, yes, that's perfect."

He thanked Dalrymple and hung up, staring back at Fuller with malicious eyes.

"If you want a fight, you're going to have it, because you're now in command of *49* at Hell-Fire Corner."

"Where in hell is Hell-Fire Corner?" Fuller asked, unfamiliar with the term.

"Dover, you damn fool, Dover!" Welman exploded. "Now get out of my office!"

As observed by authors Brian Nolan and Brian Jeffrey Street, in their book *Champagne Navy*, "For once, Fuller did as he was told".[41] Rather than head across the Irish Sea, his new orders were to return south and report to HMS *Lynx*, but not before taking a few days leave in London. He didn't request and receive approval for the time off – he simply showed up late to his new post. In normal circumstances this would render one as 'absent without leave' and guarantee a reprimand, if not outright arrested by MPs, but Fuller knew how to exploit the system. "On all these transfers you quickly caught on to the fact that you never showed up until ten days late because the draft tickets never caught up with you," he later explained. Adding a few buffer days was a common practice and Fuller enjoyed his short holiday in London.

On March 31, he reported to *Lynx*. The base served as one of many coastal forces' establishments along the English Channel, separating the British Isles from the rest of occupied Europe. Those serving along the coast simply referred it as the 'Narrow Seas', a quasi 'no-man's land' where both RN and Axis ships clashed for dominance. After the fall of France, many of these shore establishments began springing up along the southern and eastern coasts of England. HMS *Lynx*, commissioned in 1939, would be where Fuller would finally get his chance to engage the enemy.

As was the practice, his accommodations were located outside the base, in this case the Lord Warden hotel. By English standards, the building was relatively new, dating back to the mid-1800s (there were pubs in the area centuries older than Canada), and showcased a regal façade and stunning interiors. At the outset of the war, it served as a stop/resting centre for soldiers on leave, as well as for politicians and journalists, but by September 1940 the RN, as with so many nearby locales, requisitioned the building to serve as the coastal forces HQ in Dover. Renamed, HMS *Wasp*, it provided adequate space for planning, administration, plotting rooms, and signals, as well as billets for MGB/MTB crews when ashore. The boats themselves were kept in the Camber, mere steps from the buildings entrance.[42] *Wasp* also housed members of the Royal Norwegian Navy who would assist coastal forces during routine operations and patrols. The Wrens who worked at HQ were housed at Dover College*, now part of HMS *Lynx*, and less than a five minute drive away. The proximity to his boat made Fuller's lodging at *Wasp* convenient.

---

* As it was a likely spot for a German invasion, the school was temporarily evacuated and was used by the RN.

MGB *49* was a converted MA/SB, one that Kirk had skippered before him.* Originally a private yacht built by Samuel White[43], it was purchased by the RN and commissioned on July 20, 1940. MA/SBs were MTBs equipped with asdic and depth charges, enabling them to sweep for enemy U-boats. *49* began doing air search and rescue work in 1941 and then switched to patrolling the channel for enemy convoys. Now the vessel was under Fuller's command.

Aside from a Toronto native by the name of 'Wiggy' Bennett, who was doing Air-Sea Rescue in support of operations, Fuller was the only Canadian "amongst all the Limeys" at the Lord Warden. He'd been assigned to the third flotilla and received orders to conduct his first mission the same evening of his arrival, leaving no time to break in his crew or boat. They didn't know anything about their new CO, and he wouldn't have time to adjust to the new command.

Before boarding his vessel, which was already idling along the jetty, Fuller asked for the crew to assemble on deck. Amidst the backdrop of a dawning sky, with hues of purple and pink, he introduced himself and briefed his men on their mission. He then dismissed them to their stations, spoke to his officers, and then made a quick survey of his new boat, noting the various compartments and cabins. She was older and far from top of the line, but it was his. The asdic dome had been removed, and his vessel appeared to be the only one fitted with an Oerlikon gun.[44] His last stop was the engine room.

"What are these?" he asked the MM. They were unlike anything he'd seen before.

"Scripps engines, sir."

It was an odd configuration. He would later describe them as four engines positioned "one ahead of the other, with a two-and-a-half inch jack-shaft between the two."

Rubbing his chin, he exchanged a look with the stoker.

---

* Because of this, MA/SB *49* is also commonly referred to as MGB *49*.

"I'm no MM but I'm also no stranger to boats," he said. "I'm concerned about these engines."

Fuller headed back up to the bridge, pulled on a waxed, cotton jacket, and slung a pair of binoculars over his neck. It was still twilight and he wanted to make use of the remaining light to test out his boat. He gave the order to cast-off and began zigzagging within Dover's harbour, even manoeuvring his boat between some mooring buoys. With a steady eye and exact commands to the helm, he guided *49* back alongside the dock. Overall, his assessment of his boat was far from satisfactory – it wasn't anywhere near as responsive as the vessels he trained on. The engines had a significant delay, and the steering was slow, even at higher speeds. Still, he'd have to make do. There was a severe shortage of vessels along the coast, and the RN had come across numerous challenges in implementing a rapid building program to fill the gap. Without options, many bases dealt with older, pre-war boats. They were temperamental, ill-equipped to handle rough seas, and suffered from chronic mechanical problems. That being said, even some of the newer boats were having problems, notably with their engines which were "hastily designed and thrown together".

It was time to leave. *49* slipped out of the harbour's gates and into open water. Soon, the waves began to grow, and a chill breeze blew against the bow, causing water to spray over deck and against the bridge screen. Enemy vessels loomed somewhere beyond the distant horizon, which was now barely visible in the night. E-boats were undoubtedly conducting their own patrols and the French coastline, fortified with gun batteries and searchlights, was a dangerous place. They were truly alone, vulnerable, and possibly hours away from a deadly encounter.

He glanced one last time at his upper-deck crew, noting ratings at their guns. Everything seemed in order and if any of them felt nervous or anxious, they didn't show it – not that he could see much anyway. He leaned sideways and glanced into the wheelhouse.

"It's time," he indicated. "Take us out along our course, and let's not push the engines too much straightaway."

"Aye sir," the pilot replied but then looked back and asked, "is there a concern?"

Fuller gestured with a thumb towards the stern. "I don't trust our engines."

"Right sir, nice and easy then," the officer confirmed.

Fuller nodded and brought his head back over the bridge wall just as the engines began to roar and the wind pressed against his face.

"Let's do this lads!" he called out, keeping his mouth close enough to the voice pipes so that his words carried below. They tore-off into the dark to their destination: the coastline of occupied France.

CHAPTER 5

Hell-Fire Corner

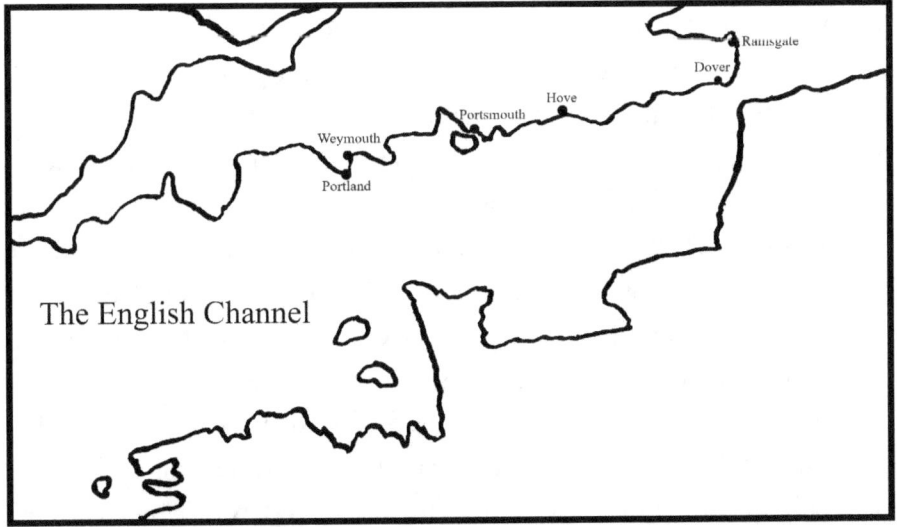

MGB *49* chugged along steadily, a barely noticeable shape cutting through the dark. Behind them, the faintest trace of white split apart from their stern, momentarily visible before absorbed by the night. Save for those closest to him, Fuller couldn't see anyone, and even those on the bridge looked more like ghosts, not quite as obscure as the blackness around them. They were travelling without illumination signals – red on the port side, green on starboard, and white on the mainmast, bow, and stern. Blackout curtains now hung from either side of every hatch to prevent any light from escaping and portholes were covered. There was a process to entering and leaving the main deck – duck under the first curtain, open the hatch, proceed behind the next curtain, and then secure the hatch before moving beyond. It was a bit laborious but necessary. Being invisible was key and during war, light on the water meant only one thing: a target. Thus, all vessels at sea moved under complete darkened conditions. If necessary, a captain might break the rule, perhaps to shine a search light onto nearby waters in search of shipwrecked survivors, but it was a risky move and placed the vessel in peril.

This was a war of shadow versus shadow, vigilant eyes searching the dark for the subtlest hint of a shape on the horizon. They also could use their ears, although their own motor often made it difficult to hear much of anything. However, sometimes a boat would shut down and drift along the waves, listening for the sound of a passing engine. A full moon, especially on a cloudless night, made most things visible from a distance. As such, most patrols avoided operating under such conditions. However, decent cloud cover could counter this and often navies took their chances. This often brought about some intense moments on the Narrow Seas – in less than ten seconds, a boat could suddenly appear under slivers of moonlight, charge at the enemy with its weapons ablaze, and then retreat into the night, vanishing from sight.

Fuller was happy that it was cloudy. So far, the lookouts had nothing to report. Still, he was keenly aware that anything could happen, especially as they were ever nearing enemy shores. While they couldn't see where they were going, detailed charts, along with navigation tools, allowed his pilot to accurately calculate their position. He'd only just been acquainted with the man, but from what he could deduce, the officer knew what he was doing. To be safe, Fuller kept checking in periodically, moving into the wheelhouse and looking over their plot. They were presently about five miles off Cap Blanc Nez, well into enemy territory. For all he knew, a squadron of E-boats could be coming up behind them. With *49*'s noisy engine, which emanated a unique gargling sound, Fuller doubted he could even hear glass breaking at his feet, never mind the distant sound of enemy gunfire. Hopefully the German vessels were just as loud.

Just then, *49*'s engines began making laboured pops and Fuller felt a sudden change in the boat – the deck started vibrating with a pronounced thumping. They were slowing and the smell of something other than high octane caught his nose. The hairs on the back of his neck felt electrified and a sickening feeling formed in the pit of his stomach.

Those blasted Scripps!

He jumped to one of the voice-pipes, flipping open the protective lid. "Helm, belay course! All stop!"

BANG!

It was too late. A loud sound erupted from deep within *49* and the boat came to a halt. The MM's voice followed, emanating via the appropriate pipe.

"Sir, we've got a problem with the engines."

"Hold on, I'm coming down," Fuller replied.

Deckhands and gunners began trading looks of concern, but Fuller drove them back to their respective tasks.

"Stay alert," he snapped. "Eyes and ears open and if you see something, don't shoot unless it's clear that they've spotted us." The last thing he needed was for a junior rating to let off a few rounds and announce their presence to the enemy. Without the ability to move, they were in no position to fight.

Fuller made his way to *49*'s engines. The MM touched his sweat-worn cap upon seeing the CO – this was the simplified way ratings paid compliments aboard coastal vessels – and wiped his hands on the sides of his dirty blue coveralls. Fuller pulled out a handkerchief and brought it to his nose to help filter the fumes and glanced at the Scripps. The issue was plain to see – the jack-shaft was snapped.

"Damn."

The MM nodded and shook his head. "I'm afraid it's gash, sir."

Fuller scratched his chin and let out a sigh. "Well, looks like our mission has changed."

"Sir?" asked the MM.

"My only concern is getting us back home."

The PO understood. If they were still without power by daybreak and hadn't already been found by patrolling E-boats, then enemy aircraft would surely spot them. And if they happened to have drifted too close to the coast, shore batteries might use the MGB as target practice.

Fixing the engines was a big task, too large to perform at sea. The best they could hope for was a patch job that could, hopefully, grant them some propulsion. The MM and his crew started working, taking the unserviceable plugs from the damaged engine, and somehow managing to use them with the still operable engine astern.[45] This resulted in the boat being able to muster almost a quarter of its original power. Considering their circumstances, it was a commendable job. It would be a slow crawl back to base but at least they would be moving.

Fuller gave the command and *49* started its journey home. They were still far from safe – at this speed they couldn't adequately defend themselves and he doubted the MM's repairs could withstand the boat making any evasive turns. The only thing they could do was to remain quiet and hope for the best. Fortunately, *49* managed to limp back to friendly waters, upon which command dispatched a vessel to tow them back to Dover.

While far from what Fuller anticipated – his first night in the channel and he'd already written off a boat – the experience provided some valuable lessons. It also tested Fuller's leadership. At no time did he lose his cool, something his new crew undoubtedly noticed. Once ashore he made his report and submitted it to the CO, noting that he "never want to see a boat again with two engines directly in line on the same shaft".

At least command took the situation seriously, immediately initiating an update to all vessels that weren't already equipped with reliable, Packard engines. In the meantime, while the maintenance team worked on his boat, Fuller took the time to rest, review the pros and cons of his crew's performance, and file some paperwork.

A few days later his CO, Cdr James Sanders, paid Fuller a visit.

"You've been appointed to take command of MGB No. *11*," he said. "I'm not sure if we'll be able to adequately repair *49*."

The news didn't bother Fuller. A new boat suited him just fine. *49* was done with coastal forces – after getting her engines fixed she would serve with the Air and Sea rescue, doing so until 1943 before being turned over to the Royal Army Service Corps.[46]

Retrieving his new boat meant going back up to *St. Christopher*. Fuller would have the opportunity to conduct workups, training his crew along the familiar waters of Loc Linnhe, before taking *11* down the Irish Sea and heading back to Dover. He imagined Welman wouldn't be thrilled to see him again, but at least he wouldn't be a student this time.

They arrived on May 27, 1941, and Fuller wasted no time putting his new boat and crew through various drills. Meanwhile, Sanders completed a standard S.206 performance appraisal on Fuller, even though he'd only conducted a single, partially completed, patrol.[47] While these reports weren't shared with Fuller, they provide a unique glimpse at the impression he made on his superiors. Within, Saunders noted his general conduct as 'Satisfactory' and described Fuller as having a 'temperate habit'.[48] The next section of the report scored him on various qualities:

Professional Ability:	7
Personal Qualities:	6
Leadership:	5
Intellectual Ability:	5
Administrative Ability:	5

Instructions for completing a form S. 206 indicated the grading system as follows:

1	=	Poor
2, 3, or 4	=	Below Average
5	=	The Average Officer
6, 7, or 8	=	Above the Average
9	=	Exceptional

The numerical system provided a common measure and assisted the admiralty when considering appointments and promotions. Fuller scored mostly average, with a few above average ratings. When evaluating Fuller's command of a seagoing ship, his SO listed him as 'good' and 'fit for more important sea command'. Below this, Sanders noted that Fuller "... is accustomed to handling small ships at sea and has a good knowledge of engines which should be valuable in these craft" and recommended him for both immediate and accelerated promotion.[49] It was a surprising proposal considering his limited activity, but clearly Sanders appreciated the coolheaded way he responded to *49*'s engine failure. He saw potential in Fuller.

During his time on AMCs, Fuller began experiencing pain in his bowls. According to medical reports, he suffered from severe constipation and concluded that his "...diet and water intake were unsatisfactory."[50] The condition unfortunately triggered other issues, notably spasms in his back. The attending physician noted this caused discomfort that "... extended through from the sternum and upper abdomen and to the middle of the back", which appeared to be "worse in the mornings and in the damp weather."[51] Despite this, Fuller kept his condition to himself, worrying that it might come across as weakness in the eyes of his crew. It was essential that he always appeared both confident and strong.

Unfortunately, these weren't the only issues he faced. Fuller was often seasick on open waters.[52] As surprising as it may seem, many famous naval officers suffered the same affliction. Even RCN legends, such as Vice-Admiral Harry DeWolf, often referred to as "Canada's Nelson" and one of the most effective Allied destroyer captains during the war, struggled with chronic seasickness. But like DeWolf, Fuller wouldn't allow the issue to keep him ashore.

Fortunately, he devised some effective make-shift remedies. The first involved snacking on greengages, which he said tasted "as good on the way up as they did on the way down"[53] but even more efficient was sipping tea and scotch whisky. How he came about this solution is unknown, but it miraculously subdued his upset stomach and prevented him from getting sick. He would later explain that it created a "neutralizing effect"[54] and allowed him to manage even the most difficult conditions at sea. Thankfully, no one was policing his activities and once his crew realized what he was doing, they quietly made certain that their CO's home-remedy was readily available, serving him "tea with a shot".[55] He rarely had to ask for someone to set the kettle – once underway, a rating would simply hand him his cup and ensured it was regularly replenished. It was an unspoken understanding and Fuller never consumed enough to become impaired. A few sips here and there was all he needed.

Around January of 1942, Fuller and his crew were done workups. Before, he'd been thrown into *49* without a chance to know his boat or crew but now, things were different. They were no longer strangers and had become a team. Leaving *St. Christopher*, they proceeded first to Poole, a coastal town in Dorset, for an appointment with the British Power Boat Company.[56] Fuller found it to be a nice town and enjoyed the quaint look of the old Georgian houses and a lively waterfront. In better times, the natural sandy beaches would be a welcome summer attraction. "A remarkable little place", Fuller would later comment.

MGB *11* was fitted with brand-new Packard engines, each boasting over 1500 horsepower. However, before they could get on their way, they required fine-tuning by a specialist, scheduled to meet them at 0900 hours the next morning. Fuller scoffed at the idea of engines needing this level of attention: "Let's see this expert that's going to tune these engines."

Fuller glanced at his watch – it was a few minutes passed their appointment. They'd all awoken early, changed into clean uniforms, and had breakfast before congregating along the company's jetty. Many of the junior ratings were sporting crisp cream-coloured turtleneck sweaters, over which they dawned dark blue duffle coats. He and his officers opted for the same sweater, but as was tradition, wore their tunics instead. It was an official dress for both the submarine service and coastal forces.

"Not the punctual type," he observed. The other officers and ratings laughed.

"I'm sure they'll be here any minute now," a company manager assured them, doing his best to appear confident. The act wasn't working – Fuller could tell the man was starting to panic. The time passed: 1000 hours… 1030 hours… 1100 hours, and still no sign of the mechanic. Fuller didn't like waiting around, but as he couldn't leave without his engines being tuned, he sent one of the ratings back into the boat to make something warm for his crew to drink.

Finally, at 1145 hours, a low-riding English racing car quickly pulled into the far end of the company's lot, drifting through the main gate in a controlled turn. The driver geared-up, speeding towards them, tires kicking small pebbles and dust into the air.

Fuller's interest was piqued – the person knew how to handle a car.

"This him?" he asked.

"Yes, yes," the manager exclaimed, looking more than a little relieved. He'd been back and forth from his office all morning, trying to reach their specialist by phone. "I'm terribly sorry about the delay but their skill is second to none."

The car was still barreling towards them. Some of the officers and crew began uttering concerns – it looked like the driver was going to drive them all off the pier. Fuller kept his cool – he knew a stunt when he saw one. At the last moment the driver hammered the brakes and turned over the wheel, sliding the car right up alongside them. Some of the men flinched, while others darted out of the way. The manager screamed but

Fuller didn't move – he just crossed his arms and frowned. The panache might have impressed him more if he hadn't been waiting for hours.

Out came the mechanic, wearing slacks and a tucked-in collared shirt with the sleeves rolled high enough to reveal the various tattoos on the arms. The person who emerged had short, wavy blond hair, sunglasses, and a mostly finished cigarette hanging from the lips. Everyone, including Fuller, stared in surprise.

It was a woman.

She gave them all a quick nod, unfazed by their looks, and then took one last, long drag before discarding the butt with a flick of her fingers. Heading to the trunk, the specialist withdrew a large toolbox and an oversized pair of dirty denim overalls, which she quickly slipped into.

"So, I'm guessing these are the boats with the new Packards?" she asked as she approached the group and pulled her front zipper up to just below her collarbone. Fuller was the only one who wasn't at a loss for words.

"Yeah," he replied, extending his hand. "The name's Tom."

She gripped it firmly and smiled. He could feel calluses on her fingers.

"Joe."

"Well Joe, how about we start with my boat?"

Fuller turned and gestured to *11*, ignoring the others who were still standing dumbstruck. Clearly, they'd never seen a woman mechanic before, but then again, neither had Fuller. However, he was eager to get back to Dover and wanted his engines checked first. Part of him was also curious – who was this tattooed woman, who spoke and acted more like an old, crusty salt than a lady? She was an exceptionally skilled driver and, based on the car, had access to money.

The woman turned out to be Marion Barbara 'Joe' Carstairs, a wealthy heiress and British power boat racer known for her less than conventional lifestyle.[57] To Fuller, she acted like one of the guys, which suited him just fine. He liked people he could easily shoot the breeze with. While Carstairs worked away, Fuller watched and took mental notes. She was quick and diligent – this clearly wasn't the first time she'd done this. He also observed that she would always set her cigarette down in the same way so that the end hung off the edge of the engine's steel casing. It was a minor detail, but Fuller had seen mechanics do this before – they worked with dirty, oily machines that were made of heat resistant materials, and prioritized keeping the part of the smoke that went into their mouth clean.

Once his new Packard's were synchronized, Fuller took *11* into the harbour to test things out. The difference in how she handled was noticeable – the MGB felt more responsive at the throttle. At last, he had a boat that was up to the task.

"That woman really knows how to tune high speed engines," he said to his XO. When they returned, he publicly commended Carstairs for her diligence and then ordered his men to cast-off. It was time to head back to the Narrow Seas – they'd been away from the war long enough.

11 arrived at Dover on February 2 and was added to the 2nd MGB Flotilla. Unbeknownst to Fuller, spring would usher in a lot more than just warmer weather – activity in the Narrow Seas was about to significantly heat up, bringing with it ample opportunity for Fuller to engage the enemy. In fact, he would establish a reputation for writing-off boats because of damage sustained in battle. According to his own naval training and experience form, Fuller commanded MGBs *13*, *11*, *9*, and *74* between the months of February and September 1942.[58] He would also serve a short stint as an acting SO with HMS *Fervent* in Ramsgate (possibly taking on a new boat in the process).[59]

Training could only do so much to prepare one for active service in the channel. While seasoned instructors were able to impart basic skills, any real refinement came on the job. Fuller may have been eager to experience combat at sea, but he wasn't naïve to the danger. He took his commands seriously and, as he did in business, sought anything he could get his hands on to increase his knowledge about tactics, best practices, and the inner workings of his vessels. Unfortunately, there wasn't much the RN could provide. While there were numerous manuals and SOPs for larger ships, print resources were slim for coastal forces. When Fuller requested resources on MGB combat tactics, he was instead handed ones for a destroyer and told to make do. Things were further complicated by rapid mobilization programs. Command was focused on increasing numbers, which meant getting new boats in the water and updating the equipment aboard existing vessels. When supplies were short, they resorted to using weapons created for other platforms, jerry-rigging them to work on their boats. And when new equipment did arrive, it often came without reference books.

For instance, during this time three Nash turrets were installed onto one of Fuller's MGBs. He approached the CPO supervising the work and asked, "where are the BRs for the turrets?"

The man turned and, noticing Fuller's rank, gave a salute before replying "they haven't been printed yet sir."

Fuller grimaced. "Well, what about for the engine room?"

"Sorry sir, but we haven't anything," he said with a shrug. "All I know is that they come from the United States and to install them on your boat."[60]

Unfortunately, this was common for most things aboard his boats. "Every piece of equipment we had, everything, no instructions, no books available," Fuller would explain. "There were no operational instructions. You were told, 'just go out and fight and do the best you can.'"

SOs would often try to fill the gap by distributing personal notes. Best practices and procedures were copied and shared between COs. While these insights were valuable, they mostly focused on combat tactics and lacked information regarding basic, yet critical things such as vessel maintenance. After the incident with 49, Fuller tried his best to be ready in case something else unexpectedly broke while underway.

Perhaps the biggest challenge for coastal forces was dealing with total blackout conditions, which made doing even the simplest task a challenge. Fuller remembered finding it hard to load a starshell*: "you'd reach for a two-star cartridge, and you couldn't see whether somebody had changed it, or what the hell hour it was and you were afraid to fire in case it might be wrong." Recognizing friend from foe was also problematic – how could one tell if a barely discernible shape on the horizon was an enemy vessel? When operating with other boats, it was nerve-wracking trying to keep track of each other. Flotillas frequently became separated during patrols and 'friendly' fire incidents became all too common. And the temptation to use lights, even for a moment, could prove fatal. As Fuller would later recount, "You'd just go to flick on your identification lights and they'd be shot away." So, he ordered his lookouts to keep the lenses of their binoculars clean and polished. Touching the glass was taboo – the oil from a finger would leave a smudge and reduce the sailor's ability to see in the dark.[61] Even the most subtle break in the distant horizon's "often indeterminate continuity"[62] needed immediate reporting.

Fuller also found the information provided during mission briefings helpful. Knowing the location of other coastal forces units operating in the area, as well as the movement of Allied convoys, greatly aided in minimizing the number of friendly fire incidents. Many times, a CO would choose to engage simply because the reported object was in the wrong spot and presumed hostile. New technology also eased some of the burden – all RN coastal vessels relied heavily on their TBS sets to communicate with one another. Fuller found this quite useful and, like many of his comrades, particularly took to using simple "ICU" (I see you) and "No CU" codes to quickly discern between friendly and hostile vessels. He would combine this with the reciprocal bearings and distances of the other boat in his message. For example, if the object was thirty degrees and approximately four miles aways, the message sent would be

---

* An incendiary projectile used to temporarily illuminate an area.

"ICU 030 4". If the other vessel replied incorrectly, "you knew goddamn well it was enemy, and you'd open fire." He noted that the enemy never quite caught on to this and would continue to "get into more civil war than you could ever imagine" during his time in the channel.

Fuller resumed patrols in February. He soon realized that commanding an MGB was not unlike being a pilot, ready to 'scramble' at a moment's notice. This made leaving *Wasp* for a night on the town difficult. As he explained, "The situation was that you went to immediate notice to go to sea, or to fifteen minutes, or to an hour." The latter was preferred as it allowed enough time to head into the city: "you could always get back from London in an hour or two." Otherwise, one was stuck at *Wasp* or, in the case of an immediate notice, aboard boat. Fuller tried his best to rest during these times, but without his usual ways of coping, namely socializing and drinking, he couldn't adequately distract his mind. Scenarios kept playing-out in his head – what would he do if this or that happened – and he could never truly rest knowing that at any moment the call to slip could be given. He would later lament, "That goddamn immediate notice and fifteen minutes notice took more out of me than any other thing in the war."[63]

By mid-March, Fuller's performance was again evaluated. The S.206 showed that from October 27, 1941, to March 19, 1942, Fuller had been in command of MGBs *11* and, at the time of the report, *13*.[64] His general conduct was still listed as 'satisfactory' and of 'temperate habit', and his scores were in line with the previous report, although his boat handling was listed as a '7' – above average.[65] *Wasp*'s CO indicated that Fuller was not yet ready to command his own squadron but, his SO, Lt George Dick 'Dicky' Kendall Richards, noted that Fuller was "a very efficient officer, possessing drive and initiative."[66] Still, Fuller needed more time-in before he could be elevated. The report recommended he be considered for promotion 'in ordinary course'.

At Dover, Fuller would meet two other Canadians, Cornelius 'Corny' Burke and John Douglas Maitland, both hailing from the west coast.

Burke, described as "impish and irrepressible"[67], would end up fighting with the 56th Flotilla in the Mediterranean and Adriatic. He knew a life of plenty in his youth, his father the president of Boeing Aircraft. Perhaps, that had something to do with his frequent rule-breaking – being rich often meant getting away with things. In fact, he even smuggled his wife aboard his troop ship by bribing one of the transport officers with a fine bottle of scotch whisky[68]. It certainly must have been of exceptional vintage.

Maitland, on the other hand, boasted a reputation for being tough, a "hard-bitten and crisp of speech"[69] boater who'd been in the middle of a sail on Cowichan Bay when he felt the call to serve. Like Burke, he also often pushed the limits of what the navy considered acceptable behaviour. Indeed, many of these 'citizen sailors'* found the overly regimented world of the RN a bit too inflexible for their taste. Naturally, the three men hit it off and would socialize during off hours (they didn't serve in the flotillas). Interestingly, Fuller's experience at *Wasp* would be quite different than his younger compatriots. While both Burke and Maitland did see some action in the coming weeks, it was nothing in comparison to what Fuller would soon encounter.

He'd wanted a real scrap with the enemy – something more than firing a few rounds at shadows in the night – and by the time May came along, Fuller he would get exactly what he'd been asking for.

---

* The nickname given to Canadians serving in the naval reserve during the Second World War. They were noticeably less regimented than their regular navy counterparts and, in many ways, refused to conform (e.g. being slacked with their uniforms while at sea).

CHAPTER 6

"Stier"

The rain splashed off the deck of MGB *13*. It hit with such force that it bounced off every surface and back into the crew's faces. Dark clouds swirled overhead, void of lightning or thunder, but stirring the sea and dropping an epic deluge. The chop jostled the boat, its bow crashed up and down on the waves, making the passage even more uncomfortable. All the pilot in the wheelhouse could see was a sheet of heavy rain outside the view screens but at least he remained dry.

Fuller and his XO stood at the open bridge. They wore rain gear but it did little to comfort them in the sloppy weather.

"I've never seen rain like this," Fuller said, pausing to find the good in it. "But at least they won't be able to see us."

Keeping close to the other vessels in the flotilla was proving a challenge.

They were on the hunt for a German ship and Fuller's boat was tasked with providing support to an attack force of six MTBs, each armed with torpedoes. Intelligence had reported that the Germans were trying to get a large ship – not quite the size of a heavy cruiser – through the narrowest part of the English Channel: the Dover Strait. The Germans decided to use the rain as cover for moving their ship in daylight. A clever idea, but *Wasp*'s radar had tipped the British off.

Unbeknownst to Fuller and the MTBs was that their prey, the auxiliary cruiser *Stier* – a former merchant ship turned merchant raider – was being ushered to the Atlantic by a sizeable escort.[70] The vessel, disguised to look like a merchant ship converted to be a minesweeper, a *sperrbrecher* in German naval terminology, was protected by sixteen R-Boat minesweepers and four torpedo boats.[71] *Stier* was also a wolf in sheep's clothing, fitted with six 5.9-inch guns, several anti-aircraft pieces, and two torpedo tubes, all hidden behind false walls which could be dropped in an instant to expose the deadly arsenal.[72]

Normally Fuller wouldn't be sent on daylight operation as it proved too risky. Without the cover of darkness, the enemy could spot small boats making them vulnerable to attack form coastal batteries, enemy ships, and worst of all, patrolling aircraft. Still, he appreciated the messy weather for the same reasons the enemy did – they were well hidden, the low clouds and rain making visibility only slightly better than at night.

The rough conditions made many of the MGB crew seasick, including Fuller, although his mug of tea laced with scotch was close at hand, protected from the rain by a makeshift shelter he'd created on the bridge. Taking a measured sip, he noted the diluted taste and sighed, enjoying some relief. The rain had been pouring since they left Dover, nearly thirty minutes ago. The scotch, even if less potent than he preferred, still soothed his stomach. He returned the mug to its place, doing his best to cover it with his free hand. If there was one thing he appreciated, it was at least being able to see where to put it. Most nights he was all but blind and had to rely on memory and touch.

Fuller checked the time and realized they were nearing their objective. He just hoped the clouds and rain would persist long enough for them to complete their mission.

———

Just over an hour into their operation, Fuller's fears were confirmed.

"Crap," he swore under his breath.

Not a good sign. The colour of the clouds started to lighten, the rain softening its assault on their boat. The seas also seemed to ease, and he could see the other boats of their task force with greater clarity. In the distance – he could actually make it out now – he noted the overcast sky started to thin. Their cover was fading.

Instinctively, he looked up to the sky, almost expecting to see the enemy bearing down on them.

"Gunners, keep your eyes peeled," he barked.

Fuller suddenly felt vulnerable.

"You thinking we'll be attacked?" his XO asked.

"The clouds are breaking, and it stopped raining," Fuller said. "I guarantee you they have planes in the sky."

He kept his eyes fixed ahead.

"Hopefully we intercept that ship any moment now, so we can hurry home."

A few tense moments passed, the entire crew seemingly holding its breath. Senses heightened; without the sound of the rain their boat's engines seemed louder – too loud. It made them feel anxious, especially as they were trying their best to go unnoticed. Of course, it was just their minds playing tricks – it's not as if a pilot could hear them. Fuller knew clear skies would provide enemy aircraft all they needed to spot the flotilla. But for the sake of his crew he kept a calm face. He felt betrayed by the weather.

Fuller took another drink. He removed his rain gear, thankful to shed the unwanted layers. They still couldn't see anything in the distance – perhaps the intelligence about the German ship had been wrong.

"Aircraft, far approaching, Green 30, angle of sight 20!"* came the call from a spotter.

Fuller quickly lifted his binoculars to his eyes to scan the horizon just off the starboard bow. He spotted a bunch of large dots through

---

* The lookout is using relative bearings; his warning means he's spotted objects in the sky, 30 degrees off the starboard bow and 20 degrees from the horizon.

a break in the clouds, fighters rapidly becoming visible as they dived on their position. The aircrafts distinctive shape and yellow-noses gave them straight away – a squadron of ME 109s.

German fighter planes.

"Action stations, all guns, fire Green 30!" he ordered. "Evasive manoeuvres!"

His XO slammed a button sounding an alarm throughout the boat. The MGB swerved, and the MTBs followed similarly breaking and adjusting speed as the planes positioned themselves to strafe the flotilla.

"Get up there number one and direct those guns!" Fuller barked.

As the officer scrambled down to the pom-pom platform, MGB *13*'s guns erupted with a chorus of muzzle flashes and sounds, the loud – THUMP, THUMP, THUMP – of his main 40mm deck gun letting out puffs of smoke with each shot. Spent casings of various sizes spilled onto the deck and bounced over the gunwales, disappearing into the waves and spray as they turned.

The planes swooped down, closing the distance and making a strafing pass on the boats. The 109s opened with their 36mm guns, forcing Fuller and his bridge crew to duck as bullets pierced the deck. Rounds splashed through the water and tore through portions of Fuller's MGB as both plane and boat exchanged gunfire.

The enemy aircraft circled for another pass, but the MGB's gunners continuing their assault, chasing the planes with their fire. Fuller's main gun switched from graze to time-fused ammunition – the latter rounds would explode in the sky, and he hoped that an airburst would down an on-coming aircraft*. The planes dove again – his guns fired, rattling the enemy, but failing to score any decisive blows. They were simply too fast.

---

* A fuse is the component of the projectile that causes it to detonate or release shrapnel when the right conditions are met. What causes the fuse to activate changes depending on the round. In this case, Fuller's boat was using both graze and time-fused ammunition. Graze-fused ammunition is triggered when something slows the round, such as hitting a target. Time-fused, as the name suggests, explodes after a pre-set time elapses.

Fuller heard glass break at the wheelhouse, and looked in. One of the Kent clear-view screens had been broken, but the pilot and cox'n remained unharmed. He popped back up.

"Take those bloody bastards down!" he shouted.

THUMP, THUMP, THUMP, his guns replied.

He stared daggers at the aircraft, thinking the 109s were "very efficient craft – not as fast as a Spit, but manoeuvrable." His appreciation for their engineering was tempered by the fact they were trying to kill him.

The German aircraft banked and prepared for a third pass. Fuller hated how vulnerable he felt, but he'd give the enemy one hell of a scrap. The boat zigzagged, alternating its speed, all guns blazing. The other MTBs faced the same challenge, but their limited fire helped to keep the 109s busy, forcing the planes to evade. They kept trading blows, but the Germans had the advantage; exactly the situation Fuller wanted to avoid.

Just then something in the sky caught Fuller's eye – more planes!

"Christ," he hissed.

One of the new aircraft crept in behind the 109s that had just attacked him, flying only forty feet above his boat. The shape and camouflage were familiar – a Hurricane.

"That's one of our planes," he shouted. "Don't shoot at him!"

The MTB gunners, however, were caught in the heat of the moment and didn't differentiate the RAF fighter from the 109s he was pursuing.

"There's friendly aircraft in the sky," he barked through his megaphone, which projected his voice across the water. "Cease fire!"

Fuller persisted until the message reached the other boats. The friendly firing stopped, but not before perforating one of the Hurricanes. The squadron of RAF fighters kept after the enemy aircraft, like sheepdogs chasing predators from a flock.

Fuller felt disappointed by the MTB's blunder, but it wasn't the first time the RAF failed to inform them of incoming air support.

"Of course, everybody informs you of nothing," he often said.

Thankfully, the combined air and surface fire tipped the odds in their favour, convincing the Germans to retreat. The flotilla suffered damage in the fight, some boats reporting injured crewmembers, but no risk of anyone sinking. So, they continued the patrol, eventually meeting up MGB *9* under the command of Lt Ronald "Ronnie" Barge.[73] The sky was still clouded and visibility remained poor despite the rain having stopped.

"She's out there somewhere," Fuller said in reference to their prey. "We'll keep looking until we find and sink her."

———

They patrolled the rest of the evening of May 12 without any signs of *Stier* or her escorts. It wasn't until about two hours after midnight that their vigilance paid off – the sounds of ships moving in the misty night.

Fuller held his binoculars tight to his eyes, concentrating as he slowly scanned the dark for any visuals of the enemy.

"I can't see a bloody thing," he complained, "but from the sounds of it, they're closing on us."

Fuller figured they'd found the convoy, but without visually confirming the presence of the cruiser, they were forced to wait. *13* and other boats slowly moved into formation, ready to pounce when given the signal.

What the coastal vessels didn't realize was that German radar had already discovered them – the enemy was well aware of their presence. *Stier*'s escorts fired starshells to illuminate the waters ahead of them, taking Fuller and the other boats off guard.[74] Blazing white streaks rose into the night, hovering in the sky and revealing everything beneath them. Although their presence was now compromised, at least they could positively identify the merchant raider.

"She's got some hefty escorts," he announced. "I think I spot torpedo boats and some minesweepers."

Aboard MTB *220* the flotilla SO, Lt Eric Alfred Edward Cornish, signaled his boats to make speed and escape into the night before being spotted. Taking on *Stier*'s escorts straight on would be suicidal – they needed the element of surprise if they were to have any chance of sinking the merchant raider.

Stier's presence was radioed back to base and soon shore batteries on the English coast began to fire at the convoy as it approached the Straits of Dover.[75] They continued to harass the Germans over the next hour but were unsuccessful in scoring a hit. During that time, the MTBs and MGBs executed a new plan to encircle the enemy and strike at the cruiser simultaneously from both sides. The flotilla split – MGB *9* went with three MTBs to creep along the port side of the convoy while Fuller and the others went to starboard. They moved slowly, careful not to give away their positions by making any loud engine noises, and by 0330 hours they were in position to attack.[76] Fuller's role was to protect the MTBs as best as he could – without torpedoes, his MGB couldn't do much to sink either *Stier* or her escorts.

Cornish raised flag four – attack with torpedoes – and the MTBs pounced. Fuller ordered all ahead full, his MGB leaping forward as his engines roared. MGB *13* kept in line with his charges, gunners at the ready. They closed quickly, the shapes and outlines of the enemy suddenly appearing through the mist and dark.

"Open fire!" Fuller ordered, hoping that his guns would cover the MTBs advance.

Red tracers flew into the night and arched towards a large torpedo boat that was shadowing the even larger cruiser. Shots splattered harmlessly against the hull and superstructure, eliciting a barrage of green tracer in response.

Up to this point in the war, Fuller's bouts with the enemy had been typical of most MGB/MTB skippers – short and sporadic trading of gunfire during night operations. He only ever glimpsed the enemy and doubted he'd ever scored a hit during any encounter. But he'd learned some valuable lessons which were now paying off. Over the previous months he'd observed that the enemy relied heavily on the use of tracer rounds during battles – bullets with a pyrotechnic charge that burned either green, red, orange, yellow or white when fired*. They assisted in helping gunners see the trajectory of their gunfire, but the Germans were using them too much.

Fuller likened it to baseball – even though the ball came at quite a speed, the distance made it possible for the batter to recognize a bad pitch and move out of the way. As shots didn't typically come at point-blank range, Fuller could spot coloured streaks coming towards his boat. He'd simply order his cox'n "hard aport" and the rounds would land harmlessly somewhere in the water on their starboard side.

In this fashion, he guided his boat to evade the return fire as the MTBs made their first pass at the merchant raider. The night and plethora of R-boats, which seemed to be now appearing all around them, made it challenging to get a clear shot. Only one MTB let loose a torpedo which missed the target.

They banked, Fuller's guns now freely peppering various vessels as they weaved their way through escorts and back to open water. Enemy starshells soared above, and combined with the gunfire, the dark waters became nearly as clear as day.[77] Circling back, Fuller could see for the first time the mass of vessels shielding *Stier* from a clear shot. He doubted they'd be able to get a run at the cruiser and weaving back into the convoy seemed impractical. Fuller made smoke to shield the MTBs' retreat, following-in behind as they sped into the night.

Meanwhile, on the port side of the convoy, the MTBs were having similar troubles – their first run had been unsuccessful and they'd also been forced by enemy fire to retreat to prepare for a second attack.

---

* There's a common misconception that the German military only used green tracer rounds, mainly due to movies, but in fact they were known to use a mix of colours. Some have suggested this was purposely done to confuse the enemy.

"We can't get that close again now that they've lit up the whole damn place," Fuller said into the wheelhouse. "Radio the MTBs to attack at a distance unless they want to be full of holes."

Coming about they prepared for a second assault, this time coming straight on as if to cross the enemy's T, but letting loose their torpedoes and turning back before getting torn apart by enemy crossfire. Once again Fuller's boat peppered the closest escorts with both machine and his 40mm guns, and again the MTBs found it difficult to get a clear shot. And so it went for nearly half an hour, the coastal vessels making their charges and then evading enemy fire as they slipped back into the cover of darkness, neither side scoring a decisive hit. But the MTBs and MGBs started to report damages and casualties, and even Fuller's boat had taken a few hits and lost a gunner. Then, just before 0400 hours, Cornish's boat was rammed by a torpedo boat and shot beyond recognition. The SO, along with the officers and most of the crew, were killed.

As some of the escorts broke formation to pursue their attackers, MTB *21* was finally given a clear shot at the cruiser. Escorted by Fuller, they pressed in, *13* strafing nearby ships while *21* launched a torpedo. It missed, passing across *Stier*'s bow, but luckily struck the torpedo boat *Iltis* amidships.[78] The resulting explosion broke the 303-foot ship's back – she sunk in two pieces, taking 115 crewmen with her.

Cheers erupted aboard both boats, Fuller again making smoke to mask their retreat. Almost fifteen minutes later, SLt Barry Easton, in command of MTB *221*, scored another torpedo boat.[79] He'd made a patch of smoke ahead of *Stier* to throw off some escorts that were in hot pursuit but waited for the enemy to creep around it.[80] *Seeadler*, a 287-type 23 torpedo boat, was the first to appear. MTB *221* launched a torpedo and, like *Iltis*, struck the vessel amidships. She rolled over and capsized before breaking apart. Eighty-five of her crew perished.[81]

Many of the remaining escorts went on the attack, determined to chase the MTBs away from *Stier*. MTB *219*, under the command of SLt

Mark Arnold Forster, took oncoming fire which penetrated his hull and damaged one of his engines. He was at half power and pursued by six torpedo boats and some R-boats.[82] They were too close for him to turn and fire torpedoes in defence and he couldn't move fast enough to shake them.[83] Shots splashed around his boat – he was in a bad spot. Panicked, he called upon both Fuller and Barge to assist, but MGB *9* had been severely damaged by this point and could not help. That left just Fuller.

Aboard *13*, Fuller received word via the RT voicepipe that Forster was in peril.

"Tell him we're on route," Fuller replied. "Sounds like he has his hands full."

At this point, MGB *13* had escorted three MTBs away from the fray and had to turn about and head back for *219*. They sped back, receiving constant reports from Forster – at one point *219* actually thought they'd managed to lose their pursuers, but a few starshells and shots landing near the stern proved otherwise. In the chaos, Fuller had trouble finding the MTB, but eventually managed to see the starshells and green tracers in the distance.

"He's really in the thick of it," Fuller realized. "Let's see what we can do."

It was a gutsy move – he'd already sustained damage and casualties aboard his boat. He'd be making himself a target to help save Forster. But that was Fuller's style. He didn't back down from a fight nor shy from coming to the aid of his comrades.

From the darkness, MGB *13* came at the enemy amidships, his gunfire likely surprising the German ships that had been focused on the wounded MTB. He banked hard, spraying the vessels with shots and then turned about, allowing his aft gun to pepper the enemy. The guerilla tactic caused confusion, allowing *219* enough respite to slip into the dark. Fuller similarly tore off and escaped – he wasn't keen to trade fire with the larger vessels. His maneuver had been so quick that Forster never even noticed it and remained unaware that an MGB had come to assist.[84]

The wounded *219* managed to meet up with the rest of the battered flotilla while Fuller's boat, having taken a bit of a detour, joined shortly thereafter. By this time the morning was quickly approaching. The sun would be rising soon and with it, the loss of their cover. They were bloodied and in no position to continue the attack – as much as it pained them, they couldn't go back for survivors*. Their only choice was to make for home. Unfortunately, despite disrupting the convoy, they'd failed in sinking *Stier*.

The sun had risen by the time they'd passed through the defence boom at Ramsgate[85], an alternate base for the 2nd MGB Flotilla. Fuller and his crew secured their vessels, moved casualties to the care of waiting ambulances, and began the business of repairs and replenishment. Not long afterwards, they received word from the RAF pilot the flotilla had shot at the previous day. RAF station Manston complained that the Hurricane "looked like a pepper pot."

Fuller shook his head, annoyed by the news, but noticed a smile creeping across the face of his twin point-five gunner.

"What's so funny?"

"Aw shucks, sir," the sailor replied. "I coulda got him. A cinch."

Despite having failed to stop the merchant raider, the battle hadn't been a total loss. Against staggering odds, coastal forces still managed to sink two vessels and damage several others. As author and MTB skipper Sir Peter Scott would later note, "it was a notable achievement."[86] The RN certainly thought so. In total, two DSCs, three DSMs, and five MiDs would be awarded "For skill, bravery and resolution while serving in H.M. Motor Torpedo Boats and Motor Gun Boats in an attack on any Enemy Convoy near the French Coast."[87] One of those DSCs would be

---

* After *Stier* arrived at Boulogne, some E-Boats went back to the scene of the attack and picked-up both British and German Survivors, as well as salvage the wreck of MTB *220*.

awarded to Fuller on July 14, 1942.[88] A naval message to NSHQ Ottawa dated September 7, 1942, confirmed that "The King has approved DSC to temp Lt. T. G. Fuller RCNVR FOR GOOD SERVICE IN ATTACK ON ENEMY SHIPS." Back home, Fuller's name popped up in some newspapers and reporters even interviewed his family. When asked about their son's action against the enemy, Fuller's father didn't have much to say; his son had simply noted at the end of a letter: "and by the way, I got the DSC a couple of days ago."[89]

Although Fuller seldom shied from taking credit for his ideas – especially the good ones – nor criticize anything he considered harebrained, he didn't like to be in the limelight. He especially detested coming off as braggadocious when speaking about his own valour, choosing instead to minimize his actions or focus on the deeds of others. He wasn't a simple man and such contradictions, being both proud and reserved, were simply who Fuller was. And although he enjoyed telling some true dits, as any good sailor does, he focused less on combat and more on the oddities and shenanigans he witnessed (or took part in) overseas. He either didn't see himself as, or didn't want attention for being, a hero.

But finally, Fuller had achieved a long sought-after goal – his first real fight against the enemy. After repeated rejections by RCAF and RCN recruiters and multiple attempts by the RN to put him in less active roles, he'd shown them all what he was made of. And from that point on, "Gramps" became a respected member of Dover patrol. But if Fuller believed he'd seen the first and last of his fighting days, he would soon be proven mistaken. Later that summer he'd once again find himself in the thick of it and at the centre of a legendary battle that would cement his reputation as one of Coastal Forces most daring COs.

CHAPTER 7

—◇◇◉◇◇—

Running the Gauntlet

The summer of 1942 came with warm air and conditions favourable for night operations – little precipitation, clear skies, and calm waters. The enemy pounced on the opportunity to ramp up their minelaying operations and supply runs, while RN Coastal Forces, flush with new vessels, increased patrols. Frequent encounters kept Fuller and the 2nd MGB Flotilla busy throughout June and July, but it seemed that things had mostly returned to how they were prior to his battle against *Stier* – the odd trading of gunfire, mostly with E-boats, which at most looked like dark shapes moving in the night. When his flotilla did come upon the enemy, usually announced by a quick burst of tracer, they'd evade, return fire, and listen to the fading sounds of retreating engines. In a matter of seconds the affair was over.

Fuller was determined to meet the enemy head-on and actively went out of his way to get into fights. He wouldn't let anyone deter him from his goal. In fact, during one of his summer patrols a senior officer, wanting to see some action, decided to join Fuller aboard *13*. However, once green tracers flew overhead the officer panicked and ordered the boat to disengage. An argument broke out on the bridge leading to the senior officer declaring himself in command of the vessel. But Fuller wouldn't have any of it.

"I hit the bugger with a number 6 Pyrex fire extinguisher," he would tell reporter Dave Brown during an interview, "[I] ordered re-engagement and stood on him through the whole action."[90]

Upon returning to base, Fuller went to *Wasp*'s CO, and admitted the whole thing without reservation.

"I had to report myself for mutiny," he explained, punctuating the sentence with a piratical "Har!"

It's a wonder that Fuller, who by the end of his naval career would be severely reprimanded on numerous occasions, was never arrested or formally punished for the assault. Perhaps the ad hoc nature of Coastal Forces and dire straits the RN found itself in during that period of the war allowed Fuller to escape unscathed. Undoubtedly, being a decorated officer and skilled skipper played in his favour. Whatever the reason, it was good that Fuller avoided time in the brig – his skills would be needed in the channel, especially when a seemingly routine operation in August turned into a brazen firefight with the enemy.

————

The day started like most. After spending the afternoon aboard MGB *13*, Fuller and his number one were summoned ashore to receive the night's orders, leaving the midshipman and cox'n to finalize preparations so they could slip upon their return. They entered *Wasp*'s operation room – rows of leather backed wood chairs facing a wall of maps and charts – and noted his SO, Lt Cdr Richards, the same person who'd completed Fuller's previous reports, sitting in the front. He was a handsome and dapper looking man, accompanied by a much younger Lt Bray, who was acting as the flotilla's spare CO. Compared to Fuller, the latter officer looked like a kid. Richards shot him one of his signature smiles – warm, confident, and genuine – and Fuller nodded in return. Another boat's command team sat a few seats away and Fuller decided to settle himself in one of the chairs closest to the entrance while his XO took the seat beside him, a notepad and pencil at the ready. It would be his task to jot down any key information during the meeting and leave the questions and talking to his CO. They barely had a chance to acknowledge the other officers in the room before Cdr Sanders entered.

"Right, let's get started gentlemen," he announced as he marched up to the lectern at the front of the room, "feel free to smoke."

A couple of officers drew out pipes, already packed to the brim with tobacco, and lit them with matches. Soon, the space filled with the familiar aromas of spice and rose, which lingered in grey clouds collecting beneath the room's lights. Sanders sorted some papers he'd brought in a folder before grabbing a long cane off a table and using it to point at an area of the large map of the English Channel, just off the French coast.

"Three boats from the 2nd MGB Flotilla will be conducting an offensive mine laying operation here," he announced.

Fuller had guessed as much – his vessel had been outfitted with mines earlier that day.

"We've received information that the enemy has been moving supplies through this area," Sanders continued. "Your mines are meant to disrupt their operations."

Fuller suppressed a sigh. Although he saw the merits in doing these missions, dropping mines was a far cry from hunting down the enemy and slugging it out with one's guns. He already sensed how the night would go – they'd head to their position, set the trap, and be back home before it was sprung. He felt deflated.

"Should be a routine mission, gentlemen," Sanders concluded, validating Fuller's thoughts. He answered a few questions before dismissing the group.

The officers departed to their respective boats. Fuller boarded his vessel and began what had now become a nightly ritual – slipping into his Ursula suit, hanging his binoculars around his neck, and putting on his cap before walking out onto the bridge.

"Let's ready to slip number one," he ordered, sounding less than enthused.

The order was dutifully followed and soon the boat gave a familiar shake as the engines coughed and roared to life, filling the air with the smell of high-octane petrol. Once *Wasp*'s signal tower flashed its approval,

Fuller gave the order to let go the spring lines and move the boat away from her moorings.

"Slow ahead together," he said through the voice pipe.

MGB *13* fell behind the other two boats which were already in line to head out the boom-gate. Richard's boat was in front and he could see the SO looking back at the other two boats through his binoculars. Shortly thereafter Richard's voice came over the RT speaker.

"Good evening captains, a surprisingly temperate night for this time in August. Lots of visibility tonight and only a few clouds. Keep in close formation and watch for my signals."

"Let's get this over with," Fuller thought.

The gates opened and the vessels left the safety of *Wasp*'s harbour, cutting deep white plumes into the fading light which sent waves crashing against the breakwater. Then, one by one, each part of the boat reported they were ready for action.

"You've got the bridge number one," Fuller announced. "I'll be in my cabin. Let me know when we're in position or if anything happens."

He went below and once in his cabin, slipped off his cap and laid on his bunk, leaving his binoculars on, just in case. The boat moved slightly, and he wedged his boot into the corner of the bed frame to keep himself in place. His eyes closed and he rested, confident his XO would retrieve him once they arrived.

———

The slowing of the engines caused Fuller to wake up. A moment later he heard a voice from the brass pipe near the head of his bunk. They were in position.

"Right, get started," he ordered. "I'm coming up."

Things were running pretty ship-shape aboard his boat – it had all become routine at this point. He even anticipated the knock at his cabin and the cup of hot tea that had been prepared for him, which he took the liberty of enhancing with a bit of scotch. That was a part of Fuller's routine. Even if the seas were calm tonight, they'd be moving slow which could upset his stomach. Better to be safe.

After taking a moment to check on the pilot and cox'n, he emerged on the bridge and was greeted by his XO who reported that they were ready to drop the first mine overboard. It was slow work – each mine not only had to be dropped in the right position but then recorded on a chart in the pilot's workstation. Keeping track of their location was critical as having a RN ship run into their own trap would be more than a little counterproductive.

It was going to be a long night but Fuller tried to make the best of it, sipping his tea and routinely sweeping the horizon. The warm and stale air felt pleasant enough – at least it wasn't humid – and there were only a few clouds in the sky, providing momentary glimpses at the moon and stars above. Unlike previous nights, he could see quite a bit more of his surroundings. Of course, that also made them vulnerable, but the passing clouds helped to reduce the light which could assist a lookout in spotting their vessels.

It was past midnight by the time the last of the mines were set. Fuller sent a message to Richards to inform the SO of his status and then looked back and imagined where the mines lay beneath the calm surface. All he could see was dark water and the small white cresting waves from his boat's wake. They were invisible.

He didn't envy the ship that would run into them.

His flotilla was only one of many mine laying operations and he wondered what the chances were of an enemy ship triggering one the explosives tonight.[91] Although Coastal Forces routinely conducted offensive minelaying operations, it wasn't a primary duty. When the right conditions presented themselves, command would jump on the opportunity. However, the main bread and butter of the RNs little ships remained the same – to engage enemy vessels. And that was what Fuller would rather be doing tonight.

"Red 10, near, multiple objects."

Fuller's senses came alive – the message had come from the forward lookout. He brought his binoculars up to his eyes and peered deep into the darkened waters. It took a moment but he finally made out some shapes, moving northbound – nowhere near the mines. Good thing his lookouts were staying sharp, they might have slipped by unnoticed.

"I think I count over seven of them," he said to his XO.

In his peripheral he could see the man conferring with his own lenses, unknowingly chewing his bottom lip as his eyes tried to confirm the number.

"More I'd say," the man replied, "but I can't make out a number. It's certainly big."

"And slow," Fuller added, "can't be doing more than 8 knots."

Although he still couldn't see specifics, he did note smaller profiles, possibly escorts flanking the larger vessels.

"I think there's an E-boat escort," he concluded. "Send word to the SO and sound action stations."

The alarm rang throughout the boat and sailors commenced a well-choreographed routine. Gunners and loading parties readied their weapons, swinging the barrels from side to side as they checked their equipment and drew ammunition from the ready use lockers. Hatches were shut and the engine room secured, the whole boat steeling itself for a possible fight.

To his surprise, Fuller had been wrong about this evening. It looked like he just might get the scrap he wanted after all.

"Right, that's enough," he said and the alarm was silenced.

Fuller's eyes never left the objects in the distance – slow convoys were bad news. Fast convoys were usually lightly defended and easier to attack, but slow ones usually meant one thing – flak trawlers. These heavily armoured tugboats were a nuisance for coastal forces, their inch-thick shielding nearly impossible to penetrate. Making matters worse, they were also well armed, including an 88mm deck gun, multiple anti-air artillery pieces (20-40mm guns), and plenty of smaller weapons.

Years later Fuller would explain the difficulty: "They could just stay there and pound the hell out of you, and all you had was three-eighths wood topside with double quarter-inch teak decks."

He lowered his face to one of the voice pipes and ordered the cox'n to turn the boat, so that the bow would face the direction the ships were passing. Although he hadn't yet received directions from the SO, Fuller anticipated that Richards would want to get a closer look and come at the convoy from the front. The darkness and their speed would allow them to surprise the enemy.

As expected, the SO ordered his boats to close in. He would need to better identify the convoy before deciding whether or not to attack. A few moments passed, the distant shapes creeping closer and closer to their position. Details gradually came into focus, unfortunately confirming what Fuller had already guessed – they were indeed trawlers but his numbers had been way off. There were twenty-two vessels, eight E-boats escorting a group of fourteen flak trawlers, divided into two columns of seven.

The three MGBs were outnumbered and outgunned.

Fuller wondered what Richards would do – would he go for it or order them to retreat?

He didn't wait long. *13* received a TBS message from the SO indicating that the flotilla would make a quick pass at the enemy.*

Fuller smiled – he liked Richards' style.

"Okay gents, looks like we're in for a fight," he called out.

From a quiet and stealthy crawl, the three boats accelerated all ahead full, moving into attack formation. At speed, they bore down on the unsuspecting ships, appearing so quickly out of the night that the enemy was taken completely unawares.

"Open Fire!" Fuller ordered.

---

* It isn't clear from the sources whether Richards' forces, despite being in such a precarious situation, decided to make moves to engage the enemy, or were spotted by the enemy and, after receiving fire, sensibly decided to flee. The former seems likely.

The deafening rattle and banging of guns interrupted. Fuller watched as bright red tracers rose and fell onto the targets as he and the other two boats strafed the enemy in three clear arcs of fire. He barely registered the sounds of shots striking wood and steel.

They'd just stirred the hornet's nest.

Aboard MGB *10*, Bray assessed the scene. Although momentarily stunned, the enemy quickly recovered and responded by unleashing what he called "the usual assortment of whizzbangs, tracers, and starshells"[92] but it was too late to catch the racing MGBs who blew past the enemy and back into the night. Richards led his flotilla away from the convoy – if they weren't so outmatched, he might have signalled his boats to make another pass but, given the odds, he reasoned they'd done all they could to disrupt the enemy this night. The flashes and sounds of gunfire faded in their wake. Eventually, the retaliatory firing ceased, the enemy realizing the attack was over.

Only then did Bray notice they were missing a boat.

It was easy to lose sight of both friend and foe in the dark. Still, Bray swore aloud in admonishment over his oversight. Richards gave him a puzzled look but before Bray could explain enemy gunfire erupted once again, tracers and starshells exploding in a distant display of lights.

"What the devil are they shooting at?" Richards spat, looking back with his binoculars.

The colour drained from Bray's face as the pieces fell together.

"It's *13* sir," he replied somberly.

Richards frowned, only now noticing that Fuller's boat was missing. "Bloody hell," he said, "did he lose power?"

It was the only reasonable conclusion – why else would Fuller's boat be there unless he suffered engine problems or the enemy had managed to score a lucky shot. Mechanical failures weren't infrequent, especially with patch jobs and hastily upgraded vessels, such as it was during Fuller's first patrol in *49*. However, *13* was a better boat – it had been converted from a MA/SB and originally fitted with twin Napier petrol engines before being upgraded like MGB *11*.[93] Still, from their vantage point, it seemed to make sense – voluntarily staying to fight would be suicide.

Both men watched helplessly at the distant assault. Little could be done now. Bray would later report witnessing "a terrific concentration of fire, all of which seemed to be directed on one spot where we thought we could see a boat."[94]

Both MGBs slowed, everyone on deck watching the demise of their ally.

"Poor old Tom," Bray remarked, "he's had it. There won't be anything left by the time we get there."

"We're going back," Richards announced, "maybe we can draw some of their fire."

But before he could issue his orders the voice of his telegraphist came up the brass pipe – they'd just received a signal.

"From who?" Richards demanded.

"From *13* sir," came the reply.

The SO and Bray exchanged looks.

———

Fuller's boat hadn't broken down. He'd stayed to fight.

As the other two MGBs escaped he turned his boat around, believing the intent was to continue the attack and just happened to position his bow right in the middle of the convoy – directly between the two columns of flak trawlers. His number one shot him a nervous look, but Fuller remained determined, a fiery gaze in his eyes. He also had no idea the other two vessels were making speed away from the convoy. Fuller figured they were both coming about for another attack, and he would be the one to lead the charge.

He also saw a golden opportunity – a chance to trick the enemy. Based on their formation, the Germans were set up to repel an attack coming from their flanks, the E-boats positioned as sentries on the port and starboard of the convoy. The idea was to protect the larger vessels but the gap between the two lines of trawlers was key. He figured they would never expect a boat to be brazen enough to attack them from the middle, sandwiched between guns with little space to move. But to Fuller, running the gauntlet made perfect sense. His MGB was fast and small enough to manoeuvre in the space. The move would take the Germans off guard, delay their response, and give him the edge.

His mind was set.

"All ahead full!" he ordered.

13's engines roared to life, his boat shooting towards the convoy at over 20 knots. As expected, the enemy's gaze still lingered to the open water and he entered the gap between the trawlers without contest, the cover of night and speed masking his approach.

At his command, all guns opened fire, spraying rounds at ships on both sides. To the port and starboard, tracers arched into the enemy, bullets ripping across decks. Confused German sailors screamed as rounds tore through flesh, others ducking for cover behind reinforced plating. Officers looked past the E-boats expecting to catch a glimpse of their attacker, completely unaware the fire was coming from the centre of their convoy. Just as Fuller predicted.

"Keep at it!" Fuller yelled, although the sound of gunfire drowned out his command. It didn't matter – his gunners knew what to do.

Aim, fire, reload, repeat.

Spent casings littered the deck as sweaty hands gripped shaking weapons, fingers pulling tightly on triggers as eyes honed in on each passing target. They were closer to the enemy than they'd ever been. In the muzzle flashes, Fuller could see moments of detail, scurrying Germans leaping for cover, awash in the reddish light of his passing tracers. This was the pitched battle he'd longed for – a real fight.

Some of the trawlers turned their guns inward to intercept the blur that shot by. With loud bangs, starshells streaked into the night, but Fuller was already out of sight. Nonetheless, the pressure to reciprocate led to a mix of red and green tracer fire that crisscrossed well behind Fuller's boat. As precaution, he ordered his vessel to begin zigzagging – a difficult feat in the limited space.

Fuller rested his hands on the bridge panel in front of him, registering the vibrations of his vessel – he felt the ship moving, the strength of his engines giving him confidence. He gave steady commands to the cox'n, watching his bow sway left and right as they slithered their way up the convoy. Looking through the gaps between the trawlers he didn't see any signs that the other two MGBs had engaged. He never expected the others to follow him through the gap but figured Richards would have attacked the enemy's flanks, drawing some of the Germans' fire and attention. Only then did he realize that he was alone.*

Fuller lifted the cover of the voice pipe that led to his telegraphist.

"Hey, Sparks," he said, "Send the following message to the SO: having lots of fun, come and join us!"[95]

Since the trawler's gunners were firing blindly into the gap they made a critical mistake – instead of shooting at the MGB, many of the trawlers fired at the adjacent boats on the other side of the column. Gunners on both sides confused their ally's tracers as that of their attacker and in short order, the trawlers began targeting each other, neither side realizing the error. As Fuller's boat breached the front of the column, his guns fell silent so that he could escape into the night, but as he looked back he was shocked to see the trawlers locked in a deadly exchange of friendly-fire.

The MGB made a gradual turn, careful to keep its distance but allowing Fuller and his crew to take in the scene. He felt ecstatic – he never anticipated his attack would be this successful.

"We'll let them shoot it out,"[96] he said.

As the friendly-fire battle raged on Fuller's crew celebrated and broke off the attack. Too late did the trawlers realize their mistake – by the

---

* In the chaos of night fighting, the SO's intent could be easily confused. The author agrees with Nolan and Street's conclusion that Richards wasn't the type to flee from a fight or abandon a friend. He was likely shocked when he realized that Fuller hadn't joined them.

time they ceased fire, they'd already inflicted significant damage to each other. The convoy would have to abort the mission and return home for repairs.

"What the devil did you do?" Richards asked once *13* met up with them.

"I'll tell you over a drink," Fuller replied slyly, "and you're buying."

It was every skipper's mission to upset enemy convoys and Fuller had singlehandedly disrupted one in spectacular fashion. Upon returning to Dover, he had quite a story to tell, but some of his crew didn't appreciate their CO's spirit. Two of his gunners criticized the attack, stating "Twenty-two to one – bit heavy in the way of odds, don't you think?"[97] Still, his crew were growing ever fonder of Gramps, and despite his toughness, even sought to stay with him as he took on other commands. Their CO might be a fire-eater, but he always brought them back home.

Fuller's decision to fight, and even the tone of his snappy signal to Richards' boat, were becoming hallmarks of his command style. As another Canadian naval officer serving at Dover reflected, Fuller was "definitely of the two-gun variety."[98] Age and experience taught him to trust his own judgment and that boldness led to great rewards. He called things the way he saw them, even if it meant being insubordinate towards senior officers, and his unmistakably cavalier attitude followed him both in and out of combat.

It had been an explosive summer but Fuller's fighting days were far from done. This was only the beginning of a truly unique naval career and engaging two convoys would not be the greatest of his wartime deeds. Indeed, the man, who would later be called a pirate by his enemies, was just getting started.

CHAPTER 8

— ◇◈◇ —

Rough Night

Fuller's solo foray in the narrow seas earned him quite the reputation. In a matter of days, everyone knew something about the daring old Canadian who singlehandedly attacked an enemy convoy. It gave him credibility in the eyes of his peers, allowing him to forge connections with the other COs stationed at *Wasp*.*

As it was, fitting in with the old guard proved a bit of a challenge. When he first arrived at Dover, Fuller found himself the odd man out. The other officers, all RN, RNR, or RNVR types, were Englishmen, and while Fuller noted that they "treated foreigners with a great deal of courtesy", he also expressed that there "wasn't any companionship or fellowship in it." For a person who enjoyed socializing, the isolation was difficult to bear. Making matters worse, his fellow Canadians, Maitland and Burke, were posted on the other side of the Thames estuary – how he missed their company during lulls in patrols.

---

* Oddly, Fuller didn't receive formal recognition for this action, despite the daringness of the attack. Some earlier publications have confused the DSC awarded in July for his actions for the evening of May 12/13 for this event, but that didn't occur until August. Honours are tricky – one must be nominated and quite a bit of paperwork is involved. Future actions will also go unrecognized or lumped together, despite being entirely different actions and in different locations.

A pecking order existed in the wardroom – while the King's commission granted an officer the privilege of entry, it didn't mean the others accepted them. A seat at the table could only be earned by proving one's mettle. COs were first and foremost hunters, united by a singular mindset which the famed MTB skipper Capt Peter Dickens, described as "the resolution to attack". Respect was granted to those who adopted aggressive tactics and actively sought to engage the enemy in combat. A formalized system of 'aces' may not have existed among the commanders of the RN's little ships, but the social hierarchy of the wardroom mirrored it all the same. Due to the way coastal forces operated, the nature and frequency of their close-quarter battles, and the cult of respect that followed battle-hardened COs, it's of little surprise why theses fast-moving vessels were often referred to as the "Spitfires of the Seas."

RAdm Sir Morgan-Giles DSO, OBE, GM, DL, who as a young Lt Cdr directed coastal operations in the Adriatic, noted that "they had as much stress and strain as any airman does," although unlike "airmen, in fighters or in bomber command do thirty ops and then are taken off" Morgan-Giles explained that "the ships company in the MTBs did... two years out there."[99]

And that's why things took a sudden change for Fuller after the attack on *Stier*. As he would later explain, his DSC "made all the difference in the world." Suddenly, the other COs no longer ignored him.

"Tom, can we buy you a drink?" they offered, extending an invitation. "We're going over to Folkstone for dinner, you must come over with us."

Just like that, he'd been accepted.

Furthermore, the daringness of his recent escapade earned a great deal of praise, elevating him to the top of the hierarchy. His moniker now became a mark of respect – just like an elder, they respected 'Gramps' for his experience and tenacity.

He continued patrolling throughout the summer, and while he frequently encountered the enemy, they were fleeting moments –

darkness, a subtle change in the horizon, volleys of tracers, and then more darkness. Often, his MGB got hit, and the sight of Gramps returning with a pockmarked boat became a common occurrence. Even Fuller confessed that his MGBs took damage "practically every time" and he noticed that repair crews were awaiting his arrival – they anticipated having work to do if the old Canuck had gone out. And if the vessel sustained significant damage, Fuller would head directly to Poole and pick up a new boat. Sometimes it wasn't even worth attempting repairs and the vessel would be written-off.

Command encouraged this aggressive approach. Proactive methods were needed to disrupt enemy operations, and damaged vessels were simply a cost of doing business. Rather than discourage innovation, SOs were given a fair bit of room to experiment, and Fuller was the sort of skipper who constantly worked new angles.

For instance, he invented a unique way to use depth charges against large surface ships. Ever since his first encounter with flak trawlers, Fuller kept trying to find a way to neutralize this threat. The guns on his boat were too small a calibre to penetrate them and while a torpedo could easily do the trick, he lacked the required qualification to use them. So, until he found himself enrolled at the RN's torpedo school – the prerequisite for commanding an MTB – Fuller needed to make do with what he had. And the only thing with enough punch to sink a trawler was a depth charge.

While his boat was armed with four Mk VI depth charges, they were designed to attack submerged U-boats. The bomb would roll off the side or stern, sink to a pre-set depth, typically anywhere between 30 to 300 feet, and then explode. If dropped in the right place, and configured to detonate at the correct depth, the explosion would rupture the submersible's pressurized hull. However, if set shallow, the charge could also damage a surface vessel. The trick would be figuring-out a way to deploy the charge – to position the bomb close enough to the enemy to breach its hull while also avoiding any repercussions from the blast.

Unlike corvettes and destroyers, MGBs didn't have side launchers that could propel a depth charge through the air, and while they could easily drop one near the target, the bomb might explode before they could achieve a safe distance. And a Mk VI, with a 300-pound charge, could do substantial damage to an MGB caught within the blast radius if the MGB were travelling at less than 12 knots when the charge was dropped.

Problems were opportunities for Fuller, and he tackled this one with his usual vigour. He ran daytime experiments outside Dover harbour, using practise targets to simulate enemy surface ships. After some trial and error, he devised a solution using shallow-water pistols and some extra line. It went like this: a line would be fixed to both the MGB and the depth charge. Upon seeing a target, the drum would be put over the stern and dragged behind the MGB, about twenty-five feet under the water. They would then cut across the enemy's bow and release the drum, the shallow settings on the pistol causing it to explode almost immediately. The line not only kept the charge level, preventing it from prematurely exploding, but also a safe distance away from the MGB. A simple, yet efficient solution.

It had Fuller written all over it.

Naturally, everyone took interest in Gramps' project, including command. The concept impressed and the decision was made to issue MGBs with an alternative explosive, specifically designed for surface ships – floating contact mines. Known as R mines, they were all linked by a few lengths of cable and equally spaced apart. When the first mine went over the side, it pulled the others with it, whereby they would spread apart. The soluble plugs around the protuberances – the horns jutting out from the mine – would gradually allow water to seep in, causing the weapon to sink just below the surface and arm itself. When the bow of an enemy ship pushed against the cable, it pulled the mines against the hull, triggering one or more of the horns. The resulting explosion would nearly obliterate the vessel.

Fuller wasted little time putting them to use. While conducting a routine patrol circuit, he came across a lone flak trawler in the channel – the perfect opportunity to test the new weapon. Breaking off from his flotilla, he circled behind the trawler and passed it on the starboard side. Then, cutting across her bow at a forty-five degree angle, they released the R mines directly ahead of the ship. It was a textbook move – even if the trawler tried to evade, they were too close to avoid the trap. The hull caught the line and pulled the explosives in....

WOOF!

The dark made it difficult to see the explosion, though the sound and concussion allowed his imagination to fill in the gap. Fuller waited for the waters to settle before raising his binoculars up to his eyes. Expecting to catch debris on the surface he was surprised to see that the trawler was still intact.

"It's still there," he muttered. "All ahead slow number one – I want to see what happens."

The boat slowed and he took a sip of his drink before fixing his binoculars again on the vessel. A few minutes passed and still the boat hadn't sunk. His mood darkened.

"What gives?"

He wasn't the only one confused. Beside him his XO shook his head – as far as he could tell it had all gone according to plan. Fuller knew there was no point lingering around; E-boats were likely inbound, so he gave the order to head home.

As the MGB sped through the night, he kept replaying the incident in his head. He reasoned something must have gone wrong – why else hadn't the trawler been destroyed? Although stout vessels, a water mine should have easily torn open the hull.

That's when he remembered something about the explosion, particularly the way it looked. A blast below the surface shot water up and into the sky, creating what looked like a white plume in the night. But that wasn't what he saw – the explosion looked dark, meaning the

R mine must have detonated before it sank. And if it didn't explode underneath the trawler, then the heavy side plating might have absorbed enough of the blast to keep the ship afloat.

It begged the question: how did the weapon arm itself if the water hadn't yet dissolved the plugs?

The next morning, Fuller addressed the problem with his officers – he wanted to hear what they thought. His midshipman offered a suggestion: "Sir, I think we should test the water mines."

"What's your idea?"

"Take the boat out into the channel and drop one mine over the side and observe what it does in daylight," he replied.

The idea had merit, and so Fuller decided to conduct the experiment. He requested and received permission from the SO to perform the test, and in short order they found themselves in their MGB, idling outside the harbour. A mine was lowered into the water, remaining secured to the boat by a cable. The midshipman, stopwatch in hand, began to measure how long it took to sink while Fuller sipped his special tea. After only three and half seconds, the R mine sank.

Fuller nearly spat out his drink – that shouldn't have happened. The process was supposed to be gradual, not immediate. "That isn't good," he said. "Heave the bloody thing back up and let's have another look at these damn mines."

Carefully, the explosive was lifted back to the surface and onto the deck. Fuller leaned in to conduct a closer inspection of the protuberances. It took him a few seconds to notice that something was missing. A look of alarm shot across his face.

"The plugs are all gone under the horns," he exclaimed, stepping back from the mine. "The goddamn thing is armed!"

If only he'd known before deciding to bring it back aboard. Now he was staring at fully armed sea mine, laying precariously on this deck. It was too late to put it back in the water – they were lucky that it hadn't already detonated – so Fuller decided to cushion it to help prevent it from moving. He then sent word ashore before gingerly making his way back to port. Thankfully, the sea was calm that morning.

Much of the harbour had been cleared by the time he passed the gates, and a small crew of sailors awaited along the jetty to assist with disarming the mine. Thankfully, they were able to avoid a disaster. An investigation soon discovered the problem: before being stored in a box by the dockyard, the plugs had been made in a dry environment. However, without any climate controls, the plugs were subjected to humid days and cool nights. This caused condensation on the metal, which slowly began to dissolve the critical water soluble plugs. By the time they were mounted on deck, little soluble material remained and when the MGB went out to sea, the spray from crashing waves took care of what remained. It was a wonder none had already exploded.

Despite having narrowly avoided a disaster, Fuller wasn't ready to give up on the mines. Instead, he decided to find a way to waterproof them. His solution worked like a charm, even if a tad unconventional.

He used prophylactics.

It made perfect sense – condoms were already shaped to cover the cylindrical protuberances and the rubber prevented the plugs from getting wet. They could safely transport the water mines without fearing they would arm themselves during transit.

"I need you to go up to the base and get a gross of condoms," he told his midshipman. The young officer, who Fuller described as a "pink-cheeked Englishman", just stood there, face reddening with embarrassment.

"We're going to put them up over the horns on all our mines," Fuller continued, ignoring the reaction. "And make it quick – I want them ready for tonight."

"Uh, just to be clear sir, you said condoms?" the midshipman questioned.

"Yes, condoms!" Fuller snapped impatiently. His bark put the officer to flight and as he watched the man hurry ashore, he shook his head.

Years later, he would say that he "wasn't a dummy, although I thought he had no brains at all."

Half an hour passed before the midshipman returned.

"Did you get them?" Fuller asked.

The man avoided eye contact and tugged nervously at his sleeves, like a child preparing to admit a wrongdoing to their parents.

"Well, there's only Wrens in the supply base," he explained.

"I sent you to get condoms," Fuller growled, "go and bloody-well get them."

The midshipman's face grew an even darker shade of red, but he said nothing – he knew better than to argue. Instead, he gave a quick salute and headed back to base. When he returned, he had a brown paper bag in his arms.

"You got them," Fuller concluded.

"Yes," he replied, handing over the bag, "but as I was going out the door, one Wren took a look at the other and said, 'Now there goes a man!'"

———

Fuller could be tough on his men. He kept a tight boat, sharpened his crew's skills, and utilized every opportunity to practise, even on patrols. For instance, whenever they reported in to Ramsgate, he'd make his gunners fire on the wrecks on Goodwin Sands, a ten mile beach situated about six miles of the coast of Kent. It didn't matter if they'd just been in combat or were on the last leg of a twelve-hour stint at sea – Gramps would have them fire off their remaining rounds at the rusted, dilapidated hulls as they passed.

"Starboard attack angle!" He'd shout once their targets became visible. "Twin point-fives open up and hit the wreck up above."

This wasn't standard gunnery orders but something unique that Fuller devised. The speed and loud engines of an MGB made it inefficient to give constant adjustments to his gunners. He likened it to "trap shooting with one arm tied behind your back," explaining that "rapid transit and trying to shoot at a target while you're moving past it is almost impossible." Thus, Fuller devised a system that greatly enhanced the accuracy of his fire. It involved keeping his guns in a fixed position – rather than order his guns to move to various angles and heights, he'd simply reposition the boat so that their shots landed on the target. To achieve this, he created an interesting way to aim: he took "the centre of the Kent clear-view screen in the wheelhouse when alongside a harbour wall and moved the midships gun until it hit the depression rail." Once in place, he moved it off two inches and then asked his gunner: "Well, what are you looking at now?" The gunner indicated an object in the distance and the cox'n lined his eye with the object and the middle of the screen. A sailor would then go out onto the deck with a marker and the cox'n would direct him where to place it.

"Right, you're in transit now," he'd say once the marker lined up with his sights. They would then screw a brass rod into the deck and coat it in luminous paint – a marker for the gunners. The process was repeated for the other side of the boat, although Fuller noted that "The brass rods weren't the same on both sides because the Kent screen was off-centre."

So, when Fuller gave the order 'starboard attack angle', the cox'n repositioned the boat so that the desired wreck on Goodwin Sands was centred on his viewscreen marker. At the same time, each gun moved in line with the respective luminous brass rod, and when instructed to fire, rounds immediately tore through the salt worn heaps.*

---

* Naval historian Gordon Laco's observations about Fuller's system is worth sharing: "[this] is exactly what Captain Broke of HMS *Shannon* used during the War of 1812 to devastate USS *Chesapeake*," he noted, explaining that Broke "had wooden battens fixed to the deck by each gun such that the guns all aimed at a single spot about 400 yards out from the ship. The outermost guns fore and aft were inclined inwards slightly, and so on to the midships guns which aimed at 90 degrees to the keel." Lastly, a wooden sight was "attached to the bulwarks of his quarterdeck and used that to aim his whole battery from there. With three broadsides so aimed, he literally blew the midships section of the American ship to smithereens then took her by boarding. The

One time, this practise nearly doomed his boat. They were travelling into a strong wind when he ordered his point-fives to fire at the remnants of a broken cargo steamer. Immediately, an odd buzzing sound caught his ear.

"My God," he thought, "the flies aren't bad in England but there's a lot tonight."

Then he realized it couldn't be flies – he wouldn't even be able hear it over the deafening sounds of gunfire and engines. His eyes turned to the small, capsized dinghy that was on deck. It looked like someone had flicked a wet paintbrush at it. But the dark shapes couldn't be paint...

"Jesus!" he exclaimed, putting it all together. "The whole thing is full of holes!"

Shrapnel holes to be exact. And now he noticed that his windshield was also perforated.

"Cease fire, cease fire!" he started shouting.

They'd narrowly avoided a catastrophe. Fuller later put it together: "we had graze-fuse ammunition in the point-fives* and we were firing forward. Our spray was setting them off about eight feet ahead of the bow and this was all the shrapnel coming back. It's a wonder we didn't kill ourselves."

Since his arrival in England, Fuller hadn't taken any leave and decided a holiday was long overdue. He sent a request for sixty days – enough time to head back home to Canada – and quickly received approval from his CO. Arrangements were made for someone to replace him as CO of his MGB and Fuller informed his crew that he'd be leaving. He doubted any of them would miss him.

"I was the roughest commanding officer of anybody," Fuller admitted, "you might say a perfectionist."

---

whole action took minutes." Interestingly, fighter aircraft would also use this technique during the Second World War, a system known as 'harmonizing'.
* Fuller likely meant to say his 20mm or pom poms as point-fives do not fire explosive ammunition (Laco).

He demanded that his crew act like a well-oiled engine – you could count on it to start whenever you turned the key. Although he was never cruel, nor did he resort to belittling behaviour, but he was tough and accepted nothing less than the best from his men. There was no patience for slackers. And while Fuller went out of his way to get into fights with the enemy, many of his men didn't share his enthusiasm for combat. He began to fear they were growing to resent him and started taking precautions. For instance, when he needed to visit his boat at night, he made certain that the OOW accompanied him, not least because the man was armed with a pistol.

"I figured that if I went down by myself with no officer there as a witness, the crew would have thrown me overboard," he explained, adding "they hated my guts so much."

After making the announcement, Fuller retired to his office ashore to complete paperwork and tie up loose ends. He felt eager to get home – he needed some time to recharge his batteries. Before coming to the office, he swung by the heads and glanced at his face in the mirror. He'd grown a thick, black beard and his face looked thinner than usual. His hair was becoming unkempt, and the bags under his eyes looked darker and more pronounced. It was the face of a man who'd been deprived of sleep for many months.

As he started into a report, a knock at his door drew his attention to the entrance. There stood his cox'n, who came to attention and gave a salute.

Fuller nodded in acknowledgement of the compliment and then instructed the man to come in and stand at ease. A tinge of concern formed in his gut – he hoped there wasn't anything wrong with the boat.

"Is everything alright?" he asked.

"Yes sir," the cox'n replied, removing his hat, and running a hand through his hair. "I understand we're paying off?"

"That's right," Fuller confirmed, "I've got my ticket and I'm off to London."

"Will you head back to Canada?"

"Been about two years now," he said, leaning back in his chair. "About time I paid everyone a visit."

The man nodded, fidgeting with his headdress.

"Would you take requestmen?"

The question surprised Fuller. Usually these happened in the morning aboard the boat.

"Now?"

"Yes sir."

Fuller sighed – he didn't want to do extra paperwork.

"Can it wait?" he questioned. "I really haven't got the time – I'm more than halfway done packing."

The cox'n looked concerned, so Fuller added: "Look, you'll get a new skipper soon but until then the base captain will take your requests because our boat is actually paid off."

"Please," The cox'n insisted, "I make this request, please take it sir."

Fuller caved and reached for a notepad. "All right, but not too long," he warned. "Who are the requestmen?"

"Well Sir, I'm number one requestman."

Fuller hadn't expected that. "Right then," he acknowledged, jotting the man's name down. "What's the request?"

"Sir, we understand this ship's paying off. When you recommission a ship, I'd like to serve again with you, if I may." The man rethought his words and came to attention. "I make the request to serve with you again."

Fuller's pencil hovered over the notepad. He didn't doubt the man was being serious, but he couldn't understand why he was making the request. Weren't they relieved to be rid of him?

"Very well," he finally replied, "I'll see to it."

"Thank you sir."

The cox'n saluted again before turning about and marching out of the office. Just as he exited another sailor showed up with the same request, as did the next sailor and the one after him. Fuller didn't know the entire crew had lined up outside his office. Eventually, he caught on when the MM entered. As he later explained "it hit me, because he was the Motor Mech, and he was a fellow that I was really laying for." Fuller looked the man straight in the eyes and asked, "Why the hell do you want to serve with me? You know I'm the roughest CO in the whole outfit."

"Well, sir," the MM replied, "we might be badly damaged, but you always bring us back to port, and that's what we want to serve on, a ship that always comes back."

After the last rating exited his office, Fuller took a moment to reflect on the morning's revelation. He'd been way off in his assessment. Despite his convictions, his men didn't despise him. To the contrary, they respected him for his firm, but fair, approach to running a ship. They could see past his tough exterior, and while Fuller believed his temper and self-proclaimed perfectionism bred resentment among the crew, they knew it stemmed from a place of genuine concern. Their safety was paramount. Furthermore, no sailor could abide a pompous, self-serving officer, especially one incapable of operating outside of SOPs and regulations. That wasn't Fuller. Common sense, functionality, and hard work were what mattered to him. After all, he was a successful businessman, and in business nothing mattered more than results. He demanded commitment from his subordinates and, in return, gave them his very best. If they needed something, Fuller made it happen, even if it meant breaking the rules to get it.

"If you try to curry favoritism you don't always end up the personality boy who's a jolly good fellow," he later concluded.

Most crews became fiercely loyal to their CO, even excusing some of their faults. In Fuller's case, it was his temper, while for others it could be a personal vice. He recalled one CO who was a known alcoholic. "… a drunkard," he explained, but also "the best seaman and the best fighter that there was." Often, the officer became so inebriated that he couldn't manage to climb down the ladder to board his boat without assistance.

"They would come up with the heaving lines, and put them around him, and lower him down to the deck of his boat to go out to sea and into action."

Eventually, overdue mess bills caught up to him and command considered re-assigning him for "alcoholic excess". His men closed ranks and defiantly proclaimed: "We would sooner go to sea under our CO dead drunk when he can't even stand up than we would with any other officer in the RN." In the end, command acquiesced.

Fuller finished the remaining paperwork and was about to arrange for a cab to pick him up when Cdr Sanders appeared.

And it wasn't to wish him a safe travel.

"Sorry old boy but I need you to stand in for another CO this evening," he relayed.

"Sir, I'm about to go on leave," Fuller protested.

"There isn't another spare," Sanders replied with a sympathetic smile. "I'm afraid you're the only one who can take it. I'll see you for the briefing."

He turned and left, leaving Fuller brooding at his desk. "So much for an easy evening," he thought glumly. With a heavy sigh, he dressed into appropriate clothing for the night's expedition, folding the leave ticket and slipping it into one of his top pockets.

During the briefing, Fuller learned he would be part of a flotilla tasked with intercepting a group of German ships near the French coast. He would likely end up in a scrap tonight. Regularly, he'd relish the opportunity but tonight he would command a different vessel and men unaccustomed to his tactics. It took weeks of training to turn his crew into an efficient team, including developing his own unique gunnery style. Not tonight – he would board the MGB and immediately head out to sea. It reminded him of his first patrol in *49* and that ended up a disaster.

Years later, Fuller described the patrol as "… one of the roughest nights I ever had." A bright late August moon hung in a cloudless sky, significantly increasing visibility in the English Channel. Furthermore, when they came upon the enemy E-boats, shore batteries spotted the MGBs and opened fire. These were large guns, capable of shredding his boat to pieces.

"Evasive manoeuvres!" he shouted as flak from the coast began to rain down. "Speed-up and move!"

The E-boats turned and closed on the MGBs. Fuller noticed and barked "all guns, starboard attack an –" but stopped before completing the command. These men didn't know what that meant. Resisting the urge to swear, he instead corrected the command "fire at the E-boats and move away from the coast."

Bright green tracers arched past the starboard bow.

"Hard aport!"

Seconds passed before the MGB finally lurched left, but not before a few rounds caught them near the stern. Fuller didn't have to see it – he could feel the thumps vibrate through the deck as bullets punched through wood. By now their own guns responded, spewing red tracers back at the enemy. The E-boats, having anticipated the retaliation, easily evaded the return fire. Search lights were now sweeping along the water while coastal guns continued their barrage. Around them, the sea turned to a boil from the assault. One well-placed shot on their engines and they'd be goners.

Oddly, despite the chaos, Fuller thought of the paper folded neatly in his pocket. "I should already be in London!" he sulked. He noticed the boat straighten. "Zigzag," he shouted down a voicepipe. More rounds peppered the hull, one shot striking the bridge. It barely missed Fuller and the 1st Lt. He scowled. If this had been his boat, they would have already crippled if not destroyed a few of the enemy. Now he'd be lucky if he got out of this alive.

He glanced behind and judged it was time. "All ahead full!" he ordered. "Make speed and get us out of here!"

The boat sped off into the night. Thankfully, the E-boats decided to break off their pursuit. Fuller didn't say much on the trip back. He felt sick in the stomach – another drawback of the trip: no tea and scotch. It took a lot of focus and willpower to stave off the need to wretch over the side. Moreso, he felt unusually anxious. Once they returned, he found a private place ashore to calm himself and reflect.

Something about how things unfolded this evening – going from a state of relaxation only to be thrust into battle with men he didn't know or trust – took a toll on his psyche. He'd been in far worse situations than this and yet none rattled him quite the same.

"I didn't like that at all", he would later explain. "I got shot up and went for leave."

CHAPTER 9

Swinley's Circus

Having survived his eleventh-hour patrol in the Narrow Seas, it was time for Fuller to say goodbye to Hell-Fire Corner. He immediately finished packing his kit and proceeded with haste to London. During his time at Dover, he'd gone through four boats, fought handfuls of firefights, and distinguished himself in major battles. Even his last skirmish, albeit a negative experience, fittingly brought a close to his most active period in the channel. Fuller wanted to play an active role in the war and he'd already managed to see more than his fair share of action. Now, the man who many mocked for being too old to serve, would be returning home a hero. The gadflies at the Britannia yacht club would trip all over their jokes now.

In London, Fuller went to visit Capt Frank Llewellyn Houghton. As the senior ranking Canadian naval officer in England, he needed to approve the travel back to Canada. Entering the office, Fuller snapped a salute and went straight to business.

"Sir, I understand I'm entitled to a month's leave in Canada," he said. "I'd like to have it, because my ship's been paid off."

Houghton, an old-schooled officer who'd commanded ships and served quite a bit of his career with the RN, didn't reply. Instead, he turned to a filing cabinet, opened the drawer marked D-F, and searched the folders until he found Fuller's. He withdrew the file and looked through the pages, which were fastened by a metal prong. The Capt frowned.

"You're on loan to the Royal Navy and there has been no request for your leave," he replied with an apologetic tone. "I'm afraid I can't do anything about it until the Royal Navy comes up and says that you're entitled to leave and that you're available."

Although Fuller felt annoyed by the revelation, it only half surprised him. Paper roadblocks were far too common in the service. At times, it seemed like red tape purposely permeated all forms of military administration – experience taught one how to cut through it.

"Ah, I see," Fuller replied calmly. "Would you mind sir if I made a phone call – I believe I can sort this all out."

Houghton shrugged and spun around the phone of his desk for Fuller to use. He scooped up the receiver and waited for the operator to answer. Time to play an old ace he'd kept up his sleeve.

"Yes, may I have the second sea lord's office?" he asked and was promptly transferred. After a moment the phone rang.

"Second sea lord's office," a woman's voice responded.

"Bingo", Fuller thought – he'd been counting on hearing a lady's voice. "Miss Dalrymple?"

"Yes?"

He allowed himself a smile. Ever since hearing her name in Welman's office he'd committed it to memory. Now he hoped she'd be able to help him sort through this. "Good day ma'am. It's Lieutenant Thomas Fuller and I'm hoping you might be able to help me."

She took a moment to confirm his identity and position before proceeding to hear his request.

"I'm in a captain's office and he doesn't understand things too well," he explained. The comment elicited a stern look from Houghton but Fuller ignored it. "My ship's shot up, as you know, and I want a month's leave in Canada. Will you speak to him and tell him it's all right to go?"

"Who the hell is Miss Dalrymple?" Houghton blurted out angrily.

Fuller turned and held out the handset.

"She runs the second sea lord's office, sir, and she wishes to speak to you."

Houghton eyed him suspiciously and cautiously brought the phone to his ear.

"Captain Houghton speaking."

Fuller observed the one-way conversation. The Capt listened while the secretary explained that she'd send a telegram approving Fuller's leave. The woman was efficient – Fuller had waited less than half an hour outside Houghton's office when it arrived. Years later, he would muse about Houghton being "a little bit slow to get around to things."

His leave secured and overseas passage booked, Fuller set off to Cardiff in Wales, where the Swedish passenger liner *Vallaran* awaited. He enjoyed the trip back home. The convoy travelled at a steady 8 knots, and while the journey provided ample time to relax and catch up on sleep, it more importantly presented a chance to enjoy the ship's cuisine. Unlike commonwealth ships, the food aboard was delightful. "I never did get to sit down to dinner, because I never could get past the smorgasbord that they served before," he remembered, also noting that he "put on twenty pounds in twenty-eight days going across the Atlantic."

He arrived in Halifax on September 8, 1942, and, after reporting to *Stadacona* and obtaining Foreign Service Leave, he went straight to the train station and booked passage to Ottawa. In all he had nearly two months of free time ahead of him – he wasn't due to head back to England until November. Unfortunately, his time home didn't quite go the way he imagined it. Due to a stroke of bad timing, most of his friends were away. He'd been looking forward to partying, attending clubs, drinking to excess, and finding all sorts of trouble with his mates, but instead found things to be quiet and subdued in the nation's capital. It proved anticlimactic, and while he did enjoy visiting family, it didn't satisfy his need to let loose and have a grand ol' time. Even the Britannia club felt less populated – on the evenings he went, he spent most of the time chatting with the barkeep. It wasn't the sort of shenanigans one found at the Kit Kat Club back in Brighton.

"I got bored," he would later explain.

Not even a week into his leave, Fuller decided to change plans. He couldn't stand the quiet and stillness – it was too sudden a change from the regime he'd grown accustomed to overseas. So, he contacted NSHQ: "I've got three weeks here in Canada and nothing at all to do," he explained. "I want a job." The navy leapt on the opportunity to use a decorated officer to help drum up recruitment for the RCN's own coastal forces. The next day, Fuller began a goodwill tour of all fairmile manufacturers and, while a far cry from the holiday he'd envisioned, at least he was busy and met some interesting people.

"It was all right," he later admitted, "they were paying my hotel bills and I was traveling around, given expenses."

Fuller spent most of November travelling to England. During his transit, he reflected on his naval career – the battles, close-calls, and challenges – and concluded he needed a change. While an MGB proved sufficient to tackle enemy E-boats, they were near useless against larger, heavily armoured ships in the channel. When he returned to Dover, he reported to Cdr Sanders with a request to attend the RN's torpedo course at HMS *Vernon*.

He wanted to command a MTB.

Depending on the model, these vessels were fitted with two or four large cylinders, from which a torpedo could be jettisoned into the water. Some hulls were even augmented with recessed grooves to prevent the warhead from striking the deck when it flew out of the tube. MTBs still carried various calibre guns, mostly as a defence against air attack, but their main weapon provided enough punch to sink even flak trawlers. The next time Fuller came across one of those detestable ships, he would turn the tables.

Sanders readily approved the request and Fuller informed his crew, who were much relieved to have their old CO back, that they would be heading to Brighton for training. The Admiralty's Torpedo, Mining, and Electrical Training Course, often referred to as "Swinley's Circus" after the commander in charge, had been temporarily relocated to the Roedean Ladies' College on the South Downs of Sussex. For Fuller, that meant being close to Brighton's core and his favourite haunt, the Kit Kat Club. Perhaps this course would make up for his lackluster holiday.

The campus proved more impressive than *King Alfred*. It featured red brick buildings with off-white bath stone dressing and steep, triangular roofs adorned with sloping tiles. It was spacious and blended nicely with the downs, especially when viewed from the water. A courtyard, along with immaculately kept greenery, completed the look, giving the space a regal feel. More to the point, it suited *Vernon*'s needs. For safety, the school had been temporarily relocated away from the coast, so it was already vacant and, as a boarding school, provided ready-use accommodations and space for instructions.

Fuller arrived at the main entrance and glanced up at the large guild clock on the building's southern face, above which the numbers 1898 appeared in gold. He was standing on a large open quadrangle at the foot of the main entrance, which appeared to have been designed to accommodate the student body for important announcements. At its southernmost edge, a stone balustrade offered an unobstructed view of the coast and a flagstaff featured on the terrace. He noted the White Ensign beset by a crisp blue sky and figured it now represented *Vernon*'s quarterdeck.

The building had served as the administrative centre and central residence of the school – it would now play a similar role for the RN. He proceeded up to a large, varnished wood door, flanked by carved stone pillars and a guard who paid his compliments. Entering *Vernon*'s orderly room, a bell chimed as the door opened. Immediately, a Wren sitting behind a large counter looked up and smiled.

"Lieutenant Tom Fuller," he announced, "here for the torpedo course."

Crossing out his name and lodging on sheet affixed to a clipboard, she stood up and gestured to a hallway.

"Welcome sir, if you'll follow me?"

The Wren led him through the building, pointing out key features – classrooms, messes, facilities – as they made their way down the corridor and up some stairs.

"And here we are," she announced upon reaching his room. A key dropped into his hand and the Wren hurried back to her desk.

Compared to the underground parking garage at *King Alfred*, these accommodations were exquisite: decently furnished, spacious, and comfortable. But there was a problem, and it wasn't the quality of his quarters but the location of the building itself. Isolated by design, the solitude and quiet might have been advantageous for an all-girls' school, but not for Fuller. He craved something with energy, drink, and a thriving social scene, precisely the vices the campus tried to avoid.

He placed his bags onto the bed and glanced around for a phone. There wasn't one, but an enameled plate on the wall near the headboard caught his attention. Leaning in for a closer look, he read the words inscribed above a button: "If you feel faint or require the services of a mistress push the button." He laughed and said aloud "well, well, a naval establishment!" Of course, he understood it meant the aid of a female teacher, but the innuendo still brought a smile. Rummaging through a bag he found his ditty-box and withdrew a nail file. Slowly, he worked the tip along the edges of the plate, gently breaking the bond with the wall. He figured it would make a nice souvenir from his time at *Vernon*.

Fuller returned to the main floor and asked to use a phone. He dug a hand into his tunic and withdrew a matchbook from the Kit Kat Club. Inside the flap he'd written down the number of the manager, Josey, who he befriended during his initial officer training at *King Alfred*. A well networked individual, he hoped she might know of somewhere he could stay in town.

Josey answered the phone and at once recognized his voice – the Canadian accent was a dead giveaway. He explained his situation, and, to his delight, she offered him a room at the Club itself. Ending the call, he informed the Wren that he would be lodging off campus and commuting from Brighton each morning. He then arranged for a cab to pick him up.

It was a slow first week. Fuller found himself attending lectures in classrooms and while other candidates keenly took notes and asked questions, he found it hard to remain attentive. Lack of sleep, as well as the odd hangover, didn't help – he was paying the price for prioritizing evening shenanigans at the Kit Kat. Thankfully, after a few days, they broke from the classroom and travelled to the 'Dreadnought' garage, a site located two blocks east of *King Alfred*, for some hands-on torpedo training. Here the instructors walked them through the various parts and functions of these deadly cylindrical warheads, allowing students to learn by practising with dummy models. This sort of learning suited Fuller, who eagerly explored the innerworkings of this new weapon. However, there was only so much one could manage hands-on – candidates were assigned nightly readings and were expected to study. Daily assessments, in addition to a condensed schedule*, meant students had little room for leisure. Fuller's nightly socializing resulted in him performing dismally on written tests and he ended up failing the first phase of the course.

"I managed to get a zero on the examination," he admitted.

He'd put himself in a tough spot. Technically, he wouldn't be allowed to advance to on-water training. Another officer might have resigned themselves to their fate, but this was Tom Fuller - fighting was in his blood.

---

* Classes ran all day Monday to Friday, including a morning lesson on Saturday morning.

The lead instructor, a former destroyer captain, addressed the issue in private.

"What happened Lieutenant?"

Fuller didn't beat around the bush. "Sir, I'm not one for studying, I learn best by doing things – I believe my track record speaks for itself. If you'd be willing to read a few of my action reports, I think you'll see that I'm worth passing on to the next phase of the course."

As the man considered the request his eyes noted Fuller's DSC ribbon. His expression softened.

"Alright," he agreed.

After studying four of Fuller's reports, he granted the Canadian a special exemption.

Fuller and his crew arrived at Weymouth to conduct work-ups the following week, and while this meant leaving the Kit Kat Club, being back on the water was a good trade off. At last, he would have a chance to set foot upon a proper Dog Boat – the iconic Fairmile D. It took Fuller little time to adjust to the larger and more powerful craft. After only a week, he'd transitioned from being the worst candidate to top of the course. He excelled on the water, easily passing successive performance checks. It also helped that he was no longer staying up socializing all night.

A few things still bothered him, especially mandatory gunnery lectures by Whale Island instructors*. Fuller viewed these as both tiresome and unpractical. Everything they covered had already been done at *St. Christopher* – he thought the whole point of Swinley's Circus was to familiarize themselves with the use of torpedoes. Making matters worse, their teachers insisted on candidates using standard gunnery procedure, which irritated him to no end. He'd already realized the folly in trying to apply techniques designed for larger ships on coastal vessels. Gramps wasn't impressed.

---

* The RN's famed gunnery school had been established at HMS *Excellent* on Whale Island in the late 1800s.

"Stay to the back of the room boys," he told his men as they readied themselves for more gunnery lessons. Typically, ratings sat at the front while officers positioned themselves along the back, but Fuller wanted them close so he could covertly whisper in their ears throughout the lesson. "I doubt this is going to be useful."

The teacher, a RN Cdr, waited for everyone to settle before commencing and Fuller crossed his arms in a gesture of defiance. As anticipated, the instructor delved into traditional methods of issuing gunnery commands. Not even five minutes into the lesson, Fuller felt compelled to lean forward and whisper, "it's all balls, don't pay any attention to it." A few of his men had to stifle laughs which thankfully went unnoticed. Meanwhile, the Cdr was amidst explaining that "up 200, right 200" were examples of proper gunnery orders.

"A bunch of pukka Whale Island garbage," Fuller thought, before again telling his men, "it's all balls – pay no attention to him." He glanced at his watch and frowned – they weren't even a third of the way through. The instructor rambled on and, gradually, the insistence on proper, time-tested practices and gunnery jargon started to bother his men. Fuller could see them shifting in their seats and looking agitated, which made him concerned. The last thing he needed was for their heads to get filled with a bunch of nonsense. "It's all balls boys," he insisted, this time a little more forcefully. "Don't listen to what he's saying." But his words weren't reaching all of them.

"Proper commands will ensure the swift destruction of the enemy," the instructor continued unawares, "and let nothing convince you otherwise."

Fuller decided to risk raising his voice: "it's all balls – pay no attention to him."

Unfortunately, he was too loud and realized it immediately. The room fell silent, and the instructor paused mid-sentence. Heads turned and eyes fell upon the Canadian leaning back in his chair. Fuller felt his stomach sink.

He was in trouble.

Again.

In short order, he found himself in Swinley's office, standing at attention as the instructor furiously relayed the incident. "… in front of the entire course, I might add!" he fumed, finger outstretched and pointing at Fuller like a lawyer in court. "I've never been so humiliated!"

Fuller remained silent.

"I demand he be severely reprimanded for this insubordination," the Cdr concluded, nearly breathless from his rant. To his credit, Swinley appeared unfazed by the emotional display. He'd remained seated at his desk, calmly listening to the instructor, and now looked at the Lt standing before him.

"You're on a rather serious charge here," Swinley explained. "And you admit you said it?"

Fuller, couldn't deny it – everybody heard him.

"Yes, I did", Fuller replied, "because what he is saying 'is' all balls."

The unapologetic admission left the instructor gobsmacked. His face reddened and fists clenched, shaking with rage. Thankfully Swinley held up a hand to calm the man before asking Fuller to explain.

"Sir, I apologize for saying that aloud," Fuller admitted. "I never meant to embarrass the commander, only calm my crew. The instruction wasn't making sense – these aren't destroyers and those commands don't work for MGBs"

The Cdr scoffed in indignation.

"Look, it's very simple", Fuller continued, ignoring the man, "let's go out and have a shoot in Weymouth Bay. I'll turn the crew and everything over to him. We can try it his way and then do it my way and you'll see what I mean sir."

Swinley looked intrigued. The Canadian's confidence made him curious. "Very well, Lieutenant, let's put it to the test."

———

The water was choppy in Weymouth Bay, force 3 under mostly clear skies. The motion upset Fuller's stomach, but as Swinley and the Cdr were aboard, he acted unphased. An old CPO, the principal gunnery trainer for the course, also joined them aboard the MGB, the same vessel Fuller and his crew had used to travel to HMS *Vernon*. The school's MTBs were strictly for training and, considering the nature of the challenge, using his MGB made the most sense.

Fuller glanced at his number one and said, "we came here to shoot torpedoes and now we're doing a gun demonstration."

The XO smiled but refrained from making a comment. "Smart choice," Fuller thought.

An old dingy sat at the back of the boat, ready to be dropped overboard and serve as a dummy target. Fuller looked aft and gave a signal. A few ratings pushed the boat off the side, while another used a baring-out spar to push it away. Fuller then ordered the MGB to move, distancing themselves from the target.

"Well sir, you're up first," he said to the Cdr. The man confidently walked up to the front of the bridge, although Fuller doubted he'd ever commanded an MGB.

"What course do you want to steer and how many knots?" Fuller asked.

"Thirty knots will do," the man replied. "Now watch and see how proper gunners do it."

Fuller ignored the man's arrogant tone – he would eat his own words soon enough – and ordered the cox'n to throttle-up. The engines roared and the boat bolted forward, forcing the Cdr to grab the bridge wall for balance.

"Put two rounds up the spout of the Oerlikon gun," the Cdr instructed, who then proceeded to order the gunner to fire one round at the target. It landed about forty feet away from the dingy, making a moderate-sized splash. The Cdr corrected the angle, "up 400."

The gunner adjusted and fired the second round, but Fuller didn't notice where it landed – clearly not on target. The MGB shot past without scoring a hit.

Of course, none of this surprised Fuller. He'd been through all of this before. That's why he created an alternative system.

Fuller turned to Swinley.

"Now, can I show you how I think it should be done, sir?"

There was no objection so Fuller moved his boat off into the distance and prepared his crew for another attack-run, this time using their usual method.

"Let's show them how we do it lads," he yelled out. "Load up all the guns, all catches off, and train all guns port attack angle."

They wouldn't be firing two shots – he planned on blowing the target to bits and pieces. He ordered all ahead full and moved his mouth to the wheelhouse voice pipe.

"Port attack angle, cox'n."

"Aye sir," came the reply, and using the port-side mark on the wheelhouse's view screen, the boat positioned itself so that the floating dingy and guns were in line with the make-shift sight marker drilled into the port side of the boat. They were closing fast – 800 yards, 700 yards, 600 yards, 500 yards...

"Open fire!" Fuller ordered. The guns erupted to life, a cone of tracer streaking out and descending onto the target. Sure enough, as Fuller observed, "the goddamn target disintegrated."

The guns fell silent and the MGB slowed back down. Triumphant, Fuller congratulated his men and then turned back to an impressed Swinley.

"That's the way to fight your ships," he concluded, "not your 'up 200 and right so much' and all the goddamn Whale Island stuff."

Despite the Canadian's brashness, Swinley couldn't help but smile – he'd seen enough. Although he still didn't approve of Fuller's outburst in class, the demonstration proved the inefficiency of standard gunnery commands for coastal boats. The Cdr, on the other hand, wasn't gracious in defeat. He'd turned to his trainer, the old CPO, and asked him to back-up his method. The chief scratched his chin and looked out to where the remains of the target floated on the water.

"You know, sir," he finally replied, "the Royal Navy travels on four hundred years of tradition, but goddamn little efficiency."

CHAPTER 10

————— ◇◇◉◇◇ —————

Call Him Jock

With his torpedo course completed, Fuller returned to Dover and discovered that he would be given command of MTB *654*. It was one of eight Dog Boats comprising the 33rd MTB Flotilla under Lt Cdr Ron Ashby.* The new vessel didn't disappoint – Fuller noted "she was a new 'D' class hundred-and-twenty-footer with 6,000 horsepower." Longer than his previous MGB, *654* featured a doubled plywood frame at the bow, reinforced by steel angle bars. She was a steady gun platform, and, of course was fitted with torpedo tubes. Four propellers were beneath her stern not only making her faster than other coastal vessels, but, in conjunction with greater fuel storage, gave her greater endurance and the option to travel further distances. This ultimately meant *654* could conduct longer patrols without having to refuel. As for design, it was a beamier boat, and while the increased width made for a stouter looking shape, internally it afforded more space and comfort for the crew.[100] The aesthetics didn't bother Fuller – if his craft could bring the fight to the enemy, it suited him fine.

---

* The 33rd would comprise of MTBs: *649* (Archer), *651* (Horlock), *654* (Fuller), *655* (Green-Kelly), *656*, (Tate, Hughes, Masson), *665* (Thompson), *667* (Jerram), *670* (Ashby).

While pleased about the MTB, he didn't anticipate leaving Dover. The 33rd was tasked with joining the Allied fight in the Mediterranean Sea. Dog Boats had been operating in those waters since early 1941: the 10th and 15th MTB Flotillas patrolled the eastern part of the sea near their base in Alexandria and, in 1942, were joined by the 7th MTB Flotilla. They provided coastal support to the British Eighth Army in North Africa and, in September, assisted in a raid on Tobruk to the west of Alexandria.

The latter proved a challenge for the flotillas. Under the codename "Agreement", the operation launched amphibious and land assaults on the German controlled port city. While Fuller began his leave in Canada, a combined British, Rhodesian, and New Zealand force prepared to spring their assault. The results were disastrous; without air support, German and Italian dive bombers attacked the Allies with impunity. Hundreds were killed and/or captured, and in total, one cruiser, two destroyers, six MTBs and dozens of small amphibious craft were destroyed.

Still, continuing pressure managed to push the Germans and Italians further west, and coastal forces subsequently relocated to Malta. After the successful British-American invasion of French North Africa in Operation Torch, Sicily became the next target. The island supported German forces in Tunisia – the Luftwaffe controlled the skies in this part of the Mediterranean, especially the Straight of Messina. It was a narrow band of water between the North-Eastern Sicilian coast and the mainland of Italy known to MTB skippers simply as 'The Narrows'. Allied shipping through this area proved hazardous, especially by day, and MTBs were needed to assist in making the passage safe. Preparations were being made for an all-out invasion of both Sicily and the Italian mainland, and the 33rd, along with the 32nd MTB, 19th MGB, and the 20th MGB Flotillas – a total of sixteen MTBs and sixteen MGBs – were to be part of it.

Of course, getting there was easier said than done.

The distance to Gibraltar was significant and required moving through enemy infested waters. Many of the crew had yet to experience the notorious swells of the Atlantic, and their boats weren't suited for heavy seas. It wouldn't be a comfortable transit. Also, unlike larger surface ships, which patrolled for days and weeks before returning to port, coastal vessels usually only went out to sea for a few hours at a time. This trip would take about seven days, easily the longest stint any of them would experience aboard their vessels. To make matters worse, MTBs and MGBs didn't carry enough fuel reserves to manage such a long trip, nor did their galleys provide regular meals. Most boats didn't even have a qualified cook aboard. And they wouldn't be afforded much time to train their crews at their new base at Milford Haven; once the boats were converted to carry additional fuel tanks and the weather warmed (they couldn't manage the trip in winter), the flotillas would take turns heading south, escorted by two trawlers to guide them to their destinations.

The plan didn't excite Fuller. Without a tow, his boat would need some crafty engineering to make it even possible to carry enough fuel for the voyage, and his MTB didn't exactly have a lot of extra space. He figured additional tanks would be fitted on deck, crowding an already cluttered area and making his vessel top-heavy. "Weight in the wrong place,"[101] as observed by Derrick Holden-Brown, 1st Lt on *655*. The excess high-octane petrol, already volatile compared to the diesel used by E-boats, transformed these ships into veritable floating explosives with limited manoeuverability. Fuller also feared that a crowded deck would restrict the movement of his guns.

Despite his reservations, *654* left for Wales and travelled upriver to the docks at Pembroke. There, final preparations and modifications to his MTB would commence. His predictions proved correct – workers installed fuel drums to the upper deck. It took months to refit all four flotillas and by completion, *654* carried an additional 3,000 gallons of high octane petrol, increasing the MTB's total fuel capacity to 8,000 gallons. Unfortunately, he'd also been right about the guns; arrester bars normally fitted to limit arcs of fire had been altered to further restrict their movement to prevent gunners firing into one of the tanks. It made sense, but still diminished his boat's ability to defend itself. Even moving about on deck now proved tricky.

To preserve fuel and keep pace with the slow-moving trawlers, the convoy would travel at a maximum of 10 knots, a painful crawl for coastal vessels. This would make conditions aboard even worse – the MTB's shallow draft, combined with large waves and slow speed would make the vessel feel like a cork bobbing on water. Only one engine would run at a time, which added even more limitations on their guns. Fuller explained the problem: "all of the guns worked on swash-pumps which ran off each motor. You only had two guns that you could operate with the one motor that was running. The rest had to be put on manual."*

Nature also worked against them. The spring ushered in a series of storms, resulting in days of strong winds, which even made their downriver return to Milford Haven a challenge. As Fuller brought 654 into the bay's inner basin and secured his boat, a large storm hit.

"It was force six to force eight and in the Bay of Biscay was force ten," Fuller recalled. "We waited and we waited and we waited in Milford Haven."

What else could they do? They were stuck aboard their boats, bracing as fenders repeatedly slammed against their respective docks. And while it proved more than a little uncomfortable, Fuller feared it would pale in comparison to the conditions they would experience in the Atlantic. Here at least they could stomach a bit of food – he doubted that would still be the case when they made for Gibraltar.

One small concession was that each boat had been issued with a generous ration of canned beer. It helped the crew pass the time but,

---

* Laco elaborates on what Fuller refers to as 'swash pumps': "What he [Fuller] means is some of his larger gun positions were actuated by hydraulic motors. With only one engine running to power the hydraulics, only two gun positions were powered. The rest, some manual and some hydraulic, could still be operated manually, but only two would be powered until other engines were started up."

because of the foul weather, most ratings disposed of their empties by shoving them out of the boat's scuttle. The other boats were doing the same – nobody wanted to head out in the rain and wind – and so he didn't give it any thought.

The next few days passed without respite. Finally, the weather began to improve and, taking advantage of the break, a tug decided to enter the bay. It came alongside and gave a blast of its horn – a request for the gates to be opened. Conditions continued to rapidly improve, and as the tug passed through the entrance, the water began to suddenly recede. Fuller had been sitting in his cabin when he felt his boat drop as if a trap door had opened under *654*. The ferocity of the winds had caused the harbour to swell – now they were returning to their normal level, but at an abnormal rate. *654* started listing to one side and at once Fuller realized the danger. In order restrict movement during the storm, their mooring lines had been secured tightly, but now that the water was rushing out of the bay, the boat was starting to hang from the jetty. Springing from his cabin, he clambered up to the bridge shouting "slack off the lines, slack off the lines! The whole basin's dropping!"

The crew darted to both the bow and stern, hastily removing lines from double-bit bollards, mere moments before they became too taught to adjust. Slowly, the boat settled back into the water although it continued to receded and eventually *654* bottomed out in the mud. Fuller glanced up at the exposed wall of the jetty and then around the basin. Other MTBs had also found themselves in muck, including the tug.

"I guess we'll all just sit in the putty until the tide comes back in," he said to his XO. The smell of the basin floor caught his nose and he recoiled from the stench. Pulling a handkerchief from his pocket, he brought it to his nose before observing, "Luckily there's enough mud not to affect our screws."

The clouds were breaking, and something glinting in the sunlight caught Fuller's eye. Along the bottom of the sluice gates were hundreds of empty beer cans, which prevented them from closing after the tug entered. He groaned, gesturing at the mess: "all the cans have jammed the goddamn gates." Now he understood why the waterline dropped as quickly as it did. Eventually divers were dispatched to clear the obstruction, but only once the tide returned.

Ashby informed his boats that they would soon slip and begin their journey to the Mediterranean. Over a thousand nautical miles lay ahead, and Fuller felt eager to get it done and over with. For safety, the boats would travel in batches – too many at once would make for a large convoy, and possibly easier to spot by patrolling aircraft. If something did go horribly wrong during transit, going separately would at least mitigate the loss. Two MLs would also accompany each group, adding some additional guns in case they were attacked. Half of the 32nd departed on March 4 followed by six more on the 16th. Five more began their trek on the twenty-third and then another five on April 6. By the thirtieth, the largest group, consisting of the 33rd and boats of the 20th (including Canadians Maitland, Burke, and Ladner), left Milford Haven escorted by four trawlers. It would be the last convoy to leave.

Fuller felt concerned, particularly because of the fickle weather. It proved hard to predict what conditions they would find themselves in – at present, heavy winds awaited.

"Right boys, looks like we'll finally be heading to the sunny med," he told his men with his usual bravado. "We'll show everyone how things are done."

They cheered, exactly the response he expected. Beside him his 1st Lt shot him a subtle look – he knew what really awaited them. And as they left port along with the other boats of the 33rd and 20th, only the experienced sailors had some inkling of how perilous their journey could be. The MTBs and MLs filed out in line, and Ashby sent them all a cheerful message over his speaker.

"Sir?" The voice came from the hatch leading to the wheelhouse. Fuller noticed a rating holding out a cup of steaming tea, which he gratefully accepted. Blowing to cool it, he took a sip and smiled at the taste of scotch. His stomach relaxed almost immediately – truly a wonderous cure.

"Just the way you like it, sir?"

Fuller winked at the young man – he'd grown quite fond of his men. "Just the way I like it."

————

With two hands gripped firmly on the bridge wall, Fuller threw out his legs and found something solid to plant his feet against. It was all he could do to keep from falling over.

"Put your feet there," he said to his XO, who'd just drawn himself back up. Three days at sea with rough weather – nothing but stomach-churning swells that grew worse the deeper south they went. After leaving Wales, their trawler escorts led them first up the Irish Sea, sensibly distancing themselves from possible enemy patrols, before cutting west and wrapping around Ireland's northern tip. From there it had been a straight line towards the Spanish coast, although the moment they were clear of the British Isles, the weather pounced – a prevailing easterly wind, which kept pushing against their freeboard and rocked each boat like a seesaw.[102] They were now halfway to the Mediterranean although Fuller wondered if his boat could survive the abuse. Waves now pushed his already top-heavy MTB nearly ninety degrees onto its sides. Everyone was seasick and scared, including Fuller. As a precaution, he instructed everyone on deck to fasten lifelines around their waist and all ammunition removed from both the guns and ready-use lockers so that they could be stacked along the boat's keel to help keep it steady. While it meant they would be delayed responding to an attack, at the present he felt the priority was remaining upright. Besides, not even a mad man would be stupid enough to hunt anyone in this weather.

One of his feet slipped and his shoulder dropped roughly into the side of his 1st Lt, causing the man to drop the binoculars he was holding and tumble back down to the deck. Fuller fell on top of him, but both men quickly recovered, steadying each other as they clambered back up to their feet.

"Sorry," he apologized before quickly turning his head and dry heaving – there was nothing left to expel. The man shook it off, ignoring the sight of his CO being sick to prevent himself from retching. He again raised his binoculars to his eyes in attempt to track the other boats in the flotilla, making it harder for him to keep his balance. It was a wonder that he managed to see anything in these conditions. At present, Fuller envied his sea-legs, which were obviously better than his own.

"We're keeping pace with the other boats," he reported.

Fuller nodded. Earlier, the weather disabled a couple of the boats in the flotilla, forcing them to raise the 'Harry Four' flag to indicate all four engines out of action. It was a small relief that their own engines were still working. Supplying fuel to the motor proved a challenge in rough waters – he pitied the ERAs working below deck in these conditions.

The worst part of their journey was at night. COs needed to ensure they stayed within a cable length of the boat ahead of them, as well as a single cable length to the boat at their port or starboard (depending on where they were positioned in the column).[103] Without the aid of running lights, it was far too easy to get separated.

For the first time, galleys were bustling with activity, prepping regular meals, even though the present weather made appetites modest at best. Turbulent conditions made it difficult to keep generators running, and a crew of thirty-five men were limited to 125 gallons of fresh water for the week. How anyone could manage a kitchen in this weather was beyond Fuller. He couldn't even keep a cup of tea handy without it smashing on the deck. The whole flotilla endured incredible hardships – travelling from England to the Mediterranean in vessels designed for shore-based operations proved a momentous feat of willpower, nerve, and seamanship. L. C. Reynolds, at the time serving in MGB *658* – one of the boat's that travelled to the Mediterranean with the 20th MGB Flotilla under 'Corney' Burke – insisted the journey would have "… tested experienced crews in tried boats."[104]

Water sprayed over their heads from a wave crashing into the bow. It wasn't raining although it might as well have been – everything above deck was wet. Fuller glanced at both gunners and loading numbers, who clung to their covered guns for balance. Fuller doubted any of them were keeping a lookout. At least the spray washed the vomit off the deck. He longed for a hot tea, but the weather made it impossible. When he could, he'd go below deck and take a swig directly from the bottle in his cabin.

"This is getting old," Fuller grumbled, again adjusting handholds. "We're rolling from rail to rail."

On queue, the contents of his number one's stomach burst from his mouth, covering his oil skin in puke. "I'm regretting my choice to join the navy," he admitted, wiping his mouth with the sleeve of his coat.

"What, and miss all this fun?"

Before the man could reply, more water sprayed off the hull and into their faces.

————

Relief finally came about an hour later. The wind gradually eased, and with it the incessant jostling of their boats finally subsided. Morale immediately shot up – appetites returned, and the galley began producing heartier food. Better yet, Fuller could manage a cup of tea, the hot, alcohol-laced liquid making him feel human again. He even ate some greengages and biscuits, which he soaked in his drink before consuming. Ammunition was brought back to the ready-use lockers and guns uncovered and reloaded.

Using his binoculars, Fuller scanned the area around them. Vessels were much easier to spot – the four trawlers herded the convoy, two in front and two behind. Those ahead provided navigational signals, which were then passed down the line. Two columns of MLs were sandwiched between the MTBs and MGBs who in turn made up the flanks. Ashby's

670 led the starboard side of six MTBs while four MGBs and the remaining MTBs took up the port.[105]

The improved weather did have a drawback — they were a sizeable convoy and more likely to be spotted. They were also nearing the mainland and that meant increased air patrols. Long-range German reconnaissance planes were known to be in the area and could report their position to nearby enemy vessels.

Gramps rubbed his eyes and stifled a yawn. He'd spent most of the trip on the bridge, unable to stand long periods below deck, which only made his seasickness worse. Naturally, getting any sleep proved next to impossible but now that the waters were calmer, he felt fatigue creeping up. He swallowed the last of his drink and then nudged his 1st Lt.

"I'm going to get some sleep," he said. "You've got the bridge – let me know if anything important happens."

Seconds later he was in his cabin, sprawled out onto his bed. He didn't even bother to remove his footwear and fell into a deep sleep the moment the damp hairs on the back of his head touched the pillow.

———

Fuller awoke to the sound of a voice near his ear. It echoed through a brass pipe, connected to the bridge above. Still drowsy and feeling disoriented, he forced himself up.

"On my way," he replied, his voice coarse sounding. How long had he been asleep? As he hadn't undressed, he simply lifted his cap from the deck – he didn't even remember taking it off - placed it on his head and stumbled towards the hatch. In short order he was back on the bridge. It was still daylight.

"Report number one?"

"We've got company sir," the officer replied, gesturing to the sky. "A German reconnaissance plane."

Fuller lifted his binoculars, adjusting the sighting until he could see the aircraft. It had long wings and four props – a Focke-Wulf Condor around 20,000 feet up. And it seemed to be coming towards them.

"Not good," Fuller thought, before telling his XO, "Looks like he's coming for a closer look, have the gun take aim and let the SO know about our new friend."

As the 1st Lt readied the gunners and relayed the message to the radio room via voice pipe, Fuller kept his eyes locked on the aircraft. Aboard the other MTBs, MGBs, and MLs, similar preparations were made. Lower and lower the plane came, until it leveled off just out of range of their guns.

"He's going to bomb us," Fuller realized.

He didn't have time to warn anyone else as a 250 kilogram bomb loosened from a crutch attached to one of the Condor's wings. It fell towards them but thankfully overshot the convoy, exploding some distance from the lead trawler. The pilot broke off and pulled the plane back up to 20,000 feet, whereby it maintained a holding pattern, circling the flotilla. Every CO knew what it meant – their position was being reported.[106]

"What are your thoughts, sir?" his number one asked.

Fuller scratched the beard he'd been neglecting to trim. "Expect company," he replied. The Condor continued to circle them until sunset, whereby it broke-off for the mainland. Its departure didn't make Fuller feel any better. He felt confident that the enemy – whatever that may be – was presently on route to intercept the convoy. And as darkness fell, his gut warned that it would happen soon.

––––––

A line of tracer fire shot out from the night. It came from the port and while it missed the trawler and *654*, it caught Maitland's MGB, igniting one of the surplus petrol tanks. Through his binoculars, Fuller sighted flames aboard *657*. Exactly what he feared – the extra tanks made them easy targets. Despite the danger, Maitland's vessel returned fire, shortly followed by even more enemy tracers. Unfortunately, the fire raging on *657*'s bow made for an easy target and one of his turrets was hit.[107] The rounds came low and horizontal to the water, and Fuller deduced that they likely came from something with little to no freeboard.

A U-boat.

Meanwhile, Maitland, whose seamanship skills were second to none, kept his cool. Despite the danger of the inflamed fuel canister on his deck, he turned his bow into the sea, allowing the waves to wash over the tank and extinguish the fire. He then resumed course.[108] Fuller caught the whole thing and let out a laugh.

"Atta boy, John!" he exclaimed, enthusiastically smacking the arm of his number one. "He just broached to and took about a thousand gallons of water on and that put the fire out."

Whoever did attack *657* didn't stick around. No other activity followed.

"Lookouts, keep your eyes open," he cautioned. "That jerry might just be prepping for another attack."

"How do you know it's German, sir?" A midshipman asked. He'd been a last-minute addition, joining before they left Wales, and was helping to sweep the area for enemy vessels. The more eyes the better, Fuller reasoned.

"The pauses between their gunfire," he explained, lowering his binoculars but keeping his eyes focused on the open water. "They always use clips rather than drums, so they need to reload more often."

"Always?" the young man sounded suspicious, which Fuller liked. He wanted his officers to say what they were thinking.

"They're a regimented bunch," he explained, his face looking reflective. "Learning their patterns can work to your advantage. We used to trick them back in the channel – E-boats fired vertical shots of tracer to indicate 'I'm friendly', so we did the same. They wouldn't attack, thinking we were friendly, and it gave us a leg up. They never caught on." He gestured out to sea. "This guy isn't an E-boat and knows who we are. Stay sharp – this night's far from over."

The midshipman brought his binoculars back up to his eyes. "Aye, sir," he replied.

For hours they kept up their vigil but never once spotted anything on the horizon. Fuller wondered if *657* scored some hits, enough to deter a second attack. Unbeknownst to the convoy, two U-boats had converged on their position – *U639* and *U439* – and were preparing for another strike. At 0030 hours, green tracers again shot at Fuller's side of the convoy.

"All guns, green 30!" Fuller commanded. "Cox'n, take us in!"

The other MTBs did likewise, as well as the lead trawler *Coverley* – the entire starboard column was on the offensive. *654* sped into the unknown, hull bouncing off waves as gunners leveled their barrels on their respective markers. Unfortunately, their torpedo tubes weren't loaded. While Fuller regretted not having a fish handy to fire into a U-boat – one alone would certainly do the trick – they were already top heavy with fuel. Still, he found it ironic that his first action commanding an MTB restricted him to using only guns.

"Wreckage in the water," a lookout called. "Dead ahead."

Fuller traded a glance with his number one – no one had attacked yet. He glanced over the side and, sure enough, noticed debris floating past.

"What the…?"

Just then a noise caught his attention. He stood up and signaled with his hand for the XO to slow their engines. As the boat responded, he closed his eyes and focused. He heard it again, clearer than before. Something like wind blowing through a tube.

"Hear that?" he asked, and the 1st Lt nodded, looking puzzled.

"Light spotted in the water, near," the bowman relayed. Fuller moved right up to the bridge wall for a better look. Using his binoculars he identified the source – patches of burning oil on the water's surface.

"All ahead slow," he ordered.

The sounds grew louder and more distinct – life jacket whistles.

"We're going to find men in the water," he warned, "standby to assist."

More debris passed along the port and starboard sides of the hull, including small patches of fire. Dark clouds and the smell of burning oil waft over them and then the sound of something soft and heavy striking the hull. At once, Fuller grabbed a torch and shone it over the side.

Bodies.

Among the dead, a group of seamen floated in the water, huddled tightly together. Some were injured. While he couldn't identify their nationality, Fuller assumed they were shipwrecked merchantmen. After all, they hadn't destroyed any enemy vessels, and it was entirely possible that the U-boat sunk a merchant ship in passing prior to the flotilla's arrival. Regardless of who they were, his duty was clear.

"Bare a hand, bring them aboard," he ordered. Easier said than done – the chop and darkness made it a challenge. Fuller explained, "… with no-displacement boats; you can't stay head to wind." His options were limited: keep his stern to the wind and manoeuver towards the men or get windward of the survivors and drift towards them. The latter option made the most sense, lest some men found themselves chewed up by *654*'s props, and he positioned the MTB so that the swells brought him sideways to the men.

"Alright, this is how we do it," he shouted, using the portable speaker to project his voice. If some of the men in the water heard him, the better. "We're adopting the broadside-to approach: when the boat rolls down the wave, I want all ratings to reach over the gunwales and grab a man, then lug him aboard when the boat roll's back up. Use the momentum to help you."

Ratings assumed a post wherever they could find an empty space that wasn't already taken-up by empty torpedo tubes or additional fuel tanks. The bobbing shapes drew closer and closer, until it was possible to make-out details – oil slicked hair, eyes, hands, and orange life preservers stained by the spill. As the boat rolled towards them, hands reached out to grab anything that provided a firm grip, usually the strap at the top of the neck support, but sleeves, armpits, and belt loops also worked. As the boat teetered back, they heaved the men, heavy water-logged clothes and all, up and onto the deck. Two men were needed in some cases.

The sheer volume made it impossible to bring them all aboard at once. As the waves continued to push the MTB, men were forced under the hull and across the keel, only to be propelled back up to the surface by their buoyant flotation devices. Fuller observed their heads popping-up like a wack-a-mole carnival game, and he repositioned his vessel to make another pass. This continued a few more times until twenty-six sailors were rescued, nearly doubling *654*'s compliment of twenty-nine*. This concerned Fuller – they were some eight-hundred miles west of Cape Finisterre, a rockbound peninsula west of Galicia, Spain, and Gibraltar was still very far away. There was only so much room below deck and supplies were dwindling.

A rating approached, touching his cap in a nervous salute. He looked scared.

"Sir, none of them speak English – what if they're not friendly?"

"The subs sunk a ship," he assured him. "They're probably Lascars from a Limey freighter. Don't let that worry you."

Then the torpedo officer appeared, looking even more alarmed.

"What is it, Torps?"

The man came close and, in a hushed tone, reported, "captain, sir, I must warn you before you bring any more men on board. We've got German submariners, and furthermore, we've got two crews that don't know each other. They're not from the same boat."

Fuller stared at him. "How do you know that?"

"I speak German Sir – I recognized they were speaking it and eavesdropped on their conversation."

---

* Fuller carried one more person than the other torpedo boats, the flotilla torpedo officer.

"How the hell did two different U-boat crews end up on my bloody boat?"

Torps shrugged and then offered, "I can question the crew if you'd like sir?"

Fuller shook his head. "Not yet," he replied, rubbing his beard. He needed to re-evaluate the situation now that POWs were aboard. "Right, things just got a bit dicey. We've drifted well astern of the convoy and need to catch-up. Let the SO know of our situation and break off the search – we need to get back in formation. I also want the main mess deck cleared for our 'guests'."

He glanced over at the German sailors sitting on the deck under the watchful eyes of his gunners. "In the meantime, search them all thoroughly. I don't want to take any chances so confiscate anything they have – even their belts."

"Belts?" number one questioned.

"If it can be used as a weapon, take it," Fuller insisted.

Paying their compliments, they set off. Commanding a floating gas cannister was dangerous enough but turning their MTB into a brig made things even worse. There wasn't an abundance of free space aboard *654*. Fuller took additional measures, ordering tape to be placed over all water taps. Fresh water needed to be carefully rationed to avoid running out before reaching their destination. Once the POWs were settled in the main mess deck – the largest open space aboard – Fuller addressed them, Torps serving as translator.

"You are prisoners and will remain under constant guard," he explained. Pointing to a faucet he warned "if the tapes on any of these water taps are touched by any of you, we'll just take two of you on deck and shoot them. Straight."

By the looks on the men's faces, they didn't take this to be an idle threat. However, they were still relieved to be saved and understood the need to ration supplies. They were a disciplined lot and Fuller later noted "they were pretty honest about that and they were well trained, extremely well trained."

One of the POWs revealed that he spoke English and in a thick German accent, asked "Where are we heading to, sir?"

"Well, where do you think this ship's going?" Fuller asked in return.

"Oh, Gibraltar of course," the prisoner replied.

Fuller couldn't help but shake his head. Clearly the enemy knew quite a bit about their mission. "So much for operational security," he thought. The man followed with another question.

"What's going to happen to us?"

While not obligated to say anything, Fuller gave an honest response. "I don't mind telling you this, that no submariner who is a prisoner of war is kept in England or Ireland, or any European country at all... They're all sent to Canada, so you'll probably finish up in there."

A look of relief came over the man. "Oh, I'd like to see Canada. I've heard a lot about it."

Fuller raised an eyebrow. "Why, who would be telling you?"

The submariner shared that his aunt lived in Ottawa on 'Flora Street'. Fuller later made a note of this, along with the name of his relative.

It would be some time until anyone learned the truth of what happened that night. *U639* and *U439*, the very same vessels that attacked them, wound up colliding with each other shortly after the second attack.[109] Fuller's boat had the bulk of German POWs, while Jerram's *667* rescued an additional two. Jerram lucked-out in more ways than one – not only did he have far less prisoners to contend with, but one of them was a gifted baker. For the next three days, *667*'s crew enjoyed fresh bread![110]

Not all was lost for *654*. Among the POWs was a skilled cook, who happily volunteered his services in the galley. The man certainly knew how to operate a kitchen and soon ran it alone, making and serving all meals including snacks and kye. Mild in nature, caring nothing about the politics surrounding the war, he developed a rapport with all the officers and crew, even speaking bits of broken English. Fuller and his men never ate so well at sea – it would be a shame to lose his culinary abilities, a rarity in coastal forces – so he adopted a business approach. If the man agreed to serve as their cook, he wouldn't be turned over with the rest of the POWs.

Three days later, when MPs escorted the prisoners out of the MTB, they were short one. Decades later, Fuller casually explained that "he decided he'd rather join the Royal Navy than be a prisoner of war, so we signed him on as Able Seaman 'Jock MacPherson' and put him on the payroll."

No small matter. Grave consequences would befall either party if authorities discovered the scheme. Even though Fuller had no real authority to make such an agreement, German command would still view Jock's move as defection and execute him for his crime. As for Fuller, he along with his officers and men, would likely find themselves charged with knowingly harbouring an enemy sailor. To make matters worse, they also passed him off as a British national and member of the RN. Crown law explicitly stated that providing "aid and comfort in the realm, or elsewhere" to "the King's enemies" was an act of high treason.[111]

Fortunately, these things never came to pass. Also, it's important to apply a wide lens to this action – to date, Fuller consistently demonstrated, in the highest traditions of the RN, commitment to duty, conspicuous gallantry, and unquestionable loyalty to his comrades. Realistically, Jock could do little in his position: even if he harboured dubious intentions, the shrewd, quick-witted Fuller kept him firmly under close watch. Still, the risks associated with this decision were severe.

In the end, it's a wonder that Fuller managed to pull-off the things he did with little to no consequences. Perhaps his confidence and trust in his own judgment in part explain why he proved himself such an effective CO. In fairness, he didn't always succeed avoiding consequences when breaking the rules but always managed to come out the other side unscathed. Things might have been different during peace time, but considering the grave situation the world was now in, the navy likely didn't want to bench one of its key players. Love him or hate him, there was no denying that Fuller was the sort of person coastal forces needed in command.

CHAPTER 11

The Med

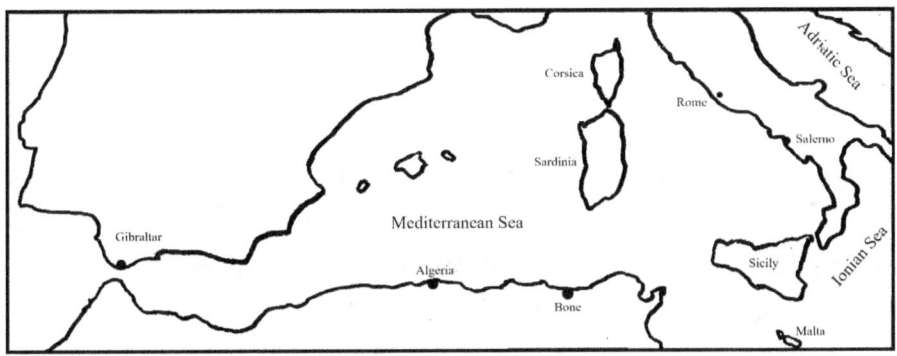

In May 1943, Fuller and the rest of the flotilla finally passed through the Strait of Gibraltar. Miraculously, despite the weather and contact with not one, but two U-boats, the entire convoy completed the long and arduous journey without the loss of a single vessel. To their relief, the waters here were calm and their rendezvous contact, a flotilla of RN destroyers stationed just off the coast, were close by.

MTB *654* came alongside the flotilla's lead O-Class destroyer, HMS *Onslow*, and although it would only be a brief pit stop, they could finally unload the POWs and replenish some of their stores. More importantly, it was a chance to shut off the engines, which had now been running for nearly a week straight. The persistent rumbling had blended so much into the background that nobody consciously noticed – now the sudden absence of their sound made things feel oddly quiet.

Fuller took in the various greys that made up the destroyer's disruptive camouflage, accented by streaks of burnt-orange rust. Soon, the 33rd would continue west along the North African coast to Bone, an Algerian seaport city under Allied control. It would be there that his boat would finally have the extra petrol tanks and arrester rails removed and torpedo tubes loaded.

Onslow dropped ladders over her gunwales, the cargo nets unravelling as they unfurled along her hull. Lines were also passed to *654*, the deckhands using them to secure the MTB to the larger vessel.

"Right, let's get our guests up the ladders," Fuller ordered.

In line, the POWs clambered up, a struggle as their belts hadn't been returned. A few failed to keep their pants from falling around their ankles, and one even lost them entirely. Once on deck, they were corralled and assessed by the ship's doctor before being moved to the brig. Of course, Jock remained in *654* and out of sight. If forced to speak, his accent would be a dead giveaway. Once the last prisoner ascended, Fuller, accompanied by a few ratings, proceeded to board the destroyer. He would need to make a report to *Onslow's* captain before departing.

"I take it that you've had quite the journey," an officer observed as Fuller stretched his legs.

"You don't know the half of it," Fuller replied, voice horse and tired. He then followed the officer who led him and his number one into the ship. As they walked, *Onslow's* intelligence officer caught up and confirmed that the POWs were indeed from two U-boats, although erroneously concluding they were from *U437* and *U534*. At the time, the belief was that the trawler *Coverley* managed to ram one of the U-boats, causing significant damage. As for the other, it had been sunk earlier from a Sunderland aircraft.[112] While Fuller nodded along politely, he knew better – Torps had already questioned the survivors and discovered that both U-boats were surfaced and going with the wind when they broached to, collided, and were fatally damaged.

They removed their headdress and entered the wardroom, taking seats and helping themselves to some refreshments. Compared to the MTB, the space felt palatial. The captain soon entered with some of his senior officers. Spirits were high and Fuller got the sense they were looking to be regaled with tales of their passage. Later, he would explain that the destroyer "had sour lemons for a month and a half and hadn't seen a goddamn thing to shoot," so the sudden presence of prisoners caused quite a stir throughout the ship. Truth be told, Fuller didn't feel like going over any of it – a stiff drink and sleep were what he craved. Still, he made nice and relayed what happened, not that it was much of a tale. Besides poor weather, miserable conditions, and one bomber attack, they hadn't even fired a gun. It didn't compare to Fuller's other skirmishes.

"Surely you fired your torpedoes at the enemy?" the captain asked.

Fuller shook his head. "We didn't even get close enough to drop depth charges," he answered, "and before we knew it, we'd come across survivors."

"But your torpedo tubes are empty," the captain countered. "My OOW noticed your cook up on deck and drawing a bag of potatoes from the back tube."

Fuller hesitated – it could only be Jock. He felt his chest tighten but remembered that Torps had scrounged up some spare pieces of kit and managed to dress him in a passable uniform.[113] Relaxing, he replied, "they were never loaded to begin with." When he saw the confusion on the captain's face, he explained "because of the extra fuel tanks needed for the journey, we couldn't carry them without being too top heavy. And someone back in England told us that there was apparently a scarcity of potatoes in the Med, so we decided to store a few extra bags in the tubes."

His audience laughed – if there was one thing the RN hadn't run out of, it was certainly potatoes. The question abated and they all enjoyed some sandwiches and coffee. As he finished the last of his drink, a messenger knocked on the hatch and relayed that one of Fuller's motor techs – Forder – had suffered an injury while servicing 654's engines. Springing to his feet he rushed back to his boat, picking up additional details while on route: Forder had been lying on his back, working on a hose connection that happened to be under too much pressure. When loosened, it blew off and struck the man in his eyes, scalding his face.

"Get him to my cabin," he ordered, heading first to his medicine chest. Moans emanated from Forder as he was brought in and laid onto the CO's bed. Fuller rummaged through the kit until he found some atropine. While not a physician, his father had suffered from eye problems in the past and through necessity, Fuller learned how to administer various remedies. Of course, he never would have guessed he'd be using that knowledge aboard an MTB.

After sanitizing his hands, Fuller carefully opened Forder's wounded eye and applied the atropine. The man groaned as the droplets dilated the pupil, but Fuller eased him, saying, "easy, it's going to help." Next, he took a small vile of clove oil* – a pain killer – and then prepared fomentations, infusing the cloth with boric acid before soaking it in a bowl of hot water that Jock had brought from the galley. Carefully, he rolled back the eyelid, dropped some of the oil, and then covered the injury with the warm compression. Again, Forder moaned but soon relaxed, his body sinking into the thin mattress.

654 departed with the rest of the flotilla for Bone, although Fuller spent most of his time caring for the wounded man, popping up to the bridge for brief reports before heading back to his cabin. Every four hours, he would re-apply the atropine until Forder's pupil extended to the very whites of his eye and then refresh the fomentations. None of this was missed by the crew who silently acknowledged their CO's

---

* According to Fuller, it contained both cocaine and opium, among other ingredients. He later learned that his boat was the only one in the flotilla with both atropine and the clove oil.

attentiveness. While at times brash and foul-tempered, he clearly cared for his men. And the treatment he provided proved critical. Once in port, Fuller sent Forder to an American hospital with a note stating, "home atropine every four hours and hot fomentations, cocained the eyeball."

Sometime later, Forder's doctor paid 654 a visit.

"How's my man?" Fuller asked after greeting the American.

"He's well," the doctor replied, surprised by Fuller's accent. "I take it you're not English?"

"Canadian."

"I should have guessed," the man admitted. "I actually came to see your doctor – you're lucky you just happened to have an eye specialist aboard. Is he around?"

Fuller chuckled, "I guess you're looking for me."

"It was you?" the doctor questioned, giving the CO an incredulous look.

"Picked up a thing or two helping my old man before the war," Fuller explained.

The physician pursed his lips and nodded. "Well, I gotta say, that I'm impressed – he's likely going to make a full recovery. Should be fit to return in a few weeks."

While Forder recovered, the MTBs and MGBs had the cumbersome extra fuel tanks, arrester rails, and other modifications cluttering the upper deck, removed. Torpedoes were also loaded into the tubes and gunners reported, with much relief, that they could again move their weapons without any restriction. Fuller's MTB was now fit for battle.

Upon arrival, all COs were warned to keep a watchful eye for looting. NAAFI ships were regularly unloading crates onto Bone's dock and the rate of deliveries, in addition to the sheer volume of supplies – these were big vessels and carried quite a bit of cargo – quickly overwhelmed logistics ashore. Men would be in the middle of moving one load when another ship would arrive and begin unloading even more goods and equipment. With limited numbers, it became impossible to keep up. Boxes piled along the shoreline and with little oversight, sailors could pillage rations, equipment, alcohol, and tools with relative ease.

In hindsight, it might have been better not to share this information with coastal forces personnel. Out of necessity, many COs had already taken to stealing gear and rations to ensure their ships remained properly equipped and operational. Some even purposely conducted raids on their own supply depots, sneaking sailors ashore to grab what they needed and then darting back to sea before anyone noticed. And if discovered, apologizing after the fact still proved more advantageous than going through proper channels, which inevitably meant copious forms and administrative delays.

One evening, after running some errands ashore, Fuller returned to his ship and found a few ratings lingering about the gangplank. They appeared to be keeping an eye out for someone, and when they noticed their CO, rushed up to meet him.

"Sir, there was an accident and someone injured his leg."

"Christ, another injury?" Fuller groaned. "Where is he?"

"He's aboard the boat sir," reported an AB, "and a doctor is looking at him."

Fuller nodded, feeling some relief. "Okay, let's go check on him then."

"Wait, wait sir!" the men protested, blocking his path.

Wrong move.

"What the hell are you doing?" he barked, "out of my way!"

"Sir don't take the doctor to your cabin!" they pleaded, but Fuller cut them a look that silenced them mid-sentence. Thinking better of it they stood aside, and their CO stomped towards his MTB, looking like an angry drill instructor. Nervously, the men followed.

"Why wouldn't they want him taken to my cabin?" he wondered as he boarded his vessel. After the main mess, it was the next largest space and offered a large table and bed. Typically, during a battle, a CO's cabin doubled as a sick berth.

He met the doctor on the upper deck, along with his patient. They were waiting for transport to the base hospital and Fuller was grateful to discover the injury wasn't severe. He chatted with both men until the ambulance arrived, then went straight through a hatch and into the wheelhouse. He slipped down a ladder and then reached for his cabin's door, which opened a mere foot before bumping against something on the other side.

"What the?"

He tried again but the obstruction didn't budge. Temper rising, he slowly turned to see some of the crew crammed in the tight space above him as well in the entrance of the mess deck, situated almost directly across from his cabin. They looked like nervous children. He turned back to the entrance and glanced through the tiny opening, which was just large enough for him to fit his head. Piles of boxes, one stacked atop the other, took up every inch of free space he could see. They were on the floor, bed, table, and desk, and went from deck to deckhead. Labeled across each were the words: "Clark's Pork and Beans." The pieces fell together.

"Listen, if you're going to go on a looting party, for Christ's sake why Clark's Pork and Beans?" he chided, turning again to face his men. "You realize they've got crates of scotch piled-up out there?"

"They're not pork and beans sir," an LS replied, gesturing to one of the boxes. "Notice the green shamrock on the top corner?"

Taking a second look, Fuller indeed noticed the marking.

"What does that mean?" he asked.

"They're actually full of cigarettes."

That took Fuller by surprise, but he still disapproved of their choice. Before he could say another word one of his deckhands warned that another CO was approaching the boat. Fuller sighed and yelled "gangway", prompting his men to scurry out of his path to allow him back up the ladder. The last thing he needed was for someone to come aboard and find his cabin crammed to the brim with stolen goods. He intercepted the visitor just as he boarded.

"Hey Gramps," he greeted, and then asked, "can you spare a moment?"

"Sure, what's up?"

The man removed his cap to wipe the sweat off his brow with a handkerchief.

"I've got about a thousand cartons of cigarettes aboard my boat," he shared, careful to stay quiet, "and some of my men say your boat has the same. What are we going to do about all of this?"

"My guys picked-up Armour brand corned dogs and Clark's Pork and Beans," he lied, "but let's keep this to ourselves. Putting it back would be too risky and it might help having some stuff to trade later."

That appeared to do the trick – the officer left, allowing Fuller to resume scolding his men for their lack of foresight. "Let's get some good stuff," he said, "get rid of these cigarettes and find something we can really use. There should be a lot of tinned fruit and stuff that we haven't seen for a long time." From the looks on their faces, he could tell they were grasping his logic. One of the LS organized some men to remove the boxes from Fuller's cabin, which were temporarily placed in the main mess. While no one spoke a word of it to him, he knew what would transpire – a few ratings would covertly head out that night and swap them for something better. That's why he wasn't surprised to find boxes of tin fruit and other decent rations stowed away the following morning. Yet, when he opened his cabin's hatch he was startled to find a container just outside his quarters. No note was attached, but looking inside he knew that it must be a gift from the crew – a full shipment of scotch.

After a month at Bone, orders came to continue east; the 33rd along with the 14th PT Squadron were to head to Malta and assist operations in support of the invasion of Sicily. They reached the island on June 17, 1943, and marveled at the sight – shores of soft, golden-beige limestone, rising steeply from crystal waters into ancient fortifications that blended seamlessly with the land. These were once the bastions of the Order of St. John, and as they neared the eastern coast, more of the island's architecture became clear. Densely packed buildings and streets emerged behind medieval defences, and like everything else, were made of stone. It made several of them wonder if they'd somehow travelled hundreds of years into the past. Had a knight suddenly appeared on a wall, clad in armour and heraldic trappings, it wouldn't have looked out of place.

For thousands of years, Malta had been a strategic naval base and occupied by many nations before becoming a British colony. And once again, the island's location proved vital, this time as a launching point against the Axis' hold of the Italian mainland.

HMS *Gregale*, a relatively new shore establishment, had been established in late December 1942. Private housing and garages, situated among four villas on the Ta' Xbiex terrace, were requisitioned by the RN, and a handsome, small, two-storey, stone house, served as HQ for the Captain Coastal Forces Mediterranean.[114] The hilly peninsula provided a commanding view of Marsamxett harbour in addition to ample mooring points. Garages under the main road outside the HQ made for convenient workshops to service boats and other equipment.

Fuller berthed his MTB alongside the rest of the flotilla and joined Ashby and the other COs ashore. A short walk up some stairs took them to the main road and directly to the front entrance of the HQ. Ashby would conduct the S.206 evaluation of Fuller's command, one of his last duties as SO of the 33rd before being re-assigned in July. The report, dated June 22, 1943, is revealing:

Professional Ability:	7
Personal Qualities:	7
Leadership:	8
Intellectual Ability:	8
Administrative Ability:	7

Fuller's scores had greatly improved.* Moreso, Ashby noted his ship handling as "Very Good, Indeed"[115] and commented "I consider that in the next few months this officer would make an excellent SO of a Coastal Forces Flotilla preferably 70 ft. Gun Boats and consequently I recommend that he be promoted to the rank of Acting Temporary Lt Cdr RCNVR."[116] He ended by highlighting that Fuller "has drive, experience and is a born leader".

In July, Fuller moved to MTB *655* and began preparing to conduct patrols near the Sicilian coast, which, at cruising speed, would take three to four hours to reach. Recent intelligence reports indicated that enemy activity would be heavy. Coastal Forces increased night patrols along the eastern part of the island in June and observed an increase in enemy shipping. By the end of the month, they had extended their sweeps to the west port of Marsala before being tasked with defending anchored ships. Operation Husky began on July 10 and four days later, Fuller was confirmed as the flotilla's spare CO, now under the command of a Lt Cdr Edward "Tizzy" Green-Kelly.

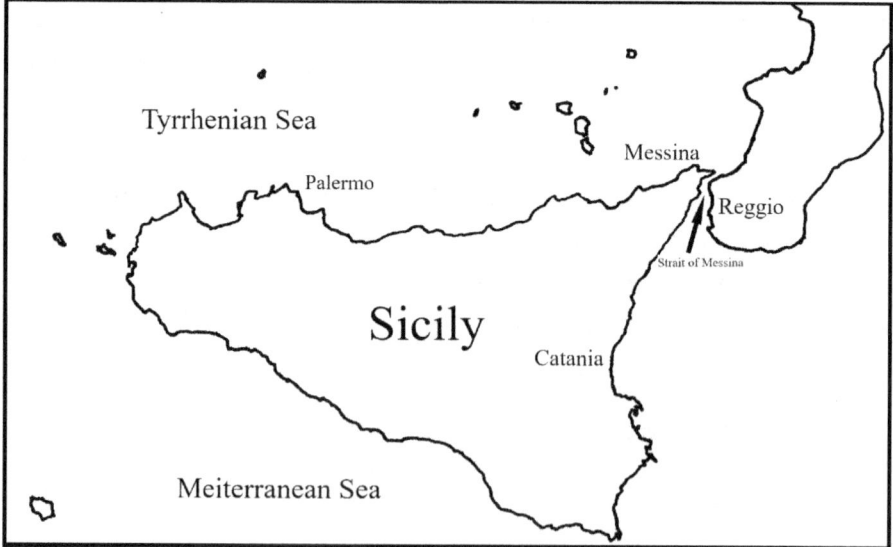

---

* It is unclear why Fuller's scores changed. The rankings are subjective and ultimately reflect the disposition/opinion of the SO compiling the report.

Three MTBs were dispatched to the Straits of Messina, the narrow strip of water separating Sicily from the Italian mainland. *656* (Lt D. Tate), *633* (Lt A. B. Joy), and Fuller's *655* were to conduct a night patrol. As spare CO, Fuller would have Green-Kelly aboard his boat. The SO would coordinate the flotilla while Fuller skippered the vessel. The trio would follow on the heels of the 24th flotilla, consisting of MTBs *81* (Lt L. V. Strong), *77* (Lt J.B. Sturgeon), and *84* (2nd Lt. G.R. Smith), which had departed for the same area fifteen minutes before. SO Lt Christopher Dreyer, aboard *81* led the boats and made a preliminary sweep of the area.[117]

At 1300 hours, the 33rd left *Gregale* and took up the rear guard. For the next few hours, they proceeded across crisp, blue waters, that separated the two islands. The fifty-three nautical mile journey across the Sea of Sicily was peaceful, the temperature warm and inviting – in no way alluding to possible dangers ahead. *655* led the way east towards Acid North Beach, the place where Allied forces had made landfall. From there they continued up along the eastern coast, nearing ever closer to the strait.

The C-in-C Mediterranean, Admiral Cunningham*, deemed the operation a "high risk" and cautioned SOs to be on guard. The Strait of Messina was a volatile choke-point – forty-five high powered searchlights and fifty gun-emplacements poised along either side of the channel. To make matters worse, the strip tapered to just about a mile in width, providing nowhere to retreat if discovered. If searchlights locked on an MTB, the crossfire would certainly destroy them.

Blood would be drawn that night. Per Dreyer's plan, the 24th entered the straits as the sun dropped below the horizon. He'd observed on a previous patrol that "the period lasting about half an hour between dusk and full darkness was a very effective one in which to operate."[118] The waning light made starshells and searchlights ineffective, and

---

* His nickname was 'ABC': Andrew Browne Cunningham.

spotting a Dog Boat by eye in the twilight wasn't easy. He deduced that it would allow his flotilla to enter and operate in the strait virtually undetected.*

At a steady 10 knots, they made their way to Reggio, whereupon they reduced speed to 6 knots. With quieter engines, they slipped into the darkening waters of the narrowest portion of the straits, where the thinning channel turns almost directly east. All engines were silenced, allowing the three MTBs to wait for unsuspecting enemy ships to cross them. They would pounce, launch torpedoes, and then beat a hasty retreat south.

Around 2215 hours, Dreyer's patience was rewarded when a lookout on the mainmast spotted an object approximately three-hundred yards off their starboard bow. It turned out to be U375 moving south to hunt for ships in open waters.[119] A prime target. Dreyer sent the signal "nuts to starboard", nuts being code for enemy, to the C-in-C and throttled up to engage.[120] The sound of their engines alerted the enemy and the U-boat defensively maneuvered towards them to narrow the target area. In response, the MTBs moved astern to reposition themselves but now 81 was too close to fire torpedoes and needed to distance itself from the U-boat to increase sea room. As they pulled away another shape became visible – another U-boat directly behind the first. 81 turned about, increased speed, and shot from the hip, launching a torpedo a mere one-hundred yards away from the enemy. It raced towards the target and struck true. U561, the boat in question, exploded in a brilliant show of fire, smoke, and debris.[121]

The battle had commenced.

Dreyer signaled the others to engage the remaining U-boat. Both 77 and 84 managed to straddle the enemy who "had jinked to starboard

---

* Dreyer wasn't new to operating near enemy shores. He'd led one of the MTBs at Dunkirk under orders to "nip over… and see what you can do." He towed several small vessels out of the shallow waters and was blown-off the MTB when he tried to scuttle his crippled vessel by firing his pistol into his engine room which had filled with fuel.

when his partner was blown up".[122] Unfortunately, *77* suffered a double-misfire and, although in perfect striking position, couldn't launch a torpedo to take out the submarine. *84* managed to hastily fire off its own torpedoes, just as U*375* dived, the shots passing harmlessly overhead. Smith immediately commenced a depth charge attack but was unable to score any significant hits before the U-boat fled back to port. Dreyer would later apologize in a communication to Cunningham, stating "Two U-boats engaged in position. Regret only one sunk."[123] At the very least, their attack had interrupted its patrol, which meant two less submarines would harass Allied shipping that night.

Shortly after sweeping the area, Dreyer's lookouts noticed a squadron of German E-boats moving with haste down the Calabrian coast. By this time, Fuller and his comrades had positioned themselves in a holding pattern to intercept any vessels that slipped passed the 24th. Dreyer made a hasty attack, launching a port torpedo from eight-hundred yards, which missed wildly. They radioed a warning to the 33rd to expect company.*

Aboard *655*, Fuller received Dreyer's message: "E-boats spotted heading south traveling at 25 knots."

"All ahead full," he ordered, urging his gunners to "keep sharp – we're hunting E-boats tonight."

Green-Kelly signaled for the other two boats to follow on an intercept course. At speed they moved up the strait, and Fuller raised his scotch-tea to his mouth, savouring both the drink and thrill of the hunt. They were pushing 20 knots in starboard line formation. At 2340 hours, Fuller's lookouts spotted the E-boats, moving in line at 6 knots.

"Slow to 8 knots," he ordered before looking back at Green-Kelly, who stood just behind him. "Let's let them come to us?"

The SO nodded his approval.

---

* *81*, *84*, and *77* proceeded back up into the straits but were soon picked-up by enemy searchlights. Six of them fixed on the trio and opened fire, but Dreyer employed an old trick Fuller recounted earlier in this text – launch a three-star red signal into the air, which made the enemy believe they were friendly.

Fuller waited about four minutes, right until the enemy came within one-hundred yards – too close to escape. He then gave the order to throttle-up, bringing *655* into firing range. The sudden appearance of three MTBs took the enemy completely by surprise. Fuller targeted the rear boat while Tate and Joy focused on the other two. Lines of tracers shot out as bullets ripped through enemy vessels. It took a moment for the E-boats to respond, by which time it was already too late. They fired a few wild shots as their boats turned back for the Sicilian coast, which was only three-hundred yards away.

"Looks like they're running for it," Green-Kelly observed.

"They can try," Fuller replied.

The MTBs made a sharp starboard turn and pursued the E-boats, their guns continuing to nip at the enemy vessels.

"Keep them in your sights and adjust your speed cox'n," Fuller cautioned through the voice pipe. As with his previous boats, the wheelhouse viewscreens were marked to correspond with the brass poles affixed to the deck. All the pilot needed to do was keep the marker on the enemy. The adjustment was made and *655*'s guns tore through one of the E-boats, shredding its stern and setting it ablaze. Their rounds had struck the engine – the vessel lost power and drifted towards the coast, running aground, guns silent.

The SO raised his eyebrows – he'd just experienced firsthand the effectiveness of Fuller's gunnery scheme, and it impressed.

With one down, Fuller turned his attention to another E-boat, which proved easy to spot as it too was on fire, although not yet disabled. It moved north in a desperate attempt to escape, riding low in the water and firing towards them with only a single gun.

"Keep us at 8 knots," Fuller directed, "and continue firing."

Again, Green-Kelly witnessed the lethality of Fuller's gunnery scheme – despite having been bruised by *656* and *633*, it was Fuller's guns that expertly finished them off, ripping open the side of the E-boat and silencing her remaining gun. They passed by the wreck and observed the boat sinking from the stern, her entire upper works ablaze like a giant floating funeral pyre.[124] It too drifted ashore, leaving two fires raging just off the coast. The MTBs pulled away.

BANG!

A single round shot overhead. Fuller spun around and brought his binoculars to his eyes. Despite the flames, one of the E-boats still defiantly fired at them. Something about it stuck with Fuller.

"And people say that the Italians have no guts?" he noted to Green-Kelly. "That gun crew's still manning that gun on the after-deck, despite the fact that their deck's below the water line." He dropped his binoculars, and despite respecting the display, observed "lucky for us their aim is piss-poor."

Several shore-based searchlights flashed alive and began sweeping the area with their lime-white beams.

"Time to go," Fuller said.

Batteries along the coast began opening into the waterway, causing large splashes of water to erupt nearby.

"Good idea," the SO agreed.

WING!

Something struck the bridge wall, causing both Fuller and the SO to duck. Keeping their heads down, they traded puzzled looks.

WING!

Another shot, striking even closer.

"That's not coming from shore batteries," Fuller observed, catching something odd in the sound. "That's rifle fire."

He popped his head through the wheelhouse hatch and yelled, "now's really a good time to leave!" 655 sped up, and Fuller chanced bringing his head just high enough above the bridge wall to glance back with his binoculars.

WING!

He flinched but still caught the muzzle flash along the shoreline.

"It's a goddamn sentry with a rifle," he noted in amazement. The soldier was close to where the two E-boats had beached themselves, near the mouth of a tunnel and hidden in the shadows.

WING! Another shot struck the bridge, and this time Fuller went back down.

"By God, that fellow is accurate!" Fuller said to the SO.

He wasn't going back up until they were well out of range. That last shot really shook him and he reached for his drink and took a long pull, hoping the alcohol would help calm his nerves. Years later, he would admit the sniper fire convinced him to leave. "He was only firing at the bridge, and I'm telling you that it was real hell, because he had no tracer ammunition." Fighting against E-boats had made Fuller used to tracer fire, which partially allowed him to 'see' an attack coming. But this was the first time he'd been shot at and couldn't tell where it was coming from to evade. "Rifle fire is something else," he explained. "You can't see anything; all you hear is WING! WING! and it gets you pretty jumpy after a while."

All three boats continued south while coastal batteries on both sides fired aimlessly into the waters. The shots all fell short as the MTBs were now well out of range. With the element of surprise gone, it didn't make sense to continue the hunt. Dreyer was also still above them, so Green-Kelly decided it best to head for open water. Soon, the Messina Strait gave way to the Ionian Sea, the eastern shoreline receding and pulling back as they slipped beyond the southernmost part of the Italian mainland. With it, the gunfire began to simmer down until it ceased altogether, leaving only the sound of their deep engines. The quiet of the sea and night returned, as well as the peace of tranquil waters.

Things weren't yet over for the 33rd. As the flotilla passed Cape Allessio, *655*'s man up the mast alerted them that two Italian MAS-boats* were approaching from the south. Fuller couldn't believe their good fortune and didn't even await the SO's approval. "All ahead full," he barked, "and let's see if we can add a few more to the count!"

Leading the charge, all three MTBs closed on MA/SBs starboard side. The enemy was traveling in line and moving at speed – easy targets

---

* Motoscafi Anti-Sommergibili (MAS-boats), the Italian version of MTBs.

if the British managed to intercept them in time. Fuller squinted through his binoculars, trying to judge the distance. He wished they were closer, but just maybe…

"Open fire!"

655's guns erupted, sending arcs of well-trained tracer towards the vessels. Fuller kept his eyes fixed on the fleeing boats, coaching the cox'n so that the shots landed just ahead of their target. Experience paid-off – rounds punched through enemy hulls, prompting the Italians to return fire. But the MA/SBs weren't interested in a fight. They stayed on course, determined to outrun their attackers. The MTBs turned to pursue but lacked the power to catch-up. Gradually, the gap between them grew.

"Are we full out?" Fuller asked, referring to the engines.

"Aye sir, moving as fast as she can go."

The distant shapes of the MA/SBs continued to shrink and so the 33rd broke off the pursuit. While Fuller felt disappointed – he would have preferred adding a third boat to the tally – at least they roughed them up. Two minutes passed when, to their surprise, yet another seven MA/SBs appeared just off the starboard bow, similarly heading northwest.[125] This was turning into quite the night.

Naturally, Fuller pushed his vessel back to 22 knots and directly at the enemy flotilla. *655*, well ahead of the other two boats with an eight-hundred-yard lead, closed on the flotilla which were, again, moving in line. He knew he'd only get one chance and was determined to hit as many as he could.

"Aim for the lead boat and work your way down!" he shouted.

His guns opened, followed shortly by the other two MTBs. They riddled a few of the fleeing boats, but the MA/SBs remained undeterred. Even though they outnumbered their attackers, the enemy was set on returning to port and soon vanished into the strait. Fuller didn't even bother to give chase this time.

"Send word to Dreyer," he told Sparks. "Maybe he'll have better luck."

In fairness, the three MTBs had done plenty for a single patrol, taking out two ships and engaging at least ten more.

The 24th received Fuller's alert around 0445 hours, but by this time the vessels were already heading back south. The first hints of daylight were appearing on the horizon and soon the cover of night would be gone. Still, Dreyer pushed his boats to 20 knots in hopes of intercepting the MA/SBs before the morning sun made things too perilous to continue. They first noticed two MA/SBs and while Dreyer moved to cut them off, they caught sight of the other seven. He didn't like the odds. In his action report, he would later explain "They were not a pleasant sight at the time of the morning, since they were faster and much better armed than us, and the odds were three to one and we were a long way from home."[126] He made the prudent decision and ordered his boats to pull away, watching the enemy as they "passed on opposite courses at about [a thousand] yards range." Dreyer held his breath, uncertain if the MA/SBs would suddenly turn to attack, and was grateful they decided to remain on course. "It was quite amazing that they let us do this," he would comment, "but we accepted the situation thankfully. As we passed, they opened fire and we promptly replied, all the shooting being pretty ineffectual."[127]

Unlike Fuller, Dreyer took his boats to the advance base at Syracuse while the 33rd continued all the way back to Malta. All in all, the 33rd had sustained some damage to their vessels but nothing that couldn't be patched-up during the day.* The 24th on the other hand suffered one casualty, although thankfully the injury was considered minor.

Some interesting insights emerge from comparing the amount of ammunition the 33rd used that evening: *655* fired 168 rounds from their 2-pounder, 800 from the Oerlikon, 1800 from 0.5-inch, and 800 from the .303-inch gun. In comparison, *656* had only fired 56 rounds from the 2-pounder, 180 Oerlikon, 700 0.5-inch, and 250 .303-inch gun while

---

* Sadly, Green-Kelly would be KIA some months later in another action.

633 had fared slightly better, firing 720 2-pound rounds, 280 Oerlikon, 1000 0.5-inch, and 350 .303-inch gun.[128] Not only was Fuller the clear aggressor, his tactics allowed his gunners to 'let loose', confident their rounds would land on target. The results certainly speak for themselves.

CHAPTER 12

◇◇◉◇◇

With the Brass

The actions of July 14 and 15 didn't go unnoticed by command. To the credit of Fuller and his comrades, enemy vessels were unsuccessful in disrupting Allied amphibious landings along the southern Sicilian coast. Shortly after returning to *Gregale*, and after some much-needed sleep, Fuller received word that the C-in-C wanted to see him. So, he dressed in his cleanest uniform and hitched a ride across Marsamxett harbour to Valletta, disembarking and making his way passed churches, restaurants, and various older buildings until he reached "The Gut", the nickname British servicemen gave to Strait Street. Fuller was quite aware of its reputation as a red-light district, having spent a few evenings with comrades at some of the clubs. Not that one could tell at this hour – the street was quiet, free of boisterous and drunk sailors or pilots stumbling their way down the thoroughfare.

He appreciated the stroll, taking in a few sights along the way, which the island had an abundance of. Narrow streets, packed tightly with sandstone buildings replete with fine masonry, eventually led him to the lower end of South Street where a two-storey baroque building served as the C-in-C Mediterranean's office. Admiralty House consisted of large halls that surrounded a central courtyard, an impressive and large building that once served as the private residence of Fra Jean de Soubiran di Arafat, a Knight of the Order of St. John.

Fuller walked up the dark stone road that connected to the foot of the entrance – Malta didn't have sidewalks – and glanced up at the large door sandwiched between two tall limestone pillars, which supported a closed balcony. The place looked like a palace.

"Nice office," Fuller thought as he entered the building's main hall. Ahead was a large free-standing stone staircase – he'd never seen finer – with thick polished stone rails and steps. As he ascended the stairs, he noticed two ivory marble tablets on the wall upon which the names of all C-in-C of the Mediterranean fleet were inscribed. As a man who not only ran a construction company but came from a line of architects who'd designed some of Canada's finest buildings, Fuller was quite taken by it all.

On the second floor he entered an antechamber and reported to a Wren sitting at a lovely wood desk.

"Lieutenant Fuller, the admiral sent for me."

"Yes sir," she replied, checking his name off a handwritten list. "Please have a seat – I'll let him know you're here."

Fuller spotted a nearby bench along the opposite wall and sat down as the woman opened a set of double doors and entered an adjacent room. While he waited, he glanced around at the art and details of the beautiful and intricately carved painted ceiling. The high walls and large space evoked a feeling of importance. After a bit, Fuller decided to stroll around, looking at vases and other artifacts but began to grow impatient. He made his way back to the desk, and out of curiosity and restlessness, risked peeking through the open doors of Cunningham's office. The Wren and C-in-C were busy dealing with something and so his eyes lingered back over the secretary's desk. That's when he caught sight of a bunch of rubber stamps and a pile of stationary.

A thought occurred – this was where all memorandums and directives from the C-in-C Mediterranean were drafted. He again glanced back into the admiral's office before darting behind the empty desk.

"I did a very astute thing," he would later say.

Even for Fuller, this was taking a big risk. Grabbing one of the rubber seals from its ink well, he pulled out a notepad, flipped it over and pressed the stamp into the cardboard backing. Dissatisfied, he picked another and tested it. By the fourth try, he finally found what he'd been looking for - Cunningham's signature. Then something clicked. "In for a penny…" he thought as he took a piece of paper with official C-in-C letterhead. Carefully, he pressed the stamp at the bottom of the page and then beheld his work. It was basically a blank cheque – he could type whatever he wanted into the body and far as anyone would know, it was an official directive from the admiral.

A sly smile crept upon his face as he repeated the process five more times. He then took all six sheets, folded them on the desk, and slipped them into his tunic pocket. Returning to his seat, he crossed his legs and leaned back.

"This is going to be all right in the future," he thought.

Eventually the Wren returned, apologizing to Fuller. "I'm so sorry about the delay, but the admiral will see you now."

"Don't mention it," Fuller replied, adding a wink before strolling into the office. Cunningham sat with his back to a large, open-curtain window which made the paint of the spacious and regal room look brighter than it actually was. The admiral sat behind a large, dark wooden desk that looked as old as the place itself, carved and beautifully stained. A portrait of the King hung on one wall while a wide map of the Mediterranean adorned the other. Cunningham, an older thin man with receding white hair, sat straight, his forearms resting on the desktop and revealing a multitude of gold bars – the highest naval rank. He squinted at Fuller and reached for his pince-nez glasses, which he rested on the bridge of his nose.

The Canadian came to attention – his hat was under his left arm, so he didn't salute.

"Lieutenant Fuller reporting sir."

"Ah yes, Thomas, is it?" Cunningham asked, his voice giving off a dignified and pleasant sound.

"Aye sir," Fuller replied, taken aback by the use of his first name, "although I go by Tom."

"Tom," Cunningham repeated with a nod. "My friends took to calling me ABC in the service, because of my initials of course."

Fuller was aware; everyone referred to Cunningham as 'ABC', although few did so in his presence. He was the admiral of the Mediterranean fleet afterall – with the exception of a select few, 'sir' was the only appropriate form of address.

"A lot better than my nickname, sir."

The admiral arched an eyebrow, his magnified eyes looking intrigued.

"Gramps," Fuller revealed, "because I'm older than the other COs."

Cunningham chuckled and added "well, with age comes wisdom and resolve." He stood from his chair and straightened his tunic. "So, I've heard you had a busy night," he said as he rounded the desk and stopped in front of Fuller. "Tell me, did you get their balls?"

Fuller laughed, despite himself. Was this really the Cunningham he'd heard about? Not that anyone had shared specifics about his personality but Fuller, admittedly, assumed he'd be stuffy and self-absorbed. He was glad to be wrong – this man was relaxed, down to earth, and somewhat juxtaposed to his formal surroundings.

"Aye sir," Fuller finally replied, "I guess you can say we did."

Cunningham extended a hand. "Well done, Tom. Because of your actions, we managed to land our forces without being harassed by the enemy."

Fuller shook his hand. "Thank you sir, although I was only doing my job."

Cunningham smiled and went back to his chair, removing his glasses and picking up a memo on his desk. His voice now assumed a formal tone. "Back at it, Tom, plenty to do before this war is won. Dismissed."

And just like that the meeting was over. Fuller snapped back to attention, turned about and left the office, feeling a bit perplexed. "He was a very peculiar man," Fuller would later say. Making his way back down the stairs and out the front doors, he traced his steps back to the docks, keenly aware that in his tunic rested, "little papers… which were very useful."

A letter dated July 27, 1943, from the Captain of Coastal Forces in the Mediterranean to the C-in-C Mediterranean (with a copy going to Fuller) responded to Ashby's recommendation to have Fuller promoted. While the Capt disagreed with the SO's request, stating "I am not prepared to recommend this officer for promotion to Lt Cdr until he has proved himself as a Senior Officer of a Flotilla", he did move on making Fuller a QO Coastal Forces. Also, as 655 suffered some damage during his last patrol, he was provided MTB 313, which he assumed command on August 10. Fuller took his new boat for patrol along the Sicilian east coast, observing a bustling enemy rail station north of Catania. From what they noted, it appeared the enemy was moving supplies, possibly to help counter an Allied invasion. Fuller felt his squadron could successfully disable operations, and after receiving permission, conducted a night assault. It was a relatively smooth mission – the yard wasn't properly equipped to repel an attack from the sea.

The destruction of the rail station would be the last thing Fuller did to assist operation Husky. By the seventeenth, the Allies gained complete control of the island and turned their attention to the Italian mainland. Intent on continuing the pressure, the idea was to follow up with an immediate advance, but plans changed when Mussolini lost power. With the dictator overthrown, Allied commanders decided upon a more ambitious plan: in addition to crossing the Strait of Messina, they decided to add additional landing points to the north at the Volturno River and Salerno. The invasion of Italy would commence in September and Fuller would be there to assist.

On September 3 the Allies crossed the Strait and punched through the toe of the Italian boot at Reggio. Fuller, along with five other boats, formed a coastal bombardment line near the port of Taranto, assisting the British 1st Airborne Division. During the night, they noticed a stream of lights moving in unison towards Taranto's southern coast.

"Jesus!" Fuller said, moving his binoculars from his eyes – even without their aid he could make out the lights in the dark. "Look at all the traffic, with their headlights on and going like hell."

He ordered his boats to move in slowly, gradually coming within five-hundred feet of the coast.

"Well, they've got to be going thirty miles an hour with full headlights on," Fuller noted, looking at his 1st Lt. "It's got to be Germans in retreat." The man nodded and Fuller instructed him to "inform the other boats – we attack on my signal."

They adjusted into line formation, parallel to the coast, ready to give a full broadside. Although they couldn't possibly destroy every truck, it didn't matter. Some wreckage would be enough to clog the road and stop the enemies dead in their tracks.

"Sir!" a voice echoed up the voice pipe.

"What is it Sparks?"

"Pip-ink-ink-don sir, immediate!"

Fuller traded glances with his XO. Awkward timing but it had to be given priority. These messages only came from command and were related to identification.

"Bring it up," he ordered, but his telegraphist was already on his way and came out the wheelhouse hatch the very next moment. The message read: "Disregard. Disregard bombing-lines or you will have irate countrymen!"

Fuller looked back up at the moving lights.

"Christ, those are Canadian?" A sigh escaped his mouth and reached out to squeeze Sparks on the shoulder. "Good on you lad – send a TBS to the other boats and let them know."

The telegraphist went back to his post while Fuller ordered his gunners to stand down. He then turned to his 1st Lt, feeling a bit drained. "That was close."

Thankfully, since Fuller and his boats didn't engage, the Canadians were able to move thirty-eight miles that night.

On the tenth the US Fifth Army pressed on Salerno to the north. Fuller and his boats moved HQs, leaving Malta and settling in at Palermo. There he was assigned to guard the 'Banana Carrier' fleet, fast ships with refrigeration capabilities which supplied food for the invasion force. They were 'Woolworth' escort carriers that were slow, lacked protection and were extremely vulnerable to air attack. The distance from Palermo to Salerno was quite far and the MTBs once again needed to carry additional fuel – ten forty-five-gallon drums. As before, they'd have to be fitted to the boat's upper deck, but this time they'd be discarded over the side once used. To ensure they sank, each boat was issued with a brass hatchet. The admiralty felt that brass was less likely to cause a spark when striking the drum. Fuller recalled the tool: "It was the first time I'd ever had a brass hatchet given to me," he mused, "but in the admiralty they do strange things."

The second day of the Salerno invasion met with some difficulties. The German MGen Sieckenius and his 16th Panzer Division had countered the Allied invasion, almost pushing the Americans, as Fuller observed, "… back into the sea". Fuller, assisting with Air-Sea Rescue work in support of Operation Avalanche*, received word that he was to head back to base. A request had come from the US Navy Base Operations Division and Fuller's superiors decided he was the right person for the job. Coming to meet him was none other than LGen George S. Patton Jr, who commanded the Seventh Army.

Fuller didn't receive much information, just that Patton was bringing him an officer and that he was to follow his instructions. Upon returning to port, he met the general, along with MGen Lucian Truscott. Old 'Blood and Guts', as Patton was known by his men, had become a living a legend. Strong minded, tenacious, and complicated, Fuller shared many

---

* Codename for the beach landings at Salerno, which was part of the Allied Invasion of Italy.

of his qualities. They were both sure-footed warriors and more than a little egotistical. For his part, Fuller was taken by Patton's persona – a cleanly pressed uniform and a pair of pearl-handled pistols hanging from his hips.* He was also a large man – at 6'2 he towered over Fuller, who was almost 5'9 – and carried a sense of self-importance. He made his way along the jetty to Fuller's boat, seemingly ready to bulldoze through anyone in his path. Truscott followed just behind him along with an entourage of staff officers.

"You Fuller?" he asked, looking down at the bearded naval officer with an impatient and judgemental gaze. Despite the man's overbearingness, Fuller stood tall and stared him in the eyes. He wouldn't be fazed by the general.

"Yes sir," he replied with a salute.

"Good," Patton said, looking back and tapping Truscott on the arm. "I want you to take this boy over to Salerno."

Fuller nodded and said, "give me the chart and I'll ensure he gets there, sir."

Patton turned to the men behind him and reached out for the chart, but they didn't have a navigation chart, so they handed him a regular map. "We need him here," he said, resting a gloved finger at Salerno.

"Understood sir, but I need a navigation chart to get him there."

Patton sighed angrily and again looked back at his men, who shook their heads nervously. Growling, he turned on Fuller and barked "Just take him over to Salerno, take him to Salerno!"

Impatience was yet another characteristic both men shared.

"Yes sir," Fuller replied – what else could he say? Patton stormed off and Fuller went to his cabin to make preparations, which included trying to find a chart of the area. Travelling close to land without proper navigational information was more than a little risky. If they suddenly

---

* Depending on the circumstance, Patton would wear one or two guns. As explained by Whilt Collins, "When he wanted to portray the part to the largest possible gallery, he wore both, so that he would be unmistakable from any angle of observation"

ran aground, especially while moving at speed, the consequences could be fatal. Making matters worse, channel markers and buoys weren't always present during times of war, and even if they were, they might have been purposely moved to mislead the enemy.

"How did it go sir?" an officer asked upon their COs return.

"Peachy," Fuller replied dryly. "We'll be taking an American general to Salerno." He then pulled his 1st Lt close and whispered, "let the boys know – everyone is to keep sharp – and see if you can track down a chart we can use to get this VIP to Salerno."

"They didn't provide one?"

He gave him a "are you really surprised?" kind of look.

"Right," the man replied and then left. Thankfully, he did return with a chart and once everything was sorted for the trip, including extra fuel, Fuller went off to retrieve their passenger. He found him speaking to Patton, the two sharing some light conversation. "At least ol' blood and guts looks to be in a better mood," he considered before coming up and saluting.

"Sir, we're all set to take you to Salerno."

"Just a moment," Patton said, wrapping an arm around Truscott. "I want you to look after that boy." He gave the other general a squeeze and both men chuckled. "You know, we think a lot of him," Patton added.

"I'll get him there, sir." Fuller answered confidently. Patton gave an approving nod – he respected assertiveness – and left. Fuller then brought Truscott aboard his MTB, which was idling and ready to depart. The general took his place on the bridge and the MTB departed at speed across the Tyrrhenian Sea.

Fuller noticed that the MGen, not unlike Patton, sported a unique style. He wore a characteristic beaten up looking leather jacket and white scarf, which he kept tucked in his coat to prevent it flapping in the wind. An issued .45 rested in a holster on his hip and the ensemble was completed by a pair of 'pink' cavalry breeches tucked into knee-high cavalry boots. Truscott often said he felt the combination of old pants and boots were 'lucky' and he was very superstitious about his attire. Fuller wondered if US Army generals were encouraged to alter their uniforms – perhaps it helped build a persona upon which the men drew confidence?

Overall, their VIP proved pleasant. Thankfully, Truscott was more relaxed and calmer compared to Patton. While tough and confident, he didn't bother trying to show it.[129] Fuller enjoyed their conversations and respected the man's candor and straightforwardness.

313 eventually entered an Allied safe-zone – the sanctuary – and came across an American B-52 bomber in the sky.

"One of yours," Fuller noted, handing over his binoculars to Truscott.

"Mitchell," he confirmed, "likely on his way to patrol the coast."

The bomber began to turn, changing course towards Fuller's boat. Something wasn't right.

"I'm not sure he knows this is a sanctuary area," Fuller observed, a hint of concern in his tone, "or that were friendly."

"Don't worry about it boy," Truscott replied, "I'm sure he's just checking us out."

The aircraft descended and then bore down on them.

"I've been attacked by plenty of aircraft," Fuller explained, "and that's what it looks like."

Truscott brought the binoculars back to his eyes and frowned.

"What is that fool doing?"

The Mitchell's machine guns answered, sending lines tracers at the crystal blue water before them. Thin splashes, like successive rows of meerkats jumping up on their hind legs, made their way towards the MTB.

"Evasive manoeuvres," Fuller shouted, "and hold your fire, the idiot's a friendly!"

The MTB swerved to avoid the incoming fire, but the plane was primarily a bomber and dropped a single explosive. It fell towards them and, due to the angle and speed, bounced off the water like a skipping-stone. The bomb flew up and over the MTB, just high enough to avoid being caught by the radar mast. Both Fuller and Truscott followed the dark shape as it landed behind them, bouncing yet another time before finally exploding. Water shot high into the sky and the concussion rattled the boat. It hadn't been a small bomb.

"That's a first," Fuller observed. "Thankfully he dropped the blasted thing prematurely."

Truscott was beside himself, saying, "if I ever find out who that numbskull is --" but he was cut short by Fuller.

"That goddamn Mitchell is coming around," he announced, pointing up at the plane. "If he attacks us again, we'll have to shoot him down."

Truscott considered his words and then nodded. "You've got no choice."

Fuller turned to his men. "If he comes at us again, take him out," he ordered.

A few tense moments passed, all eyes following the bomber as it turned and readied itself to make another approach. Then, for reasons unknown, the aircraft suddenly broke off and abandoned the attack, resuming its original course. Fuller turned to Truscott.

"You think someone finally told him who we are?"

The general shrugged. "I don't know, but we nearly got our tickets punched by the US Air Force."

Close calls were becoming a bit of habit for Fuller. "Resume course," he ordered.

Twenty minutes passed when a lookout reported a surfaced U-boat in the distance.

"This day just keeps getting better," Fuller groaned. Prior to leaving port, he'd received an Admiralty AZ message indicating that they would pass through a submarine sanctuary area. To be safe, he double-checked with his navigator and sure enough, they were in it, which meant he couldn't lawfully attack a surfaced submarine. "Why the Christ they would have a sanctuary area for submarines at an invasion anchorage, I can't understand," he complained. It was right there, and his torpedoes were loaded – he could take it out. He turned to the general and said "Jesus, it's a sanctuary area, I know the thing is German – do I disobey and attack?"

But Truscott shook his head. "You can't do it boy."

He couldn't disobey the order, especially with a general aboard telling him not to. So, against his better judgment, he let it go, but it made him feel uneasy. "I don't like it," he voiced in protest. Truscott reached out and squeezed his shoulder. He then quoted Lord Tennyson's poem:

"Ours is not to reason why."

Internally, Fuller scoffed. The line referenced soldiers on the verge of charging the enemy, but he was no longer a soldier, and as a naval officer he very much made it his business to know the 'why' of things. He didn't blindly follow anything that didn't make sense.

Thankfully, the rest of their journey went without a hitch and they eventually reached their destination, the Barnegat-class seaplane tender USS *Biscayne* situated just off Salerno's coast. It served as the flagship of Vice Admiral H. Kent Hewitt and assisted with the invasion as a quasi-hospital and command centre. Fuller brought his MTB alongside the much larger ship.

"Well, this is me," Truscott remarked, "thanks for the passage, Tom, it was certainly memorable."

Fuller laughed, "Anytime sir."

Truscott made his way up the ship's ladder while the MTB remained tethered, topping off their fuel. Not long after, word came to Fuller that Hewitt wished to see him, which took him by surprise. He couldn't imagine what a USN admiral would want with him. Still, as he didn't have much of a choice, Fuller made his way aboard where an officer guided him to Hewitt's cabin. Truscott was also inside, sitting on a chair.

"Lieutenant Fuller," Hewitt said, getting straight to business. "What's this business about a sanctuary area?"

The question confused Fuller – why was the admiral asking him about this? "I'm sorry sir, what about it?" he asked.

"The general here told me that you didn't attack an enemy U-boat because he was in a sanctuary area," he clarified, standing to his feet. His tone was serious, which put Fuller on the defensive.

"That's right sir," Fuller replied, his voice also firm. Admiral or not, he wouldn't let this man push him around. "My Admiralty AZ message said it was a sanctuary area and we can't sink submarines."

"No such order," Hewitt countered, an icy edge in his tone.

Digging in his heels, Fuller shot back "yes, there was sir. I would have sunk that blasted thing otherwise."

Hewitt looked annoyed but Fuller pressed on before he could say anything. "Sir, I can get the message to show you?" he suggested. A reasonable enough request, so Hewitt allowed it, although as a precaution, he sent some ratings to escort the Canadian back to his MTB. With the orders in hand, Fuller returned to the admiral's cabin and held it out. "The signal, sir," he announced defiantly.

Hewitt appeared taken off guard – he must have thought Fuller was bluffing – and snatched the message from his hands. As he read it a look of concern came upon his face.

"Oh-oh," he exclaimed, before asking Fuller and Truscott to follow him. His tone and demeanour had completely changed. Leading them both to the ship's radio room he held up the paper to the telegraphist and demanded, "did you know that this existed?"

The sailor hadn't but did some digging and eventually figured out what had happened - it was an old communication which had since been cancelled but the USN had yet to update the RN about it.

Fuller growled at the revelation. "We could have had him sir," he said to Truscott. The general gave him an understanding and apologetic look.

"There's been more than one gaff this day," he conceded. "I'm sorry about the mix up son."

"Well, at least I'm not in trouble," Fuller said, which elicited a chuckle from the general. He liked Truscott, although the same couldn't be said for Hewitt, but he reasoned they may have just got off on the wrong foot. Dismissed, Fuller headed back to *Biscayne's* main deck. Enemy aircraft buzzed overhead, and the sounds of anti-aircraft fire pounded in the distance. His eyes focused on *USS Savannah*, a Brooklyn-Class light cruiser that was closer to shore (and the first American ship to open fire on enemy shore defences during the invasion).[130] Along with USS *Philadelphia*, both vessels were fending-off a squadron of aircraft and things looked to be heating up. High in the sky, safe from anti-aircraft fire, a German plane dropped a Fritz X PGM – a radio controlled gravity bomb – which exploded just shy of fifty feet from *Philadelphia*. *Savannah's* skipper ordered the vessel to take evasive action, increasing speed to 20 knots, but a Dornier Do 217, masked by the sun, moved on the ship. Although P-38 Lightnings moved to intercept, it was too late. At 18,700 feet it dropped a Fritz X PGM Bomb, striking *Savannah's* third gun turret and breaking through three decks to the ship's lower ammunition-handling room. Fuller and those aboard *Biscayne* watched helplessly as an explosion of fire erupted from her wound. Successive secondary explosions followed, but the crew, through great effort and courage, managed to control the flames.[131]

Fuller headed as fast as he could back down to his MTB. Giving the order to cast off, a return course to Palermo was plotted and the vessel slipped away from *Biscayne*. While he was partially motivated to get clear of the aerial bombardment, he was mostly keen on coming across that same surfaced U-boat so that he could blow it out of the water. Unfortunately, the enemy was long gone, but at least a friendly bomber didn't try to destroy them this time.

A week later Fuller moved to Alexandria and from late September to March 1944, he was appointed as the Senior British Naval Officer Aegean and NOIC for all Turkish ports, 'Vathy'.[132] He would report directly to Vice-Admiral Sir Algernon Usborne Willis, who as C-in-C,

Levant*, was the senior administrative shore commander in the area and directly responsible for conducting naval operations in the Aegean Sea in support of the Dodecanese Campaign.[133] The post, established back in February 1943, was the result of a decision to split the Mediterranean Fleet into two commands – one to deal with ship operations and the other with shore establishments.[134]

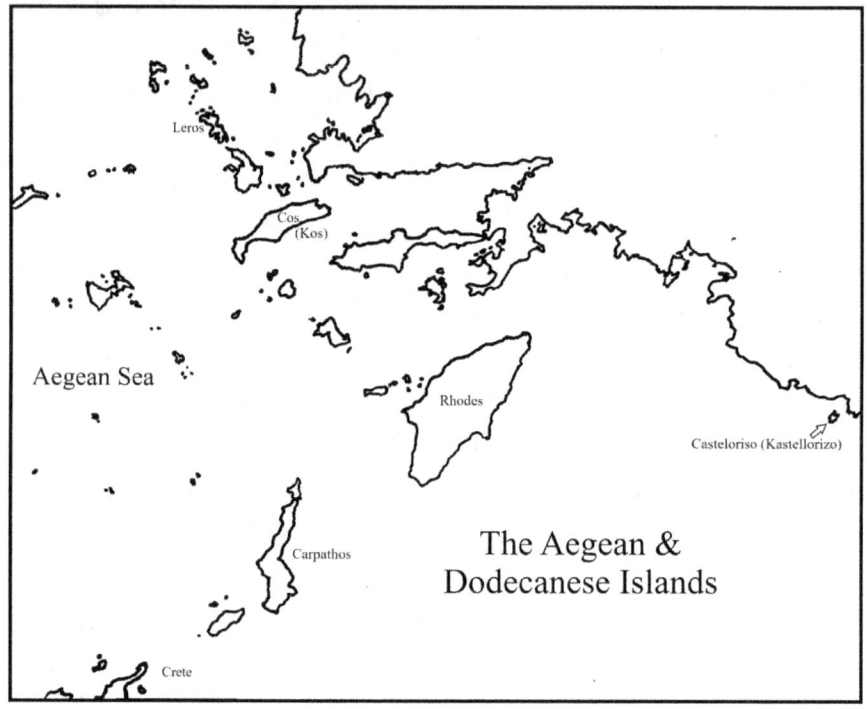

Leros

Cos
(Kos)

Aegean Sea

Rhodes

Casteloriso (Kastellorizo)

Carpathos

The Aegean &
Dodecanese Islands

Crete

Fuller, now spare CO of the 60th MGB Flotilla, was given charge of four boats. He moved MTB *313* to HMS *Mosquito*, an RN shore establishment in Alexandria, Egypt, and then on October 1, moved to HMS *Canopus*, a smaller RN training base, also in Alexandria. Fuller began conducting patrols from October 6 to 21, taking his four-boat flotilla north where they moved about islands recently liberated from Axis control. In Beirut they acquired camouflage nets, which they raised

---

* 'Levant' is a historical geographic term referring to an area in the Eastern Mediterranean (Western Asia).

over their vessels during the day to hide from enemy aircraft. Their patrol extended to Cyprus and then across the Levantine Sea to the island of Casteloriso (AKA Kastelorizo, west of Rhodes), known to many of Coastal Forces skippers as Red Castle.[135] To the north, Fuller found a small, mostly abandoned island called Cos, which became his primary base launching point to conduct raids.

He was now operating on his own and in these waters, far removed from the Allied presence to the west, patrols took on a different approach. The 60th didn't operate solely out of *Canopus*, but island hopped throughout the area, spending days aboard their vessel and replenishing supplies when needed along the way. They secured rations by developing relationships with the local inhabitants and learning how to haggle. They even brought a lamb aboard to slaughter and eat, but the crew became too attached to the animal and it was spared from becoming dinner.

On October 20, Fuller brought his boats back to Casteloriso, much to the dismay of the local inhabitants. Since their last visit, German bombers had attacked the island and the residents were concerned the presence of MTBs would attract more enemy aircraft. As the 60th drifted into harbour, villagers popped their heads out of windows and doors to yell "go away, you'll bring the bombers!" Their homes were built along steep embankments, sitting above one another like steps of a giant, dilapidated staircase.

"I'm sure they're just scared," Fuller said. "Don't worry about it; this is as good a spot as any."

They moored their vessels and raised their nets. Night came and Fuller got some much needed rest. The following morning featured a welcoming sun and clear skies. After breakfast and tea, the crew prepped for another patrol. The twenty-four-degree weather meant many removed their shirts as they went about the usual routine of cleaning the boat, guns, and checking equipment. Fuller finished some reports in his cabin and signed off on supply inventories before coming topside. He loosened his collar and unbuttoned his shirt, although a hot tea and scotch was already in his hands. The galley was busy cooking lunch and the scents wafting through *313* were making him a bit hungry – thankfully his bowl spasms had been better the last few days, which he attributed to the weather and fresh produce.

Aboard *309*, Lt Ross Campbell*, also emerged on deck and caught Fuller's gaze from across the water. He gave him a wave and the Canadian raised a hand to return the gesture but brought it back to his mouth to stifle a yawn. Fuller decided to head back to his cabin and catch a quick nap before lunch. He fell on onto his bunk and into a deep sleep.

Campbell stayed on deck. For the next thirty minutes he observed his men working and allowed himself to enjoy the weather when something in the sky caught his eye. He reached for his binoculars and studied the specs which had appeared above the horizon.

"Stukas!" he shouted, raising the alarm. A squadron of small enemy dive bombers, who had been based at Rhodes, quickly approached and began their death-dives on the harbour, directly above the flotilla. With little time, Campbell shouted at his men to slip their moorings and start the engine so that he could pull his boat away from shore. Above, the all too familiar sound of Stuka 'Horns of Jericho', as they called their wind driven sirens, filled the air with their terrible 'scream'. The German pilots kept the noses of their aircraft pointed directly on their targets, waiting to the last minute to pull up and out of the fall. Bombs fell, blowing up homes and shops around and above the MTBs.

"Get us clear!" Campbell yelled and as his boat began to move, he watched in horror as a stone building exploded and sent chunks of debris and dust over *313*. A sandy-brown cloud fell onto the water and quickly spread over the harbour, blinding Campbell and the other boats. The

---

* He would receive a DSC before the end of the war. Later in life Campbell would have a distinguished public service career working for the department of foreign affairs. He was made an Officer in the Order of Canada in 2007.

taste of stone and earth filled their mouths as the dust swallowed the vessels.

The planes continued their assault, although the blanket of debris made it impossible to pinpoint targets. Once their ordinance was spent, the Stukas hurried back to base and, eventually, the sandy cloud dissipated, revealing to the MTBs the destruction ashore.

"They smashed the place to bits," Campbell lamented. An eerie silence fell, broken occasionally by falling debris that splashed into the water.

"Bring us back in, slowly," he ordered as his eyes looked for *313*. "Tom!" he shouted, focusing on where Fuller's boat had been. All he could see was a pile of rubble. As they drew closer, details emerged – a glimpse of a hull and the odd protruding gun barrel. *313* was pinned in place, weighted down in the water, and obscured by small and large bits of stone, rock, and earth.

"Tom!" he called out again.

No reply.

"Tom!"

Finally, some of the rubble atop *313*'s bridge began to shift, stones rolling to the side as hands pushed and tossed debris to make a clearing. Finally, after some work, a bruised and grouchy, but otherwise alive, Fuller emerged from the heap of house-bits laying on his boat. He glanced around and caught sight of Campbell.

"Just like Nazi's to ruin a perfectly good day," he commented.

What Campbell didn't know was just how close Fuller had come to death. He'd been asleep on his bed when the bombing started. Thankfully, the sounds of explosions awoke him and he instinctively rolled off his mattress, landing onto the deck and clambering on all fours out of his cabin. He darted up to the wheelhouse and was about to head outside when a thought occurred to him: "Well, halfway in the armoured-plate partition is the best place to be!" So, he dropped into a protective position as darkness enveloped him, debris smashing the view screens and cracking parts of the deck head. Fuller could feel the glass falling over him and the sounds of breaking wood and thuds of debris stacking atop his boat were deafening. The vessel sank deeper and deeper into the water, as if a giant hand was trying to force them completely under. Only once things settled did Fuller risk moving from his spot under the chart table, fumbling in the dark for a flashlight. Luckily, he knew his vessel well enough to know where to search, and soon his fingers touched the familiar ribbed metal of a torch. Thumbing the switch, the light turned on and he immediately made eye contact with the cox'n who's face was mere inches in front of him. Both men screamed in fright.

"Jesus!" he gasped.

"Sorry sir," the other man apologized.

Fuller found another torch and passed it to him. "Go check on the others – I need a damage report." He then dropped back down the ladder and proceeded into the radio room.

"Sparks, you alright?"

"Aye sir," replied the telegraphist, rubbing his head. "Hit my noggin off the bulkhead but I'll be okay."

Fuller turned and shone the beam through the open hatch of his cabin. The sight chilled his blood. Later, he would explain "a piston with this goddamn twenty-four inch con-rod had come right through our deck and had gone down through my bunk where I had been sleeping."

He'd nearly been run-through. As Fuller tried to come to grips with his own mortality, Sparks appeared beside him and noticed the large metal connector piercing the bed.

"Lord, that was a bit close sir," he observed.

"Too close," Fuller agreed.

309 managed to pull *313* away from the dock, Fuller using the muzzle of one of his Oerlikons as a bollard, even if only six inches of it protruded from the debris. Once they were at a safe distance, the rubble was cleared and damage catalogued. It wasn't good – his guns were wrecked, the torpedo tubes had been knocked overboard, the deck was punctured in several places, and the hull leaking. Crew members were organized into parties and took turns pumping out the water to prevent the MTB from sinking.

"Looks like we'll be writing off yet another boat," he commented to his 1st Lt, who was supervising the clean up. Most of the debris had come from a little building alongside a diesel generating plant, which Fuller surmised was the source of the piston and con-rod that had nearly taken his life. Sparks updated command and since live torpedoes were in the harbour, the area was labelled a hazard.

Some Indian Army Engineers were able to assist and supply a four-inch pump that removed the remaining water from their hull. The MMs were then able to get the boat's engines working again. Although they were unable to fully plug the leaks, Fuller devised a workaround: ordering his number one to take the boat out of harbour, he grabbed a fire axe, bent over the side and cut a hole in the transom so that the water coming through the bottom would run out the stem. Of course, for this to work they would have to keep moving at speed to avoid having water seep in through the hole he'd just made, and the journey back to Alexandria was about three hundred nautical miles. If anything happened in transit to slow them down, the boat would sink. Thankfully, the rest of his flotilla were in decent shape, so he decided it would be worth the risk.

They waited until night before leaving, hoping to avoid another air patrol. Conditions were decent – while a bright moon and cloudless sky meant little cover, the seas were thankfully calm, which meant they wouldn't have to worry about waves. The trip took a nerve-wracking twelve hours, pushing *313*'s engines nearly beyond their limit and requiring the crew to constantly bail water to manage the excess intake and leaking.

"Thank God the sea is co-operating," he noted from the bridge. "Flat like a plate of pee."

To pass the time, and keep his officer's minds off their current predicament, he decided to start up a game of bridge. The problem was there was only three of them – they needed a fourth man – so the midshipman poked his head into the wheelhouse and asked, "cox'n, do you play bridge?"

The sailor looked back and nodded.

"Well, put a sandbag up against the wheel and come up."

And so, the cox'n and three officers played their game under the moon-lit night. It worked like a charm to keep their minds busy – in fact, they became so engrossed that Fuller recalled "we had to break up the bridge game to send the cox'n down to grab the wheel or we'd have headed right past Beacon Buoy in the centre of Alex Harbour. Nobody on the wheel for three hundred miles!"

Despite nearly missing their mark, all four boats made it back to Alexandria's harbour, whereby they sent a signal to command to have a slip ready for them at the Marizuta jetty. Unfortunately, a spot couldn't be prepared in time, forcing Fuller to turn his vessel about. Naturally, they couldn't risk slowing, which meant the manoeuvre had to be executed in harbour while moving at 30 knots. Heavy wake started bouncing boats moored along the gangways and a signal via an aldis lamp ordered them to "stop!" Fuller ignored it, but a second signal from Cunningham's very own flagship followed.*

313 was again in a tough spot.

"If I stop, I sink," they signaled back.

"Understood. Stop." came the reply.

So Fuller took his boat to the jetty, picked a spot, and brought the MTB alongside. Gear was frantically tossed ashore as the boat began to

---

* Fuller said that the ship was HMS *Abdiel*, an Abdiel-class minelayer, but it was sunk on September 10, 1943 in Italy's Taranto harbor. Cunningham's flagship was HMS *Warspite*, a Queen Elizabeth-class battleship, that was likely undergoing repairs from the damage she endured during the Salerno invasion (which would explain the concern over the heavy wake).

succumb to her wounds. Nothing more could be done for *313*: Fuller would later observe, "We just settled down and that was it."

It was now October 22. He paid off *313* and stayed at *Canopus* until the arrival of their new boat, *2106*[136], which had to be sent down from Leros. In the meantime, the crew took it easy and Fuller spent a few days resting. After nearly been blown up and skewered to his bed, he needed some time to himself, not only to process what had happened, but was still yet to come.

CHAPTER 13

Leros

It took a few days for MTB *2106* to arrive. Unlike *313*, their replacement was an older boat and required some modification to meet Fuller's specifications. He took a day putting the vessel through manoeuvres off the coast, including setting up his custom shooting markers, and practising firing at floating targets. Once satisfied that the boat could perform to his standards, Fuller took his flotilla back out to sea. Returning to Casteloriso was out of the question – the enemy would be waiting for them – so he instead travelled to Bathy Bay in Turkey. From there they swept around the Dodecanese Islands, doing their best to avoid enemy aircraft. As a safeguard, they now worked exclusively at night and remained hidden under camouflage nets during the day. The number of bomber patrols was intensifying and Fuller suspected the Germans were preparing to launch an attack, but where exactly remained uncertain.

On October 28 new orders from command painted a clearer picture: he was to move his flotilla to Leros, which needed help defending against increasing aerial strikes. Allied commanders felt the enemy were softening up the island's defences in preparation for a full-scale invasion, hence the growing air traffic. They set off immediately and arrived the next day.

Leros, a mountainous island situated in the southern Aegean Sea, consisted mostly of low hills*, rocky coasts, valleys, and secluded bays. If not for the war, it would have made a great place for a family vacation, picturesque, relaxed, and offering mild temperatures. Since the surrender of Italian forces in September, the Allies were quick to reclaim the territory and the Dodecanese Islands served as an excellent launch point for Allied strikes against German-controlled Balkan territory. Leros proved key – located 317 kilometres south-east from the port of Piraeus, in Athens, and north of the islands of Kalimnos and Cos, it was close to Bodrum and a perfect spot for a base of operations. On the fifteenth of September, British forces arrived to bolster local Italian forces but by twenty-sixth, Germans forces began pushing back, launching a series of violent air attacks from nearby Greek-held territory.

It was the start of Operation Leopard.

Generalleutnant** Friedrich-Wilhelm Müller was the mastermind behind the offensive. For locals, his name evoked fear and panic, and for good reason. An iron-fisted commander, his tactics were ruthless and without mercy. Survivors of his campaigns, be it POWs or civilians, learned quickly that anything shy of absolute obedience would elicit a fierce response. Müller cared little for the general conventions of war – he'd already orchestrated the massacres of Greek non-combatants at Viannos, Anogia, Amari, and Damasta. In fact, the dive bombers that had attacked Fuller's flotilla, turning Cos' coastal settlement into a moonscape, did so under his authority. Unfortunately, the strike proved only a prelude to something far more sinister. On October 6, after Müller's forces made landfall and subdued local resistance, over a hundred Italian Army POWs, all officers, were murdered and their bodies buried in mass graves.[137]***

---

* Its tallest mountain was only 320 meters in height.
** Lieutenant General
*** Müller also orchestrated the Holocaust of Kedros (August 22, 1944) where 164 Greek civilians were murdered. After the war he was tried by Greek Military Court and

The German presence was bad news for the Allies. Müller wielded a formidable combat force consisting of several regiments of the 22nd infantry division, paratroopers, amphibious commandos, and air support. Before the end of October, he'd managed to capture both Cos and Kalimnos, leaving nothing between him and his ultimate prize – Leros.

The island served as the HQ of the Regia Marina*, now allied with the British. There were approximately 7,600 Italians on the island, mostly sailors at the naval base, led by Capt Luigi Mascherpa. As for ships, there were several tasked with the islands defence. The 4th Destroyer Flotilla, which, despite the name, boasted only one Turbine-Class vessel, *Euro*, and the 3rd MAS Flotilla, consisting of two MTBs and six MA/SBs. Additionally, eleven minesweepers, two minelayers, and three MFPs were stationed at the island. Bolstering the Italians were British forces under the commanded by Brigadier-General Adolphus Robert Tilney and included around 3,000 men from the 2nd Battalion of The Royal Irish Fusiliers (the 'Faughs'), the 4th Battalion of The Royal East Kent Regiment (the 'Buffs'), the 1st Battalion of The King's Own Royal Regiment (Lancaster), and the 2nd Battalion of the Queen's Own Royal Kent. Additionally, upon Fuller's arrival at the island, he noted fifty commandos of the SBS.

As at Dunkirk, enemy aircraft first dropped leaflets over the island to demoralize the defenders and encourage their capitulation. The message was clear – surrender or else. Then, on September 26, Müller made good on his threat and began a vicious bombing campaign. Immediately, the Allies recognized that Leros was situated too far north in the Aegean for RAF squadrons to render assistance. This alone proved disastrous, allowing the Luftwaffe to operate with impunity. Aside from the island's anti-aircraft guns, German aircraft were relatively free to attack any target.[138] On the twenty-sixth alone, German Ju 88 bombers conducted a devastating assault, sinking a British and Greek destroyer, Italian

found guilty of war crimes. He was executed by firing squad on May 20, 1946.
* Italian Navy

MA/SB, and destroying the island's submarine base, naval barracks, workshops, and some fuel depots. The Allies, on the other hand, only managed to knock out seven bombers.

The aerial attacks continued, averaging four a day. By October the number rose to eight, allowing little time for ground forces to recuperate. Enemy aircraft became as common as the local bird fauna, although no one grew accustomed to the terrifying raids. Military installations and civilian settlements were targeted without discrimination, and the constant noise of screaming engines, anti-aircraft fire, whistling bombs, and the inevitable explosions, wreaked havoc on the mind. Casualties mounted at an alarming rate and medical centres evacuated to temporary facilities in the many man-made caves that dotted the hills around Leros City and Portolago (Lakki).[139] While these conditions were less than ideal – doctors and nurses were constantly struggling to maintain adequate power for lighting and equipment – at least the dense rock protected them from falling projectiles.

Tilney grew increasingly concerned. Without more men to repel the inevitable land invasion and, better yet, increased warships to intercept amphibious vessels before they could land their troops, executing a successful defence of the island became less and less of a reality. He would give anything for a squadron of fighter planes to clear the skies. That way he could at least rebuild fortifications and prevent further loss.

The fate of Leros, as well as other Dodecanese islands, was at the forefront of a meeting held at Tunis on October 9. There, all C-in-Cs in the Mediterranean considered what could, and should, be done in response to Müller's campaign. German forces were advancing at an alarming rate, reclaiming land the Allies had liberated only a month ago. The line had to be drawn at Leros and priority was given to resupplying Tilney's forces via submarines.[140] With some luck, they could refortify the island before Müller launched his main assault.

By the time Fuller arrived at Leros, much of the island had already been destroyed. All along the coast, buildings lay in ruins, and distant smoke hinted at further devastation over the hills. The air smelled of explosives and ash, thick enough to taste, and the soldiers along the water's edge looked battle worn and aged. They tried to put on brave faces, reassuring each other that they'd eventually be victorious, but Fuller saw right through it. As his boats crept up to Portolago's main dock, he could feel his nerves tingling. This area wasn't safe. As a precaution, he ordered his boats to raise their nets before coming alongside.

Not long ago, he'd nearly been killed aboard *313*, ran-through by a piece of debris that punctured the upper deck of his MTB. He didn't like the feeling of being stuck in one place. While being at sea felt relatively safe – their vessel could move and evade attacks – the same couldn't be said in harbour. Tethered to a mooring post along the coast of an island with inadequate aerial defences made him very uncomfortable. If enemy planes were to suddenly drop from the sky, they couldn't escape to open water in time to avoid the bombs. So, Fuller decided that he and his men would instead stay ashore rather than remain in their boats. If necessary, they could at least run for cover.

Over the next two days, Fuller witnessed firsthand the ferocity of the enemy's raids. Their barracks, dug directly into the rock along the recess slopes of the hill, provided adequate cover and the entrance conveniently pointed towards his boats. During attacks, he would keep his eyes on the harbour, worried that one of his boats might suddenly go up in flames. Thankfully, none were sunk or damaged.

During the night, MLs conducted anti-invasion sweeps of the area while the MTBs and MGBs remained close to the island. They would wait until the MLs spotted the enemy, then move to intercept. After a few days, command decided to expand the scope of these patrols to observe enemy activity in and around nearby islands, and so Fuller's boats began spreading out into the Aegean to gather intelligence. A lot had changed over the past month – friendly ports had fallen under German control, making it challenging to find safe places to restock supplies. Food and water was rationed, and fuel carefully monitored. Campbell recalled how difficult it was: "We had a bad time for food. At one point we were down to taking our last tins of bully beef and hanging bits of the beef out around the boat, then throwing hand grenades and scooping up the fish—a most sporadic source of supply."[141]

Returning to Leros on November 8, Fuller reported that an enemy invasion appeared imminent. Planes were landing daily, boosting their already impressive numbers, and troops were gearing up to board amphibious craft. He estimated the Germans would attack before mid-November, which was only days away. Tilney had already made a proclamation that the island was under a "state of siege and that "no enemy must be allowed to set foot on the beaches."[142] Easier said than done – a day ago the Luftwaffe sent close to 200 bombers to attack the island. By November 12, enemy aerial attacks increased to forty raids a day, decimating coastal defences and batteries on the east end of the island – the area Müller had selected for landing his soldiers. "They used more aircraft in Leros than they did on the whole Eastern Russian Front," Fuller would claim. "They had eight hundred and fifty aircraft overhead continuously."*

Of all aircraft, the dive bombers bothered him the most. Larger planes were easy to spot. Based on their approach angle, he would deduce if they presented a threat. However, the smaller bombers came straight down on their target, making them harder to predict and evade.

"These goddamn Stukas," he complained, "[they] put everything to the ground."

Müller's main force moved in that morning.

It began around 0430 hours with German landing craft approaching the island's north-eastern coast. Fuller's flotilla, accompanied by an Italian MA/SB, were out patrolling, serving as a first line of defence. They'd circled Leros, lookouts scanning the horizon for any sign of the enemy. Around 0250 hours they were moving up along the island's eastern

---

* Likely the total number over the four days. Between Nov 8-12, numerous enemy aircraft moved relatively unchallenged in the sky above the Island of Leros.

coastline. Fuller, positioned on the bridge, sipped the usual scotch-tea. Luckily, he'd been able to salvage a few bottles from *313*. He glanced out at the dark, calm waters and then checked the time: 0300 hours.

"Green 20, far, multiple objects," a lookout reported.

Setting down his drink, Fuller glanced through his binoculars and confirmed the presence of several bumps on the horizon.

"All stop," he ordered and the 1st Lt relayed the message to the cox'n.

2106 glided to a crawl, her bow sending gentle ripples behind them as it settled into the glassy water. Fuller remained focused on the objects and after a minute noticed even more shapes appear.

"This is it," he guessed, dropping the binoculars so that they hung against his chest. "Let the boss know that we've got company."

Sparks wired the message.

Meanwhile, Tilney was awaiting the arrival of some RN ships sent to assist in the island's defence. Unfortunately, due to problems with HQ's communication equipment, he'd not been able to contact the warships in transit. So, when he received Fuller's message, he immediately sent back a request.

"They want us to confirm if it's the enemy?" Fuller clarified.

"That's what the message said, sir," the telegraphist replied.

Fuller looked at his number one and asked, "how many RN ships are they expecting?" He went back to the voice pipe and said, "tell them that it's a LOT of ships and, again, that they are coming from the EAST. It doesn't make sense that our reinforcements would approach through enemy waters."

"Aye sir."

Fuller shook his head but didn't realize the real issue – only part of his message was being received by HQ. They maintained their watch, careful to keep a distance from the approaching force. By 0400 hours Fuller could confirm the ships were, as deduced, German and reported they were heading for Palma Bay and Pasta di Sopra. Once the message was dispatched, he ordered his flotilla to head back to the island. There would be one hell of a battle before daybreak.

————

By 0500 hours, Müller's forces were mere minutes from landing ashore. Roughly 2,000 British and 5,000 Italian soldiers held fast in defensive placements. Throughout the islands the sounds of church bells warned of an impending assault – last chance for non-combatants to seek shelter.[143] The Buffs were stationed north, the Faughs in the centre and the King's Own south near Portolago. Tilney kept the Kents back in reserve, standing by to support where needed, while highly skilled SBS commandos were scattered throughout the island. Meanwhile, the Italians manned the island's many large gun mounts, which were already taking aim at the vessels nearing the shore.[144] As for Fuller, he kept his boats near the coast between Pandeli and Alinda Bay.

The shore batteries were first to open fire. Echoes of their blasts rang down the hills and into the sea as large plumes of water erupted all around the approaching vessels. Enemy destroyers, which had escorted landing craft to the island, responded immediately, raining shells all along the coast. Muzzle flashes erupted everywhere as the remaining vessels and shore-based defences joined in. By the time the morning sun broke over the horizon, the eastern shores of Leros had already become illuminated by a terrific display of tracers, explosions, and thunder.

Incoming enemy vessels scattered to avoid the deadly Italian guns – direct hits obliterated smaller ships – but the bulk pressed forward. While the island's batteries began picking off German landing craft, there were simply too many approaching the shoreline. Moments later, hulls dug into sand to the north as well as mid-way on the island's eastern coast near Pandeli Bay. German soldiers spilled out, boots landing in water, and pressed forward into incoming counter-fire. These were experienced and battle-hardened troops who continued past over fallen comrades to face the defenders. Irish Fusiliers rushed up to block them, taking positions behind defensive walls, and firing into the soldiers storming the beach. Their marksmanship slowed the enemy, but the suppressive fire couldn't force them back into the sea. The Germans dug in and established the first of many beachheads.

Fuller could see the whole thing playing out from *2106*. The sheer scale of the battle was unlike anything he'd ever experienced – everywhere he looked, war raged with furious conviction. His MTB moved north, racing to intercept any smaller vessel they came across. Considering present circumstances, there was little else he could do – the other ships were simply too big and heavily defended to attack, and with darkness fading, only the smoke discharged by large caliber fire provided momentary cover from their gunners.

As they closed on the northern most part of the island, the flotilla began turning west to round the tip. Suddenly there appeared a convoy of twenty-five landing craft escorted by two destroyers, six gunboats, two trawlers, three MFPs, and two steamers.[145]

"Jesus!" Fuller exclaimed, "Back off cox'n, back off!"

2106 rolled hard over, the boat cutting through the water as it quickly turned about. Again, without the night as cover, his four MTBs couldn't get within range to attack.

"What now sir?" his number one asked, also seeing their predicament.

"We wait for an opportunity," Fuller replied, sounding bitter. Watching from the benches wasn't his style, but his hands were tied. Thankfully, one of the shore batteries turned towards the convoy and opened fire. The gunners were good – two MFPs exploded, forcing the rest of the escorts to scatter. Alone, the landing craft were pummeled by the defenders. Later, eighty-five German soldiers would surrender on the beach.[146]

Meanwhile, the situation south grew worse. The bulk of Müller's forces were focused midway on the eastern coast, and despite British defences, more and more enemy soldiers continued to make landfall. Eventually, the numbers became too high to repel and forced the defenders to pull back to the hills. Two shore batteries were subsequently captured.

At sea, both MA/SB *559* and *555* were disabled in Grifo Bay. To prevent its capture, shore batteries targeted and sunk *555* while *559*'s crew scuttled their boat.[147] Large planes approached from the east, flying low and over the hills. Trickles of men fell out the sides, parachutes deploying one after the other until the sky was full of white chutes.

"Fire at those planes," Fuller ordered his guns, although most had already managed to dispatch their full compliment of paratroopers. *2106*'s anti-aircraft guns swung up and sprayed red tracers into the hazy-blue morning. The other boats followed, but the planes were already back out of range. A few broke off their course, but the other pilots skillfully turned back in time to drop their remaining soldiers. The last paratroopers glided down and vanished into the treeline and hills, some much too close to the large gun batteries. Fuller guessed that their mission would be to capture or disable them.

"This isn't looking like a sea battle," he observed. "We might also have to take this fight to land."

His 1st Lt shot him a questioning look but Fuller didn't notice – two enemy gunboats were dead ahead, having just appeared around the island's outcropping.

"Open her up!" he yelled.

His vessels charged. The enemy noticed the MTBs and immediately turned around, pushing their engines to the maximum speed. Fuller and the other MTBs opened fire but couldn't close the gap to get within range. He decided to break off their pursuit and make for port. Radio communication was becoming even more spotty and he hoped someone ashore could give him an update.

The battle would be ultimately decided on land – the enemy simply had too many men, vessels, and airplanes to prevent them from reaching the island. Exacerbating matters, unreliable communication equipment forced senior officers to rely on couriers to transmit messages to and from HQ. Precious time was lost waiting for replies and the enemy pounced on every opportunity to push into towns and up hills. After a brutal, long day of unrelenting combat, Müller's forces managed to split the island across its thinner midsection, between Gurna and Alinda Bay. The Buffs and King's Own were to the South, along with Fuller and his boats, while the Fusiliers were situated to the north.[148]

Once in harbour, Fuller went ashore armed with a Thompson sub-machine gun and .45 Colt revolver. He needed to find someone in charge, and a junior officer provided him with an escort to take him to Mount Maraviglia, the location of the No. 127 battery and Allied HQ. The troop proceeded up roads and winding dirt paths that cut into the wild. Standing at 650 feet, Maraviglia looked down upon both Castle Hill and Mount Appetici which were situated across a large valley.[149] It would have also provided a commanding view of the coast if not for the smaller hills surrounding it. Along the way, Fuller noted several slit trenches dug into the slope, each large enough for one to two soldiers. He counted nearly sixty Faughs manning these positions, ready to repel the encroaching Germans. About halfway to the summit was the entrance of a tunnel, one of several created by the Italians to form a network of passages through the mountain. The Faughs had worked frantically to establish an HQ and officer quarters in these caves, and the soldiers Fuller passed looked utterly spent from the effort. Many used amphetamines – army-issued Benzedrine called 'Bennies' – to keep from succumbing to exhaustion and he considered finding some for himself.

Charing Cross HQ was situated deep in Maraviglia. Passing through camouflage netting, Fuller proceeded into the winding six-hundred-foot tunnel, using a flashlight to navigate through the dark. Further in, electric lights emerged as well as chambers jutting out from the main passageway. He spotted quarters, signalers working coding machines, a make-shift kitchen, an open fire pit, and a staff office.[150] There he found the Fusilier's CO, LCol Maurice French, looking over a map draped across a trestle table.

"What can we do to help?" Fuller asked.

"You wouldn't happen to have some rum on you?" French joked.

Fuller smiled – the man was tough and didn't even show any signs of being stressed.

"We've got to push the Germans out of Leros," French continued. "Our communications are in shambles and the Brigadier doesn't know what he's doing. First, we take a position then he orders us to fall back. They've knocked out a few batteries and we've got to prevent them from taking more. We need supplies and reinforcements." He pondered something, before saying to Fuller, "your boats' radios might be the only way to reliably communicate."

"We'll stay out of sight then," Fuller replied. "If you can send along messengers to us in Portolago, we can relay it to Alex."

French gave the Canadian an appreciative tap on the arm before turning to another officer who'd just walked in. "Right, let's drive these bastards off then, shall we?"

————

The Fusiliers managed to hold their position for three days. By the fourteenth things momentarily looked favourable for the defenders: British forces managed to repel the Germans with such efficiency that even Müller began to doubt their chances of success. Alas, by the fifteenth, the enemy countered and managed to knockout all but the No. 127 gun on the mountain. Unfortunately, LCol French was killed while defending the position with his men, and the remaining British were ordered to withdraw down the mountain, even though the Italians refused to surrender their position.

Fuller had returned to *2106*, relaying messages from French and hoping the situation on Leros would improve. A few days later, communications from HQ stopped, which he hoped only meant their radio was acting up. They spent the morning waiting, anxiously listening to distant sounds of battle and trying to guess what was happening. Then, just after noon, lookouts spotted a group of British soldiers making their way down the coastline to their flotilla. Fuller decided to go ashore and meet them halfway. He recognized them as soldiers who had been stationed on the mountain. They looked battered and bloodied.

"Where's the colonel?" he asked a Sgt.

The NCO whipped his face of dirt and replied, "they got his number, sir, early today."

Fuller sucked in his breath. The loss of French was a hard blow, and likely meant his HQ had been overrun. He looked around for an officer. "Well, who's in charge?"

The Sgt shrugged and glanced around before responding, "I was hoping you were sir."

Fuller listened as the man went over how the remaining troops had combined into composite units, most without officers or NCOs, with orders to push ahead with the Kents while the Faughs followed behind.

"Okay Sergeant," he said. "I'm going to contact base and see if I can connect with our guys to the north. What do you need? Supplies have got to be running low?"

"We're fresh out of .45 ammunition."

Fuller patted the man on his dirty shoulder and said, "I'll see to it."

Slinging his machine gun, he boarded his boat and proceeded straight into the radio room to ask Sparks to send the request. The next day, HMS *Echo*, an E-class destroyer that had been supporting operations to re-occupy islands in the Aegean, arrived to provide support. Fuller supervised the transfer of supplies then asked the ship's CO if he could spare some rum to brighten the soldier's spirits. A generous ten cases of gin were given instead, which were soon distributed to the Buffs and Fusiliers. Fuller, a soldier in his youth, developed a soft spot for both regiments. He would later commend them both as "a goddamn good regiment" and "damn good fighting outfit."

Even with the supplies, the situation on Leros remained grim. Four days had passed without word from the other side of the island. They were disorganized and without the ability to communicate with each other, unless Fuller could use his flotilla's radios to reach them. He set off, leapfrogging along the western coastline and connecting with remnants of various regiments, relaying the updates back to Alexandria. The only intelligence from Leros now came through him.

But something was bothering him. Since learning of French's death, his mind became preoccupied by the plight of those left defending the island. Their morale hung on by a thread – they were both physically and mentally exhausted, and clearly in need of a leader. Fuller wasn't only the senior man in age, but also by rank, and the soldiers instinctively looked to him for guidance. It weighed heavily on his conscience and, in the end, forced him to make a difficult decision.

One morning Fuller turned to his 1st Lt and sprang the news. "I'm going ashore to help. Keep the boat out of sight and await my return."

The XO, failing to catch his meaning, jokingly asked, "you're joining the army?"

"I'm serious," Fuller insisted, checking his weapons. "Keep an eye out – if all hell hits the fan, don't wait up for me and take the boat back to Alex." Then, before the officer could respond, Fuller hastily departed. He didn't want anyone trying to talk him out of it, nor did he want any of his men to follow him. They would be safer out at sea.

Without permission, not that present circumstances provided time to go through proper channels, he'd relinquished his command and informally became a pseudo naval/infantry officer. And considering the state the island, the defenders could use all the help they could get.

CHAPTER 14

——◇◇◉◇◇——

Buck-Private

A scratchy patch of vegetation along the berm of a beach provided ample cover. It had been a slow crawl through sand and polished stone pebbles to reach the spot, whereupon Fuller carefully entered the growth and settled flat on his stomach. Pressing the butt of his rifle into his right shoulder, he allowed his cheek to rest against the stock and focused the sight on a large boulder in the distance. The object, about the height of an average man and four times the width, rested less than a hundred yards away, on the upper wrack line of the same beach. Shallow turquoise water separated him from the object, the shoreline creating a gradual depression, like an elongated horseshoe, pitting the man and boulder on opposite ends of the 'U'. Not that the boulder was the intended target – it was the soldier taking cover behind it.

Fuller relaxed his breathing and closed his left eye. Shortly after leaving *2106*, he met up with a platoon and accompanied them up the coast. They travelled through vegetation but wound up coming under fire from Germans dug into the sides of nearby hills. Fuller knew it would be folly to take them head on and so decided to double back and follow the shoreline in hopes of finding a safer way around. When they got to the beach, they noticed a small boat anchored in the distance on the opposite side. Pressing forward, weapons at the ready, the distinctive sound of a THOOMP filled the air.

"Mortars, take cover!" someone shouted.

Fuller jumped to the side, years of army training returning in an instant. The round whistled as it approached, slamming into the beach and exploding thirty feet ahead of their position. He rolled onto a knee and brought his machine gun up, scanning the area.

THOOMP!

Leaping away, he again took cover but managed to notice where the mortar came from – a large boulder on the other end of the beach. The explosive detonated in the swash zone, about ten feet closer than the first one. Water, sand, and stone fell over the men.

"Behind the boulder!" Fuller directed, opening with his gun. The Thompson shook, spraying bullets wildly at everything except the intended target.

"What the?" he muttered, just as another THOOMP rang out. He barely dropped before the mortar exploded and this time he felt the blast against his body.

Too close.

"Christ, fall back!" he yelled as he scurried up to his feet. He didn't have to repeat the order – the soldiers worked their way back inland, leapfrogging and firing suppressive rounds to cover their retreat. Bullets harmlessly struck the boulder in puffs of dust while mortars continued to rain down, striking random locations along the shore. They moved back into the treeline.

Fuller tapped a solider on the arm and pointed to his rifle.

"Swap me your Lee Enfield for my Thompson."* He was familiar with the service rifle from his days with the signals regiment. "You guys stay put," he directed, "I'm going to find a spot up the beach and see if I can peg him."

---

* Fuller swapped weapons "because the muzzle-velocity of a Thompson sub-machine gun is only 50% of the muzzle-velocity of a revolver". In his view, the Thompson was a "useless goddamn thing", with little accuracy and a propensity for jamming. He wasn't the only one to think so – another veteran of Leros, Lt Ted Johnson, noted "… the Thompson sub-machine guns were unreliable."

He doubled back and eventually found an outcropping with some dense vegetation. He then slithered his way to his present location. Another mortar fired and that's when he noticed a German pop his head out to see where it landed. It was only for a moment, the soldier careful to remain hidden behind the boulder. Fuller deduced the German's approach – he'd launch a mortar, check where it struck, and then adjust his aim.

It wasn't going to be an easy shot. The man moved fast and didn't always choose the same side of the boulder to peek around.

THOOMP!

Fuller's finger gradually began to add pressure on the trigger. He focused on the spot where the man had last looked, hoping he'd choose the same spot again.

THOOMP!

BANG!

He fired, but the recoil of the rifle momentarily obscured his view. While he couldn't be certain, he believed he noticed the man's head fly back, but that might have been the soldier simply diving for cover. Working the bolt, he chambered another round and waited. A few minutes passed without any activity – no mortars or movement – but that might only mean the man was hiding. If the situation was reversed, Fuller would certainly avoid showing his face again. After a few more minutes, he decided to make his way back to the treeline.

"I think you got him sir," a Cpl said when Fuller arrived. "The mortars have stopped."

"Could be playing possum," he countered.

From here the trees and tall grass made it difficult to see down the beach. The only way to tell what happened to the German would be to investigate.

Carefully, the men made their way closer and closer to the other side of the shore, Fuller taking a position in the middle of the party. All the while, things remained quiet – no movement or sound came from the boulder. Finally, the two soldiers leading the group made it to the large rock and gently pressed their backs against it. Fuller watched, holding his breath and readying his rifle. The men nodded to each other and then circled around either side of the rock. A moment passed and then a voice reported "you got him sir!"

Fuller allowed himself to breath and relaxed his grip on the gun. Making his way to their position he saw the body laying beside several boxes of ammunition and a launcher, enough to keep up the assault for an hour. The round had gone right through the German's Stahlhelm and struck him in the head.

"Good shot sir," the Cpl praised.

Fuller turned and asked "who you calling sir? I'm just a temporary acting buck-private."

Some other men decided to check the boat, but found it empty.

"Let's take that with us, along with the ammo," Fuller said, pointing at the mortar launcher. "I'm sure the Germans will appreciate if we send them back."

The men chuckled and then proceeded up the beach to another hill, where the sounds of gunfire echoed in the distance.

———

The next four days were some of the longest and most difficult of Fuller's life, and on more than one occasion he questioned his decision to come ashore. British and Italian forces did what they could to keep the Germans from making further gains, but little by little, Müller's soldiers managed to secure territory and gun placements. And as the island's primary defences began to fall, larger ships moved in and began pounding the coast with their guns. Matters were made even worse when German reinforcements arrived. It became increasingly apparent that without Allied aid – and soon – it would be impossible to prevent the enemy from seizing complete control of Leros.

Fuller figured he looked as spent as everyone around him. The fighting had become worse and the frequent firefights prevented him from getting any sleep. Despite many valiant stands, the enemy kept pushing them back.

Years later, Fuller recalled the experience: "if you've ever gone for seven days without any sleep you'll know what it's like," he explained. "You get pretty heavy and every muscle aches so goddamn much." Along the way he'd managed to pick up some of those Bennies he noticed soldiers taking, which helped him to remain alert.

By November 16, it was clear to Tilney that he wasn't going to win this fight and so he made the decision to surrender. Fuller and his men were captured later in the day by enemy soldiers and brought to the town of Leros. There, they witnessed Tilney conversing with Müller on the road. The brit had a pipe clutched in his mouth and things appeared perfectly cordial between the two men, like football coaches chatting after a game. Something about it looked weird against the backdrop of POWs being corralled in ranks.

Fuller was separated from his soldiers and made to stand with the other officers. Müller then approached and the Canadian felt taken aback by how young the German looked. He guessed him to be only in his late twenties, although he was actually forty-seven years old. A pair of binoculars were slung around his neck, along with a tie, cap, and field-glasses that were firmly affixed by rubber bands around his ears. He also sported an iron cross around his neck.[151] Müller eyed Fuller's sidearm on his hip and grabbed the gun from the holster. After examining it, he unloaded the weapon and then presented it back to him.

"Your weapon," he said in English.

Fuller didn't know what to make of it but placed the empty .45 back in his holster.[152] A German Sgt then came up, saluted the Canadian, and gestured for him to follow. The treatment surprised him – this wasn't what he'd expected from The Butcher and his men. Clearly, the Germans held rank and status in high regard, even among enemies.

"I will say the Germans were that soldierly," Fuller explained. He was also provided decent accommodations in a hotel room, which included a comfortable bed with white sheets. Over the next two days he managed to catch up on some much-needed sleep. "They treated you really well, and lots of German cigarettes to smoke and everything else. I demanded coffee and a batman to look after me, and they gave me a servant (really a guard), and they served me coffee in bed in the morning." A German officer even paid him a courtesy visit, checking to see that he was comfortable, and then left without asking any further questions. It was far from the brutal interrogations he'd heard about – they left him alone to sleep, interrupted only to provide regular meals.

But despite the decent treatment afforded by his rank, his mind remained uneasy. Other men might have been content to accept their fate, perhaps even relieved to have survived, and happy to playout the rest of the war as a POW.

Not Fuller. "If they sent me as a prisoner of war to Germany and I got bombed by the RAF there, I couldn't take it," he explained. Once rested, he began considering ways to escape.

A few things worked to his advantage: the privileges of being an officer and that the Germans were not properly equipped to manage the sheer number of POWs on the island. While he figured it would be easy enough to escape into the mountains, the real problem was what to do next. Ultimately, he needed a way off the island itself, which meant finding a boat. He tried to make an excuse to visit the harbour – needing to stretch his legs – but the Sgt wouldn't let him leave his room. He needed a better plan and decided to ask permission from Müller to search the area for another officer.

Fuller met Lt Alan Phipps RN when he'd been shipwrecked on Leros during the battle. Describing the man as a "live-wire", Fuller placed him in charge of some soldiers and ordered him to repel an infantry attack. He'd not seen or heard of him since.* So, on November 18, Fuller was granted an audience with Müller and made a formal request to look for

* Fuller lamented that "I never did find out what happened to Phipps". The man's fate would later be discovered: "Phipps had been killed in action engaging a couple of

his comrade. The general acquiesced, on the condition that he be closely supervised by a guard named Fritz.

The next day, Fuller and his minder went off to Mount Maraviglia, the former site of Tilney's HQ and the area Phipps had last been seen. As they traversed the rocky path, Fuller not only searched for the Lt, but also for anything that could assist him in escaping. Perhaps he'd pass through the HQ's tunnel and lose Fritz in the dark. From there he could head for Portolago and see if there might be a vessel lying about.

As they ascended the peak, they came upon one of the island's gun batteries. He ducked a head in and noted, to his surprise, an unopened bottle of SRD-2: Rum.

"Well, I had twenty-two communicators there on the island," Fuller would later explain, "and they had their rum ration; they wouldn't have come ashore without it."

The bottle provided just what he'd been looking for. "Look what I found!" he said to his guard, brandishing the bottle. Fritz squinted at the writing, unable to read it.

"It's rum," he explained.

Fritz still looked puzzled so Fuller opened the bottle and brought it to his mouth, tilting his head back and taking a satisfying pull. He then extended the bottle to the guard. Fritz' grabbed it, took a sniff, and lit up when he realized it was alcohol. He proceeded to take a large swig and relished the sensation as it warmed his throat.

"Good rum," Fuller stressed, rubbing his stomach.

"Ja," Fritz replied, a smile on his face.

They settled down under some shade and enjoyed the late afternoon sky, stretching out their legs and passing the bottle back and forth. For now, they were just two men trying to forget about the war. It didn't matter that they couldn't speak each other's language – they simply passed the bottle in silence until it was empty. Fritz seemed intent of

---

Germans attacking the Fortress HQ. He was later buried in Leros cemetery." (Peakman, ibid)

matching Fuller's gulps, wanting to show that he could handle the drink just as well as the Canadian, but never realized he was being tricked.

"I put my tongue in it and went gurgle, gurgle, gurgle," Fuller later explained – he was only pretending to drink the rum. Fritz, on the other hand, unwittingly consumed the entire bottle, and soon fell into a deep sleep. With the guard out of commission, Fuller made his way around the mountain and headed south-west towards Portolago. He still had his personal items, which hadn't been confiscated, as well as his unloaded gun, but that was it.

As chance would have it, he happened to come across another escapee along the trail – a Maj. Together, they managed to find another six soldiers who's been evading enemy patrols. Fuller led them all to the outskirts of the town.

"I take it you plan on stealing a boat?" the Maj asked.

"That's the idea," Fuller agreed.

"Anything in particular?"

Fuller crept up to the back of a building and risked a peek down the alley. "I'll let you know when I see it," he answered. In truth, he had no idea if they'd even be able to get to the jetty, let alone steal a boat.

They continued sneaking into town, careful to remain in the shadows and avoid patrolling soldiers. When they reached the harbour, Fuller finally found what he'd been looking for – their ticket to freedom: an Italian admiral's barge.* He led the men behind some large wooden boxes close to the dock.

"That's our ride," Fuller said, pointing at the boat.

The Maj looked at him. "You can sail that?"

Fuller's beard parted into a toothy grin. "Piece of cake, but first we go to get something."

"What's that?"

---

* Possibly having belonged to Admiral Inigo Campioni who was in command of the Italian Garrisons on Leros.

"I stashed a case of Gin from *Echo* some days ago. It's just off in some bushes along the way. Let's bring it with us."

Now it was the Maj turn to smile. "What's your plan?" he asked.

"I say we just march right up the street in formation – like a work party."

The Maj blinked. "Just walk on down and onto the boat?"

"Remember, the jerries are big on rank and authority," Fuller explained, patting his gun. "I'll take the rear, like I'm in charge of the work detail. I bet if we act like we're allowed to be where we are, we can go right aboard the boat without being asked a question. And if we're carrying a box, maybe it'll help sell the gimmick."

The Maj remained silent. The plan was far from foolproof.

"If you've got a better idea, I'm all ears," Fuller urged.

"Okay, what the hell, let's give it go," the Maj agreed.

Fuller brought the men back behind the buildings and drew them into a huddle to explain the plan. They would only have one shot at this.

"Remember, just keep your cool and march like you've got a reason to be there – that's how we'll con them."

When the streets looked clear, the men moved out and formed up in ranks with Fuller behind them. They then marched in step, parading down the street with their box towards the barge. Apparently, they were quite convincing – Fuller would later share that he "even picked up four salutes from the Germans that we passed on the way down to the barge."

The crew of the barge were utterly surprised and quickly subdued by the soldiers while Fuller readied the boat. It didn't matter that all the controls were labeled in another language – he knew these waters and how to navigate. Bow and stern lines were loosened and using spars to push away from the dock, Fuller hoisted the main sail. A favourable breeze blew from the north-east and soon they were free of the harbour. Nobody realized the boat was gone until the next morning – exclusively relying on the wind to propel them out to sea meant that they didn't make a sound.[153]

Once in open water, they rounded the island and headed east to the Gulf of Mandalaya in Turkey. The barge moved through the night, silent and relatively invisible due to its low profile. Fuller was careful to avoid areas known for enemy patrols, which meant taking a bit of a detour, but in the end, he managed the thirty-five nautical mile journey without incident, arriving near the village of Bogazici. Once docked, Fuller sold-off the boat to a merchant ashore. Even in war, he was ever the businessman – why abandon a perfectly good boat for nothing when you could make some money?

"All I got was three hundred and fifty Lira," he lamented. "It was worth about twenty-five thousand, so I didn't make much on that deal."

He did, however, keep one of the German lifejackets from the boat. The fit and shape suited him, and he continued using it throughout the rest of the war, even keeping it afterwards as a souvenir.* His stay in Turkey was short – he'd just been served a complimentary meal from the locals of octopus with beans, almonds, and flap-jacks, when a RN F-Class destroyer appeared. HMS *Fury*, a ship that had been very involved in the Dodecanese Campaign and assisted in sinking a German troop convoy, proceeded into the gulf and Fuller immediately signaled the vessel. A boat was sent ashore to retrieve him and the soldiers.

And just like that, Fuller was no longer a POW on the run.

Fury's captain welcomed the men aboard and, after receiving a verbal report from Fuller, offered him the use of his day cabin to get some rest – a generous offer, which Fuller happily accepted. He entered the cabin, sealed the hatch, and happened to glance at his reflection as he passed a mirror, the first time he'd seen what his face looked like since landing on Leros. He almost didn't recognize himself. The lack of sleep, combined with days of endless fighting and hot running, had taken a heavy toll. His cheeks were sunken, his eyes baggy and dark, and his thick beard

---

* Simon Fuller, telephone interview by Sean E. Livingston, September 21, 2016.

wild and unkempt. Dirt and grime stained both skin and clothes, and he guessed that he'd lost twenty pounds. After a nap, he would be certain to use the captain's bath.

He stretched out on the bed and shut his eyelids. He was nearly asleep when a steward entered. Fuller forced his eyes back open. "What's going on?"

"Sorry for interrupting sir," the man replied. "I was hoping not to wake you. We're going into Cos to shell the harbour. I'll just take these down so they don't fall on you."

The sailor began taking down pictures from the bulkheads. Fuller didn't say another word. His head sank into the pillow and everything went dark. And as *Fury* unleashed a barrage of gunfire at the enemy, the rattling and explosions failed to wake him from his slumber.*

"I never even heard the guns go off."

The destroyer returned Fuller to *Canopus* before diverting course to the middle of the Mediterranean to escort HMS *London*, a county class heavy cruiser that was carrying Prime Minister Winston Churchill to a conference in Cairo. There he was to meet FDR and Generalissimo Chiang Kai-shek of the Republic of China to discuss the Allies' strategy regarding the war in the Pacific and postwar Asia's fate. As such, Fuller wouldn't arrive back to Alexandria until November 20, where he decided to request a few days leave to recuperate from his ordeal on Leros. He chartered a car and took a two-and-a-half to three hour drive to Cairo, wanting to get close to the conference and see the world leaders with his own eyes, but found the roads too congested.

"I got stuck in the sand by the pyramids about five in the morning."

In the New Year, Fuller was reunited with his crew. He never faced any consequences for abandoning his command and was instead given

---

* *Fury* ran into some trouble during its attack. When Fuller awoke, he heard that "somebody in their excitement put the charge up before the shell got in, and you should have seen that bridge, because the cordite burnt for a good minute and a half in the gun-barrel and a sheet of flame came back over the bridge with everybody doing a full knee-bend."

ML *337*, which he took out for its maiden patrol on January 1, 1944. He operated another small flotilla, sticking mostly to the Levantine Sea, although occasionally moving back up into the hostile waters of the Aegean. He next took *337* to Haifa where the RN established a supply depot. The flotilla was in dire need of restocking and equipment.

They pulled up to the jetty and Fuller disembarked to speak with the supply officer.

"I need some parts for my boats," Fuller said, presenting a list. "Can you help us out?"

The man looked over the list, a scowl growing on his face. "You're not going to take all these pieces," he argued. "I won't have any job here – I won't have anything to look after."

Fuller stared at him.

"I can give you one or two swash-pumps," he offered, "but I can't give you ten swash-pumps, I won't have any left."

"What the hell do you think you're here for?" Fuller barked. "We're out there fighting and need this stuff to do our job. Do yours and give us what we need!"

Despite his words, the supply officer wouldn't budge, leaving Fuller fuming. A plethora of equipment and this "guy wanted to piddle about and give them out one or two at a time!" So, Fuller directed some of his men to sneak into the warehouse and pinch it. In all they stole "fifteenhundredweight" of needed supplies, before making a dash back to Alexandria.

By January 27 Fuller moved to ML, *336*, which he stayed aboard until the end of the month. He then cycled through his boats as the flotilla continued patrolling the Levantine Sea, which took until the end of February. On March 2, just prior to leaving the Mediterranean, an interesting incident occurred. He was in Macedonia when he heard that Rome had been liberated by the Allies. On a whim, he went to Foggia and hitched a ride on an American B-17 Flying Fortress to Rome.

Another Canadian, who went by "Nation", was aboard and they decided to stick together.

"The Romans didn't know that the lira had been devalued," Fuller recalled. "For fifteen cents you could get a Black and White scotch whisky. You could get Bardolino for thirty cents. By midnight that night it was up to sixty cents a drink and the next day it was a dollar."

Somewhere along the way, Fuller and Nation bumped into Maj Anders 'Andy' Lassen – the same Lassen who received a MC with two bars and would later be posthumously awarded a VC for his part in Operation Roast on April 8, 1945, in Comacchio. A famed member of the SBS and special forces legend, Lassen was known as a brawler and for creating brief action reports, such as the famed "Landed. Killed Germans. Fucked Off."[154] Lassen had also been a survivor of the Battle of Leros, so it's possible Fuller and Lassen were already somewhat acquainted.

The whole city was in a state of jubilation. People packed bars, homes, and were even dancing in the streets. To behold a liberated city was truly a wonderous sight, and Fuller was glad he'd decided to visit on a whim. The trio ended up at an establishment along a narrow street and walked up twelve steps and down a hall to a bar packed with soldiers of the French Foreign Legion. Fuller's interest was instantly peeked.

"I've always been fascinated by these guys" he said to Lassen and Nation. "Let's sit down and talk to these fellows."

The other two shrugged – it was as good as any place – and joined a table. The Legionnaires welcomed them openly: "come, sit sit!"

Someone handed Fuller a glass of Spumante – a sparkling white wine. Before he knew it, glasses were raised, a toast made, and everyone downed their drinks. He didn't like the taste, but finished it all the same. He then reached out for a bottle of champagne, which better suited his pallet. Overall, Fuller was taken by the generosity of these warriors, supplying bottle after bottle and swapping stories, and singing songs.

Every time a glass hit the ground they'd cheer - every time a bottle was emptied, another was brought immediately to the table.

It all changed at the end of the evening. When it came time to close their tabs, Fuller and his friends were stunned when the server handed them not only the bill for their drinks, but for everyone else's too. His business senses flared, his eyes catching the sly, self-satisfied grins on the Legionnaires' faces.

Wrong guy to swindle.

"To hell with this!" Fuller exclaimed. "We're not going to do it."

"Oh, you goddamn Americans and you bloody British think you run the world," the legionnaires shot back. "You've got all the money and we Legionnaires haven't any."

"We're neither of those," Lassen shot back. "They're Canadians and I'm a Dane. We'll pay our share but you're not sticking us with the whole bill."

The table flew aside, and men jumped to their feet. Some American and British soldiers who'd also been at the bar squared off against the Legionnaires, which helped even the numbers. The server ran for the back room while the bartender took cover.

"Crap," Fuller hissed. Someone killed the lights and then all hell broke loose. Suddenly he found himself in the kind of brawl he'd watched in western-movies, a mess of fists, feet, chairs, and bottles. Fuller narrowly dodged an attack, pushing one Legionnaire into another and then punching one in the face. He caught Nation being slammed into a table, but the man grabbed a bottle and smashed it into his assailant. Just then a fist caught the side of Fuller's head, causing sparks to flash before his eyes, but luckily Lassen stepped in and dropped the attacker – even in the chaos Fuller couldn't help but admire how well he handled himself. The Dane actually seemed to be having fun.

But this wasn't a film and things were turning ugly. Some of the Legionnaires were even fighting each other, swinging razor sharp bottles through the air. Men were being cut, blood staining tablecloths and clothes. Someone was bound to get killed.

Lassen nudged Fuller and pointed to a closed window.

"Better make a run for it," he said. "I'm going through the window there."

Fuller agreed. He figured the MPs were likely on their way and wouldn't hesitate to arrest them all. "I'll follow you," but as the words left his mouth, a thought occurred: "Jeez, we came up about fifteen feet so it's going to be fifteen feet to the ground going through that window."

Too late – Lassen already pushed through the crowd and dived through the window, taking shutters with him (thankfully there wasn't any glass). Fuller waited a second to avoid landing directly atop his friend and then followed. He jumped and pulled his knees up to his chest to clear the frame. For a moment he was mid-air in a dark side street, without any sense of where or how far the ground was. He extended his legs and WHAM!

They immediately caught something solid, sending a jolt right up his spine. Unbeknownst to him, it wasn't a straight drop to the street below. Instead he struck "a goddamn flat roof about four inches below the sill." His knees were pressed back into his stomach, forcing the air out of him. "I damn near killed myself," he explained. After a moment, he was able to recover and lower himself to the bottom of the street with Lassen's help. Fuller thanked him and then glanced up, expecting to see Nation right behind them.

He never came.

"He's still in the damn place," Fuller realized.

"I have to go after him," Lassen said and without hesitation, darted back up the front steps and through the main entrance, leaving Fuller standing there nursing his knees. He admired the man's courage – no wonder he'd already won so many gallantry awards. Fuller decided to follow, pushing past the pain in his lower limbs.

Inside, Lassen found Nation holding up under a table with the tops of five bottles that he'd broken to protect himself from any would-be attacker. Lassen pressed forward, hip-checking one Legionnaire out of his way and reaching under the table with his hand. Nation took it and the two men managed to make it to the entrance just a Fuller arrived.

"C'mon," he warned, "the red caps have got to be on their way!"

The three of them made their way into the street below and vanished in the crowd. The next day Fuller would discover that four people were killed and fifty sent to the hospital. He'd later describe the event as "quite a shemozzle" and one he'd never forget, adding "I never got mixed up with the Foreign Legion after that. I left them alone."

When he returned to his command, a message awaited him – he was going to be promoted. His orders were to head directly to Malta where he'd be made both a Temporary Acting Lt Cdr and SO of the 61st MGB Flotilla.[155] Fuller had endured nearly four years of combat, arguably more than most sailors. He'd slugged it out in the English Channel, survived a hellish trip through the Atlantic, bloodied himself in the Mediterranean, been taken prisoner and orchestrated a daring escape, and even survived a bar fight in Rome. And yet, through all of it, he'd managed to make it out physically unscathed. He came to the war looking for a scrap, and he got it. What more could await him?

But something bigger always lurked around the corner with Fuller. As of March 1944, the 61st was to leave the Aegean and head north-west to the sea that separated mainland Italy from the Balkans. Fuller's fighting days were far from over – in fact, he was about to become a coastal forces legend, the man the Nazis would call "The Pirate of the Adriatic."

CHAPTER 15

Vis

The 61st Flotilla made its way through the warm, sparkling waters of the Adriatic. Remarkably clear, with captivating blue hues, the sea looked like a giant gemstone. It evoked feelings of awe and the supernatural, as if having traversed an invisible boundary that separated the real world from the sublime. Their destination, a small island just off the Dalmatian coast called Vis, was no less stunning. The majestic Mount Hum, backdropped by a clear early morning sky, dominated the horizon, below which sprawled vibrant green subtropical vegetation. Rocky cliffs adorned most of the coastline, although these receded to reveal stunning sandy bays where white buildings, with distinctive orange barrel-tile roofs, stood between ancient looking stone roadways and paths. Trees, notably palms, peppered the settlement and beaches, making it look like they were on route to a holiday resort.

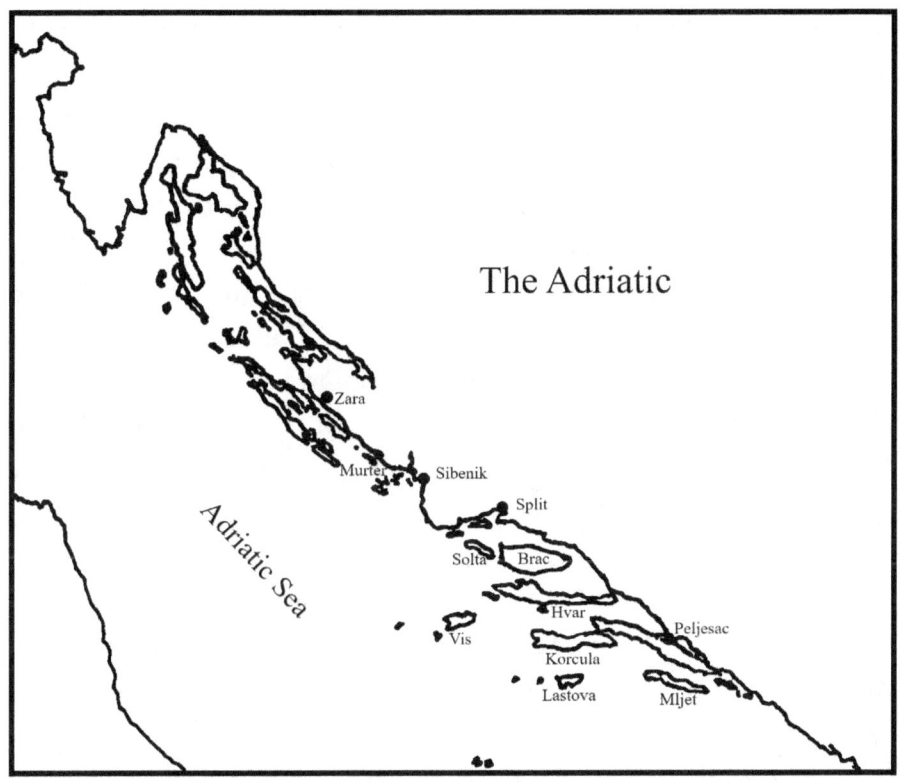

The Adriatic

Zara

Murter Sibenik

Split

Solta Brac

Hvar Peljesac

Vis

Korcula

Lastova Mljet

Adriatic Sea

Had the navigation officer miscalculated their plot? It seemed impossible to comprehend how such a place, abundant with beauty and life, could serve as a military stronghold. Surely these were hallowed grounds, off limits to the ailments of human conflict. Yet, as hard as it was to fathom, this island was indeed the location where Fuller was to establish a new home for Coastal Forces operations in the Adriatic. From Vis, they were to conduct raids against Nazi shipping in an effort to assist Partisan forces and their struggle against the Nazis. The beauty of a place factored little when it came to military planning – the island's location was of primary concern.

These waters were wasted on motors. Fuller imagined how pleasant it would be travelling in his private vessel from back home rather than in an MGB. He tested the direction of the wind – he could easily sit back and allow his sailboat to run on a broad reach. Perhaps after the war, he would return and properly enjoy the area.

Six boats – MTBs *637, 649, 651* and MGBs *642, 647, 661* – proceeded towards Komiza, a coastal town on the western part of the island. Standing along the edges of the cliff face were young, irregularly dressed soldiers, spaced approximately ten to fifteen yards apart.[156] As the vessels drew near, the closest sentry would raise their rifle and fire a single shot over the mast. While Fuller didn't know it at the time, this was how the National Liberation Army, better known as Yugoslav Partisans, identified themselves in the dark: a single shot challenge, which had to be responded by firing two shots back. Fuller's vessels would later arrange to respond by flashing the letter "A" on their hand lamp. Sometimes, the rounds came a little too close. "On dark nights it was quite hairy" Fuller recalled. "We got into a bit of civil war shortly after that." Even Partisan units wound up fighting each other in the night, convinced they were countering an enemy force. Sub-Lietenant David Conquest, who served as the navigation officer aboard *651* was "sure they had a competition to see who could get nearest to the bridge."[157] He noted that several of the COs were tempted at times to turn their pom-poms on the sentries, "saying I've had quite enough of this!"[158] One time Conquest heard a round "ping off the mast" and thought to himself, "woah, that's getting a bit close!"[159]

At the jetty, some soldiers helped to secure lines. Based on their dress and Slavic language, Fuller figured it was more Partisans. They were a communist force under the command of Marshal Josip Broz "Tito", who created the resistance movement in response to an Axis invasion of the region. Along with some British commandos, these men would be their allies. The Partisans had liberated Vis from the Italians in 1943, whereby the Allies began supporting Tito, sending first supplies, then commandos, and now Fuller and his boats.

Fuller stepped ashore and was met by a Partisan man who gave him a salute and then extended his hand. "Lieutenant-Commander Fuller I presume?" he asked in surprisingly perfect English. Fuller accepted the greeting.

"That's me."

"Happy to make your acquaintance; my name is Raphael Ivanovik and I've been assigned as your interpreter. These men will see to your things. May I escort you to your quarters?"

Fuller followed Ivanovik up a road leading into a town square. He would come to rely on the man in the coming months – Ivanovik would accompany Fuller on nearly every mission in the Adriatic, translating his commands to the Partisans, most of whom spoke little to no English. They would also grow to become good friends.

As they passed stone buildings of various heights and shapes, residents would stop mid-conversation to observe the bearded Canadian. Staring at strangers didn't appear to be a social faux pas on Vis, and while it felt uncomfortable, he reasoned the locals likely weren't used to seeing foreigners. While they walked, Ivanovik explained that Tito had insisted Fuller, as the flotilla SO, be given comfortable accommodations. A large home belonging to the owner of the Komiza anchovy-works was chosen as the site, and the fact that it wasn't vacant mattered little to the Partisans. They simply seized the building and "kicked [the family] out of their house."[160]

Morgan-Giles, the officer in charge of all RN operations in the Adriatic, was first to settle into the building. At the request of Fitzroy Maclean, he'd taken on the role of naval liaison to assist Yugoslavia's resistance to the Nazis. Coastal forces flotilla were operating independently, but Rear-Admiral Rhoderick McGrigor, who at the time acted as Flag Officer Taranto and Adriatic, decided that there needed to be "an operating authority over in these islands to be based on Vis".[161] Morgan-Giles was in the right place at the right time and was given the position.

Shortly after taking residence, he became aware of the displaced family and grew concerned for their welfare, thinking "they would have starved" if he didn't do something to help.[162] So he and the other officers took it upon themselves to sneak the family Bully Beef rations via the back door. Eventually, Morgan-Giles arranged for them to be smuggled to Italy on an MTB.[163]

Before entering the building, Ivanovik cautioned Fuller that, due to the war, construction crews were unable to finish the home before evacuating the island. Despite the warning, the main level looked to be well furnished. There were spaces for offices, a kitchen, lounging area, messing, and even a phone available near the entrance. Morgan-Giles had already set up his area, but the home was big enough so that Fuller still had plenty space to establish his HQ. Better yet, the location meant he would be close to the waterfront and his boats. Upstairs, several of the bedrooms had been converted into apartments for senior officers. And it was here that Fuller realized what had yet to be completed in the house – the stairwell.

To reach the second floor, one had to proceed over a large hole in the ground that led directly to the basement. In lieu of conventional steps, square wood timbers jutted out from the wall at regular intervals, acting as treads leading to the upper level. Without risers, balusters, and a handrail for grip, the only way up was to climb the boards. If one lost their balance and fell between the gaps, it was a long way down to the rocky cellar floor. Fuller doubted he would survive the impact.

To his disbelief, Ivanovik proceeded casually across the beams, as if he were walking up regular stairs. When he reached the second floor landing, he turned and waited for Fuller to follow. The Canadian took a moment to strategize his next move, and cautiously stepped onto the first board, leaning into the wall for support. In this way, he carefully ascended, doing his best to avoid looking down. He promised himself that fixing the stairs would be his first priority.

"I hope you'll find your quarters to your liking," Ivanovik said, leading the SO to his assigned room. Fuller's gear had already been delivered – he couldn't believe someone had hauled it up those oversized toothpicks. The apartment was cozy, offering a bed, desk, chairs, dresser, bookshelf, nightstand, lamps, and a large window. Through it, Fuller could see the shoreline as well as his boats moored along the jetty.

"I like the view."

"We thought you'd appreciate that," Ivanovik replied. "I've got to step out for a moment, but I'll be back to check on you. Is there anything you need in the meantime?"

"Wood," he answered. "Lots of it."

Ivanovik gave him a puzzled look.

"For the stairwell," Fuller clarified.

The man nodded and proceeded out of the room, leaving the SO to the view and his thoughts. Before leaving for the Adriatic, Fuller had decided it was time to use those blank letters he'd forged in Cunningham's office. Slipping a page into a typewriter, he addressed it to Hewitt, the same USN admiral who tried raking him over the coals when he'd taken Truscott to Salerno. Earlier, he'd observed that American coastal vessels were using new radars and he wanted them for his own boats. So, he began typing: "It would be appreciated if American SO radar sets could be made available to the 61ˢᵗ Flotilla."* He mailed off the letters and was happy to see the equipment delivered a week later. As he observed, "installation parties and everything else arrived right away and we were fully equipped after that." Now, all his boats were in excellent shape and the envy of other flotillas. "It was surprising what you could get on that signature," he concluded.

But it was far from a foolproof plan. It didn't take long for someone in the chain to question these requests – why would Cunningham go out of his way to do this for a single RN flotilla? And so, after some double-checking and a few phone calls, the dubious origins of these letters was discovered and MPs were swiftly dispatched to arrest Fuller.

---

* SO was one of the early S-band RADAR designations and had a 10-cm wavelength. They were typically used on American PT Boats.

He was facing a possible court-martial, but it wasn't the first time. Over his career he was penalized on three occasions for serious infractions, two of which were "severe reprimands… from the Admiralty in London expressing 'their lordships very grave displeasure' at some of his antics". [164] The first offence involved 'customizing' his boat. Without permission, he decided to add "more armament on to his torpedo boat than the manual called for." [165] The added weight compromised the integrity of his hull and the "bottom fell out of the boat". [166] To make matters worse, he turned around and blamed the RN for disaster, arguing installation crews had failed to drain the water out of the vessel prior to fitting the gear.

His next reprimand came in response to taking equipment from the supply depot in Haifa. Admittingly, Fuller half-expected a visit from the MPs upon returning to base and had been confined to quarters, which he described as "a nice holiday". He never regretted the decision and remained steadfast that the equipment ought to have been issued in the first place. A brief investigation revealed that Haifa's supply officer had been refusing to provide vessels the equipment they were entitled to and, as such, Fuller managed to avoid further punishment.

The only rules Fuller didn't find flexible were his own. For instance, during his time in the Mediterranean, he frequently operated as far as five-hundred miles outside the assigned area. "If we got an order we didn't like we'd ignore it," he said. [167] But he was also strategic in making these decision. Realizing the area suffered from poor radio reception, he would simply claim he'd never received the order, and nobody could prove otherwise. In the end, he was committed to fighting a war and believed that as long as he kept hounding the enemy, command would be willing to turn a blind eye to some of his more questionable practises.

In the distance, Fuller noticed Ivanovik speaking to some of his COs by the jetty. MTBs *649* and *651* were commanded by two experienced COs: Lt Peter Hughes of the South African Naval Force (Volunteer), and Lt Ken M. Horlock. The latter had received an MiD while in command of ML *443* during a raid on St. Nazaire. In fact, Horlock was one of the only ML's to return from the mission. Finally, MGB *661*, commanded by Lt L. Ennis*, and MGB *674* under Lt P. J. Kay, completed the flotilla. Rather than command his own boat, Fuller decided "to remain independent and ride in the boat of his choice on each operation."[168]

A sudden shrill-like noise interrupted the moment. Wincing he looked outside and even poked his head through the window to find the source but could see nothing. It was loud, and the skirl it made sounded familiar, like an instrument, although the name clung to the tip of his tongue. Approaching one of the walls of his room, he could hear it coming from the other side, the barrier doing little to mute the melody that now played. The tempo was a march and at last the name came to him: bagpipes.

Of all places in the world to come across someone playing a highland instrument, Fuller would have never guessed Vis. He exited his room and made his way to the adjoining apartment, knocking several times on the door. When nobody answered, he decided to close a fist and hammer it against the entrance, but still the music continued. Annoyed, he grabbed the handle and pushed open the door to find a British officer, in battle dress, minus the tunic, holding pipes under his left arm. Upon noticing Fuller the man allowed the mouthpiece to fall from his lips. The drones over his shoulder gradually came to rest against his body and a pathetic waning sound flooded the space as the instrument deflated into a sagging heap. Fuller noted a pair of sown-on crowns and pips adorning his epaulettes, which donated his senior rank. The officer stood confident, a steely-eyed man with an athletic build, looking to be somewhere around forty years old, with a receding hairline, slicked back hair, trim moustache, and broad chiselled jaw.[169]

"Sorry sir," Fuller apologized. "I'm the new man here and trying to get my bearings."

---

* A few months later Ennis would turn-over command to Lt. R.M. Cole, and take over *674* (Reynolds, 134)

"Ah, you must be the Canadian in charge of that flotilla I saw arrive in harbour," he deduced with a creeping smile. He settled the instrument onto his bed and approached Fuller with an extended hand. "The name's Jack – I command the No. 2. We'll be working together."

"Tom," Fuller replied, accepting the man's hand. He hardly noticed his surprisingly strong grip – the unit and name sounded familiar.

"You wouldn't happened to be the same Jack Churchill from Salerno?"

The man nodded. "I believe you were also there, correct?"

Fuller's eyes glanced back at the bagpipes, then to the rest of Churchill's kit hanging from the wall – a Scottish basket-hilted broadsword and an English longbow. Without a doubt, he was standing before the famous "Fighting Jack" Churchill, more commonly called "Mad Jack" for his daringness and combat prowess. Fuller heard stories about him – almost everyone had. His real name was John Malcolm Thorpe Fleming Churchill, although nobody called him by his given name. Even in modern warfare, he not only wore his sword into battle but also used it in combat. A general once asked him about the weapon, to which Churchill replied that, in his view, any officer who went into battle without one was improperly dressed. It wasn't the only medieval weapon he brandished. Back in May 1940, Churchill became the only soldier during the Second World War to be credited with a longbow kill. The arrow he shot landed squarely in the chest of a German Sgt, causing panic to ensue among the members of his unit.* By the time he arrived at Vis, Churchill had been recognized four times for gallantry, receiving two DSOs and two MCs.

"I was," Fuller confirmed, "although I didn't do much."

"Not what I was told," Mad Jack countered, "and I understand you had a bit of fun on Leros." When Churchill noticed the surprised look on Fuller's face, he added "Commando units talk."

---

* Churchill is also the last person to be credited with a long bow kill in a war (at least as of 2024 and information available to the author).

He went to the desk and grabbed a bottle of Rakija, a locally produced plum-based brandy, and replenished his drink, taking the liberty to pour another glass for Fuller. After they both took a sip, Churchill elaborated, "I also asked about you – I wanted to know who would be taking my men into battle. Word is you don't shy from a fight."

Fuller took another sip and then acknowledged, "I don't."

Despite having barged into his apartment, the two hit it off immediately. They were like minded individuals, although Churchill's penchant for combat far exceeded Fuller's – one would never catch Gramps leading a commando unit into enemy fire while playing the bagpipes. To be fair, few could measure up to Mad Jack, although the same could be said of Fuller. The only issue between the two was Churchill's daily practise – Fuller couldn't stand it, "especially in the daytime when we were trying to get some sleep."[170]

The next day he oversaw a work party he'd tasked to fix the stairs and decided to peek around the home's basement. There he discovered several large cisterns that had been dug into the rock to supply the building with fresh water. They'd long since gone dry, but the enterprising Canadian saw an opportunity. At the time, LST/LCTs were regularly arriving from the Italian mainland. These landing craft were designed with double-bottom hulls and Fuller asked that the next vessel fill the gap between the hull with fresh water before departing for Vis. Command granted the request and when the next LST arrived at Komiza harbour, Fuller and his crew ran a hose from the ship to the building's reservoirs and topped them all up, thereby providing his men, as well as the officers staying in the house, ready access to fresh drinking water. Whenever the cisterns neared depletion, he'd simply arrange for another LST or LCT to bring more.* It became the envy of other units. Some months later, during a bridge game at his quarters, a Capt went to the washroom and

---

* The bottom of the vessel has two watertight hull surfaces, a normal outer hull, and an inner, secondary hull, which can prevent the vessel from sinking if the outer layer is compromised.

tried the tap. To his surprise, liquid came out and after tasting it, he came running back out to exclaim "Jesus Christ, the tap has fresh water! Tile bathtub has fresh water, and all we have is a pint a day!"

Fuller made another interesting discovery. When the Italians retreated from Vis, they left most things intact, including working phone lines that connected to Hvar, a much larger island over fifteen nautical miles to the east and still under enemy control. Every bedroom had a set, so every now and then, when he felt the need to let off some steam, he'd crank-call the enemy: "the Germans would answer and then you'd tell them what you thought of them over the telephone" he reminisced, but clarified that "it was all very friendly."

Working with the Partisans proved challenging at times. While Morgan-Giles claimed that "my relationship with them was fine on a military basis", he also indicated that they were very "primitive" in terms of soldiering. Their forces lacked the benefits of radios and modern equipment – most didn't own a wristwatch, and many had to fight in snow without proper footwear. This made planning joint operations frustrating: he could always count on Partisan forces arriving either too early or too late. And since they lacked the means to efficiently communicate between units, they often wound up mistaking each other for the enemy. To keep things running smoothly, Tito gave the RN complete control of all Partisan naval activity so they could keep tabs on when and where the Partisans were operating, especially when smuggling refugees from Axis-controlled areas.

Ideological differences, along with diverging values and societal norms, proved most troublesome. When asked about his experience conducting missions with Partisan forces, Fuller cautioned "you've got to realize how completely screwy things were there." Morgan-Giles also took care to differentiate between their martial prowess and other practises. He was particularly concerned with their treatment of POWs and women. While the former were dealt with swiftly – they were all made to dig mass graves and then shot – the latter were another matter entirely.[171] Unlike Commonwealth forces, the Partisans openly integrated women into combat units. Fuller also noted the use of separate, stand-alone platoons of women, which he called "Juggarizas". Sexual relations between men and women was strictly forbidden and Morgan-Giles observed that their leadership established "a very simple rule: if there was any rolling in the hay, both of them were shot."[172]

The treatment of Juggarizas by other Partisans bothered Fuller. While women may have been allowed to fight, that didn't mean they were treated the same and an incident involving landmines on the island highlighted that inequity. Theses explosives had been littered across Vis by the Italians, which Fuller explained contained "little wires between scrub brushes and you had to watch very carefully because the wires were very, very, very thin and they were grey-coated and the rocks were grey." Merely the slightest touch of the wire could trigger the mine, and since they were connected in long strands, four or more would explode in unison. The Partisans decided to deal with the problem by marching a company of Juggarizas through various areas, purposely triggering the mines.

He also recalled an incident involving an American Army Ranger working alongside the No.2 commandos. Going by the name of Rogers*, the soldier had taken a page out of Patton's handbook and decided to wear dual, peal-handled revolvers on his hips. Between the bagpipe playing, sword and bow wielding Mad Jack, and this American gunslinger, the number of eccentric men converging on the tiny island was remarkable.

Soon after Rogers arrived on Vis, he met and fell in love with a Juggariza that he called Ubitsu.**

"He was quite sweet on her," Fuller lamented.

---

* Fuller never provided his given name during the interview and the author hasn't been able to ascertain the identity of the soldier.
** Fuller would add that "Ubitsu in literal translation means "I love you," but it also means "violet." The violet is called an "I love you", an Ubitsu". It may not have been the woman's actual name.

One day, everyone received an invitation to attend a Partisan demonstration in town. These were common occurrences and very political in nature, often replete with speeches about communist ideals. Fuller didn't even bother asking for translations – he only attended to be courteous. He stood in the crowd along with Ivanovik and Rogers, paying little attention and mostly conversing with the other two, although every now and then his interpreter would provide an update regarding important points. After the last address, the small stage was cleared to make room for a group of soldiers, who were escorting a woman onto the platform.

"Oh, they're going to decorate Ubitsu," Rogers announced, tapping Fuller on the arm in excitement. But the Canadian didn't respond – something about the scene was wrong. Her face, the drawn weapons, and the cold, grim expressions on the men's faces didn't match Rogers' deduction.

"Raph, what's going on?" Fuller asked his translator, but before Ivanovik could respond, the soldiers parted from Ubitsu, formed a line, and executed her before the crowd. The woman's body fell behind a small cloud of gun-smoke.

"No!" Rogers screamed, hands reaching for the grips of his pistols. Fuller quickly wrapped his arms around him, squeezing tightly to prevent him from drawing his weapons. He knew if Rogers drew them, he would shoot at the squad.

"Let me go Tom!" he protested, struggling to free himself.

"Easy man, easy," Fuller tried to sooth, although the effort to restrain him was taking everything he had. He cranked his head to find Ivanovik, narrowly avoiding a blow from the back of Rogers' wriggling head. "Raph, find out why in the hell they shot Ubitsu!" he ordered, and the man dutifully disappeared into the crowd of supporters that were still applauding the demonstration. Nobody even seemed to take notice of what was happening with the American. Thankfully, Rogers' rage yielded to grief and his body sank into the Canadian's arms. Together, they settled on the ground, Fuller wrapping him in a hug.

"Easy – that's it," he soothed.

"Why Tom?" Rogers asked, tears streaming down his cheeks. "Why would they do that?"

Fuller pulled the man's head into his chest and allowed him to sob – he didn't know what else to say or do. The sight of someone as strong as Rogers in such a state almost brought him to tears as well, and Fuller wasn't the type to cry. They stayed there for some minutes before Ivanovik returned.

"Well, what did they say?" Fuller demanded.

Ivanovik hesitated, glancing at Rogers before replying, "They said she had a self-inflicted wound. She couldn't fight anymore."

Desertion, cowardice in combat, refusing a command, or doing anything purposely to render yourself unable to fight, were all taboo for the Partisans and carried an automatic death sentence, but as far as Fuller could tell, Ubitsu looked in perfect health.

"Well, what did she do," he demanded, "shoot her fingers off or what?"

Ivanovik shook his head. He didn't look like he wanted to elaborate, but finally said "she was pregnant."

Rogers' head jerked up. "Pregnant?" he asked.

And then he lost it – went "nuts" as Fuller would later describe it – sobbing loudly in uncontrollable grief at the realization that the unborn child could only have been his. As a precaution, Fuller had Ivanovik take the American's guns. Eventually they got him back to his room and ensured that someone kept a close eye on him. In the days and weeks that followed, Fuller continued to check in on his friend, and while Rogers regained control, the grief remained. The woman he loved, along with their unborn child, were gone.

When Fuller related the story to Capt Lynch during his 1981 interview, he found that the memory had unearthed raw emotions he'd suppressed over the years – his disgust for what his 'allies' had done, his friend laying broken on the road, and the applause that continued around them in support of the execution of an innocent woman. He'd experienced combat, dodged death, and witnessed brutality on a scale most couldn't comprehend, but something about holding Rogers in that square affected him deeply. After a moment, he shook his head and pushed it all back down, a mental band-aid over a wound that never healed. Just as in war, Fuller did what he needed to survive, living with the shadows and refusing to succumb to the dark. So, he looked Lynch in the eyes and ended the story by saying "that was the way they played".

CHAPTER 16

Hunters

Shortly after getting situated, Morgan-Giles tasked the 61ˢᵗ with conducting nightly stink patrols. These involved incursions around the islands surrounding Vis, pressing into hotly contested waters to observe and record enemy movement. During the first months, things were relatively quiet. Unlike his experience in the Aegean, the threat of enemy aircraft was all but non-existent in the Adriatic. Still, to be safe, he routinely had his boats camouflage themselves along rocky coastlines, using their nets to blend-in with the shore. A few times, they managed to document the odd destroyer or E-boat, but mostly noted Siebel Ferries, a particular kind of flak ship consisting of a flat deck built upon pontoons. Before the war, these vessels were used to move mules and heavy equipment between the islands, but the Germans had retrofitted them with four 88mm and four 40mm guns. They were slow, hulking gun platforms powered by a single diesel outboard engine that, at best, could manage 4 knots in calm waters. However, speed wasn't the point – the stable platform allowed for deadly accurate gunnery.

Fuller's flotilla found these more than a bit challenging to deal with in combat. "[they] gave us a hell of a time," he explained, principally because they were hard to sink using torpedoes. He elaborated: "If you shot in one direction, it would go right through where there was no draught between the circular pontoons [and] if you hit one pontoon the rest of it floated—it was all pontoons underneath." Worse than these Siebel's were the MFPs known as F-lighters. The landing craft were an excellent multi-functional platform, serving as minelayer, gunboat, close escort, and transport for troops and cargo. A notable feature was their low profile, making it hard to spot them at night. The Germans also developed a simple, yet ingenious way to protect them from torpedo attack, stacking cordwood on chutes at the bow which would be released into the water like a countermeasure. The wood would float ahead of the vessel, forming a wall. "If you had a zero setting your goddamn fish went off on the cordwood before it ever reached the bloody thing," Fuller complained.

Combined, the heavy escorts, MFPs, E-boats, along with a smattering of schooners armed with 40mm and 20mm guns, made operating in the Adriatic hazardous. Luckily, Fuller, ever the innovator, discovered a solution.[173]

A primary focus of stink patrols was to ascertain if the enemy planned on invading Vis. It was the only island in the Adriatic not under enemy control, so it stood to reason that its capture would be a top priority. Back in January 1944, the Germans enacted Operation 'Freischutz' (Freeshooter), an offensive that forced the Partisans to abandon Hvar. Except for Vis, the enemy would effectively cut off any sea-based supply chain and starve their opponent into submission. However, internal squabbling stalled the plan – the Wehrmacht insisted on waiting until the Kriegsmarine provided a garrison, including a battalion and a few coastal batteries, but the German navy refused, citing limited resources.[174] Back and forth they bickered over roles and responsibilities, delaying Freischutz first to March, then April, and finally scrapping it altogether.

After a brief lull in engagements, coastal forces began ramping up attacks around mid-March, picking away at Axis supply convoys consisting primarily of schooners. These vessels were readily available, easy to navigate, and could carry a decent amount of cargo for their size.

It all started the night of March 8. Lt R "Bob" Davidson was SO aboard MGB *674* and Lt Horlock, who would soon join Fuller's flotilla, was in MTB *651*. An 80-ton schooner was spotted near Gradac, a settlement on the mainland east of Hvar. They made three passes on the ship, firing their guns into its hull and sails. Shore batteries responded but were unable to hit the small and agile Dog Boats. The two vessels snuck back into the night, leaving the supply ship in flames.

Two nights later, a 120-ton schooner was taken by Davidson and Lt P. Hyslop in MTB *85* – this time they boarded the vessel, "took off twenty-seven Germans and one Italian" before setting it ablaze.[175] By mid-March, coastal forces sank a 200-ton schooner. The golden streak halted on April 1 when Lt J.B. Sturgeon was killed aboard MTB *242* as it attacked an I-boat. Although damaging the vessel, a stray shot struck him in the fray.[176]

The following evening, Fuller took his boats out to exact some revenge. Gramps joined Horlock aboard *651* and, along with MGB *647*, now under the command of Lt M. Mountstephens, the boats slipped from Komiza just after 1800 hours. It was a calm and warm night. The two vessels first proceeded south to the island of Mljet, the most eastern and southernmost of the Adriatic islands near Vis. There they stopped their boats and floated silently near the coast, waiting for signs of enemy convoys. After failing to spot anything, Fuller moved his boats to the Peljesac Peninsula, just north of Mljet. At one point, he actually went ashore with Ivanovik to chat with a local Partisan leader who informed them about recent enemy activity they'd observed off the coast. They also picked up some American OSS* agents who had an Italian prisoner with them.

Back aboard *651*, one of the agents spoke to Fuller: "where to next?" he asked.

---

* The American version of the British Special Operations Executive. It would eventually become the world-known Central Intelligence Agency (CIA).

"Planning on heading to Zulana Harbour," Fuller replied, which was mid-way on the south side of the peninsula. "Going to strafe the local German garrison."[177]

The American shook his head. "I'd avoid it," he cautioned. "They've got a 155mm and anti-tank batteries there."

Fuller frowned. "Forget that then," he spat, going into the wheelhouse to consult the chart. Horlock joined him as well as Conquest. The men leaned over the map, and Fuller traced his finger along the Peljesac coast, east of the harbour.

"Here," he decided, looking up at both men. "Let's see what we can find."

Conquest began plotting their trip and Horlock proceeded back to the bridge. Fuller warmed up his tea in the galley, making do with some navy issue rum – he'd run out of scotch some time ago. Soon after the boats sped off into the night, pushing closer to the mainland.

————

"We're going to settle in for a while," Fuller cautioned. "Bring us along the coast and let's see if we can't catch the enemy as they pass us."

Horlock nodded and issued the orders. Soon both *651* and *647* were crawling their way up the southern part of the peninsula until they found a decent spot to idle. Their eyes adjusted to the darkness and relative quiet – even with their engines running, Fuller still caught the sound of water lapping against the hull. The sky was clear, providing a spectacular view of the cosmos, under which the bumps of land appeared black and without detail. The Peljesac coastline stretched sixty-five kilometres long, so while there was a decent chance to catch enemy movement, they just as easily could miss it entirely. An hour passed.

"Sir, should we move off?" Horlock asked.

Fuller sipped his drink. "Wait a little while longer," he replied, "I know they're out there." He didn't actually know, of course, but his instincts were tingling. Years of battles had sharpened his hunting senses.

Horlock resumed looking ahead with his binoculars. Fuller liked him – quick-witted and never shy to enter a fight. Just the sort of man he wanted in charge.

Another twenty minutes passed before they slowly resumed inching forward. As the mountainous coastline descended to meet the westernmost part of the peninsula, something along the cliff face stood out to one of the lookouts.

"Excuse me sir?"

"Yes," Horlock replied.

"That's a funny rock formation out there... it doesn't go that way, but it goes that way." The rating gestured with his hand, making a ninety degree angle. Horlock looked again and noticed that "something didn't seem quite right... it was worth turning for another look."[178] He nudged Fuller and pointed to what appeared to be "a vertical line among the lines etched diagonally in the rock face".[179] Fuller's eyebrows narrowed.

"Send word to *647*; were moving in."

Slowly, in the moonlight and gentle sea, they eventually realized there was a schooner along the mountain wall. It was a lovely 30-ton vessel – Fuller described that its "rigging was like lace, the hull like alabaster as her image moved elegantly through the water."[180] It hugged the coast, its guns pointed out towards the open water, but it hadn't spotted Fuller's vessels to her stern.

"All guns on target,"[181] Fuller ordered, but then hesitated. "Wait, belay my last."

Horlock gave the SO a confused look. "Sir?" he questioned, but Fuller held a hand to silence him, eyes fixated on the schooner. It looked to be riding low in the water.

"She must be carrying supplies," he muttered.

Vis suffered from a sever supply shortfall – the Partisans needed more of just about everything: food, ammunition, clothing, equipment, and vessels. A piratical thought crept into his mind, and he began forming a plan. Due to the schooner's larger hull and keel, the vessel couldn't position itself as close to the coastline as *651* and *647*, not without risking running aground. This provided a gap that, unlike most ships, coastal vessels could exploit.

Conquest, also on the bridge, recalled what happened next: "Tom, in his best Canadian accent, said 'well, let's capture it'."[182]

Fuller took the last pull of his rum and turned to the CO, "tell *647* to cover us in case we have company." He then spoke into the voice-pipe connected to the main mess deck, where a small team of British commandoes, along with a few Partisans, waited. "Would you gentlemen mind coming on deck?"[183] The men began making their way up, assembling ahead of the 6 pounder gun.

"We've got some fun coming up," Fuller announced to the group. "There's a boat for you to capture!"[184] Ivanovik dutifully translated while he continued: "The enemy doesn't know we're here and that vessel's got stuff that we need. I want you to take up positions on the bow and stand fast. We'll throttle-up and come alongside and when I give the word, you'll jump aboard and take the crew prisoners."

Around him the commandos and Partisans nodded and then took positions crouched along the gunwales while Fuller returned to the bridge.

"Let's do this," he said to Horlock. "All ahead full."

The CO began giving orders and *651*'s 1500 horsepower engines roared to life, the bow shooting up as the MTB launched forward. Like a grey bullet, it cut through dark waters towards the unsuspecting schooner. Fuller, now at the conn, gave steady commands to the helmsman, ensuring the boat remained just off the land side of the motionless vessel.

"Prepare to board!" Fuller yelled over the rushing wind. The message was relayed down the line, the commandos moving onto the balls of their feet, sub-machine guns at the ready. The shape of the schooner grew rapidly larger as they bore down on her stern – 100 yards, 50 yards, 25 yards…

"All stop!" Fuller ordered. "Bring the bow against her!"

The engines were cut and the cox'n turned *651* towards the enemy just as the MTB came alongside the schooner. A moment later, their wake caught up and nudged the vessel forward, slamming *651*'s bow against the larger hull with a violent 'BANG'. The schooner shook from the recoil – men aboard stumbled and fell to the deck from the sudden jolt. Fuller, braced himself against the bridge controls and ordered the helm to put the engines into reverse for a quick second burst, which had the effect of catapulting some of the commandos onto the schooner. As they leapt aboard, the few Partisans let out "blood curdling yells"[185], guns raised like swords.

A few unfortunately landed on some coiled barbed wire stored on the main deck, wincing as sharp prongs penetrated their clothing and dug into skin. Despite the less than graceful entrance, they still took the schooner's crew by surprise – four German soldiers were quickly disarmed and detained, along with the civilian crew of Italian merchant sailors. The entire boarding operation was done in a matter of seconds.

"Stay with the boat," Fuller told Horlock as he drew his sidearm and, along with Ivanovik, boarded the schooner. The prisoners watched as a black-bearded Canadian landed on deck before them. In the dark, he appeared menacing and more like a pirate than a naval officer, his deep, accented voice reinforcing the stereotype.

"Stay here," he told Ivanovik before asking two commandos to follow him below deck. They swept for any remaining crew and searched the cargo. It had an interesting manifest – aside from the barbed wire, the schooner carried explosives, landmines, cigarettes, some Bavarian ale, a jack-hammer drill, compressor, and some long overdue Christmas mail destined for the enemy garrisoned on the island of Korcula, just west of the Peljesac Peninsula.[186] The Partisans would make good use of this, not to mention the addition of a new ship. When he emerged back on deck, his men cheered.

"Wait until Tito see's this," Fuller said to Ivanovik. "Tie-up the crew and let's get going."

While the Partisans carried this out, Fuller leaned over the side and told Horlock "we're going to tow her." A bowline was secured to the *651* and soon all three vessels slipped away into the night.

———

That morning, residents awoke to find a schooner in Komiza harbour, and upon its mast, the white ensign and Partisan star flew proudly atop a Nazi pennant, announcing to all that this vessel had been taken from the enemy. News of the supplies and ship reached the Partisan's marshal himself: "we became very close with Tito and his gang," Fuller explained. Horlock would also reflect on this, stating that "obviously it was a splendid system, and it represented a double loss to the enemy. He lost a ship, and the Partisans gained one."[187] The Italian sailors were taken by the RN and returned home. Not so for the German soldiers. Instead, the Partisans dealt with them the usual way – they were put onto a boat and ferried over to a small island just off the southern coast. After digging a large hole, they were shot and buried.

As for the schooner, it became the newest addition to Tito's "Tiger" fleet and converted into a warship. Morgan-Giles marveled at how resourceful the Partisans were at doing this, even if they lacked the engineering know-how and resources. For instance, the Italian schooner *Stella Bianca*, which would be captured at the end of the month, was renamed *Crvena Zvezda*, or *Red Star**, the symbol for Tito's forces, and transformed into their primary assault vessel in the Adriatic. He described how they "lined her bulwarks with planks and put gravel in between by way of armour plating," as well as "covered her with every sort of capture machine gun so-on you can imagine", which he noted was

---

* Morgan-Giles said they named her "Stella Rosa", which also translates to Red Star, although other sources note her designation NB-11 and name "Crvena Zvezda". The ship was lost in 1945 when she entered a minefield.

"very dangerous."[188] In all, the vessel was reportedly fitted with: 1x1-2 pounder gun, 1x37mm, 7x20mm guns, and two mortar launchers. Her mast and sails were removed to accommodate the extra armament.

On the night of April 3 to 4, Fuller took *651* and *647* back out hunting. He'd briefed both Horlock and Mountstephens on the plan, careful to consider various contingencies, such as what to do if they happened upon more than one ship. In any event, capturing the schooners was of the utmost importance – Fuller cautioned that his COs were to avoid sinking these vessels, unless circumstances prevented their boarding. While destroying them would certainly deny much needed equipment, food, and weapons to enemy units operating throughout the Adriatic, the true rub came from their capture. Perhaps what drove Fuller the most was his desire to bring home yet another prize – nothing motivated the pirate more than their first real taste of treasure. Before departing, he made a wager with Morgan-Giles, betting that he would not only bring back another ship, but that it would also be larger than the first.

651 and *647* first headed south, reaching the westernmost end of Korcula. Intelligence operatives had observed the passage of numerous enemy ships around a small collection of islands known as the Prznjak, so both vessels began a slow search of the area. Conditions this evening were again favourable, providing clear skies, calm waters, and comfortable warm temperatures.

The patrol lasted a few hours, a process that involved finding suitable areas to observe possible on-water traffic, waiting to see if anything emerged, and then moving on to another spot. Tedious, but hunting required patience, stealth, and sharp eyes, especially when trying to differentiate between dark outlines making up the distant horizon.

Fuller peered into the night. Beside him, Horlock swept the area with his binoculars, looking for the slightest change in detail.

"Got something," he announced. "Dead ahead – definitely a ship."

The SO leaned into the bridge wall and, with his own binoculars, studied the area in question. At first all he could see were outlines of the hills, a common feature of islands in the Adriatic. Then he noticed it – a sleek line between the water and the island. Had they been positioned anywhere else, it would have blended in with the island's topography, but their present angle caused the man-made shape – in fact, the stern of a ship – to jut out ever so slightly from the landmass.

"Good job," he praised. "Let's go in for a closer look."

651 began to move, slowly, like a cat advancing towards a potential meal. Close behind, *647* took up the rear. It would have been premature to pounce, lest they lose the element of surprise. The type of ship, its position, and surrounding hazards needed to be considered if a successful attack were to be made. As the gap between predator and prey closed, details of the object became clearer. There were, in fact, three vessels – two schooners and a thousand-ton merchant ship. While the darkness still made it difficult to accurately judge distance, it looked to Fuller that the cargo ship was too close to the shoreline. He decided to confer with Conquest, who studied their navigation chart. Based on his assessment, the vessel appeared to be in waters that were too shallow for a hull of that size. His conclusion: it must have run aground. That would explain the presence of the schooners – they were providing cover.

Fuller smiled. Ahead lay a golden opportunity to capture not one, but two prizes.[189]

"This is going to be good," he told Horlock before ordering him to, "have Mounstephens bring his boat next to ours and prep his commandos; he's going to capture one of the schooners while we take the other."

As that happened, Fuller called the commandos and Partisans in *651* to take positions. Seconds later, Ivanovik appeared to relay Fuller's orders and *647* pulled up alongside so that Mountstephens could listen-in to the address.

"Right, we're going to try our hand at capturing another vessel," Fuller said. "They likely expect an attack, so I want everyone to stay alert." Gesturing to the MGB, he explained "we're also going to be capturing two boats tonight, so we'll have to co-ordinate our efforts to spring the attack at the same time." He paused, wanting to emphasize his final point, "we want the supplies and the ship, but if they open fire, break off the attack and open up on them."

Mounstephens nodded and moved his ship into position. On Fuller's signal, the two boats throttled up and charged into the open. As *651* and *647* broke apart, each moved to intercept their assigned target. Instinctively, Fuller's hand hovered over the grip of his sidearm – if he were the one in charge of the enemy ship, and suspected a boat was closing to board, he would play possum until the very last minute, opening fire on the commandos as they crossed the divide between vessels.

Thankfully, this never came to pass – Fuller's manoeuver was perfectly timed. They came alongside the schooner and nosed their bow into the other ship, taking those aboard completely unawares. Both commandos and Partisans pulled themselves over the gunwales, war cries echoing into the night, and landing on wood planks. Again, the crew was subdued without firing a shot, although this time nobody had to contend with spools of barbed wire. Fuller followed and found the ship to be carrying ammunition, wheat, and firewood.[190]

It went much the same for *647*. By the morning, Morgan-Giles noted two schooners in Komiza harbour. When he met Fuller at the dock, he happily paid him his winnings – a deal was a deal. Tito became the recipient of two more vessels, as well as much-needed ammunition and food.

Fuller's count had risen to three captured ships, and he was determined to increase the number.

Aside from his money, Morgan-Giles would soon share some good news – effective April 4, Fuller had been awarded a bar to his DSC "For good service in Aegean Operations."[191] A silver rose would soon adorn the ribbon on his uniform, as well as a bar on the medal itself. This only fueled the fire already raging in Fuller – he immediately planned another patrol for that very night, this time focusing on Murter Island. Situated fifty-two nautical miles north of Vis it was far from where they'd previously patrolled, which was precisely the point – it increased the probability of catching a ship off-guard for yet a third time.

Per routine, he led his boats out just as the sun began to set. He felt positively charged, excited to increase his already impressive count of captured ships.[192] They reached the island later that night, whereby they slowed, hugged the shoreline, and began to circle it, pausing for long periods to observe and wait. At around 2320 hours, under a bright moon, they spotted the shapes of two schooners near a cove, both positioned just off the coast with their guns pointed out to sea. They looked as if they were preparing to head off to deliver their supplies, both weighted down with goods. Fuller couldn't believe his luck.

"They don't seem to be catching on sir," Horlock commented.

Fuller shrugged. "It's not as if we're leaving many witnesses. As far as they know, the boats might have been sunk."

The CO considered the words as Fuller took a pull of rum.

"Alright, let's get on with it," Gramps said. "Take them on the landside."

Horlock went about the preparations and soon the commandos and Partisans were on deck. It was all starting to feel very routine by this point. The men went immediately to the bow and readied themselves like a well-choreographed performance. Again, Fuller studied the two schooners, the larger one looking to be around 90-tons while the smaller 50-tons. Neither gave any signs of being on high alert.

"Got ya," Fuller concluded with a grin. He turned to the CO, "Let Mountstephens take the big one this time."

Both vessels positioned themselves, like runners approaching an invisible race line. Fuller glanced one last time at the ships with his binoculars before finally giving the command: "All ahead full and standby boarding party."

Engines screamed, high-octane exhaust ejected as both *651* and *647* raced towards their respective targets. At that moment, something within Fuller came out to the surface, and in the rush of wind against his face and ears, he gave a loud "Yarr!" Beside him, Horlock and Conquest couldn't help but grin and trade looks. Perhaps the SO would soon insist on flying the Jolly Roger? With his shaggy black beard, Fuller looked the part.

Unlike before, the commandos and Partisan had brought hooks to toss over the sides of the enemy ships and pull themselves aboard. As both MTB and MGB closed on the schooners, the men heaved their lines, pulled, and dug sharpened claws into wood. In only twelve minutes they had boarded the vessels, captured the crew, and secured towlines. By 2332 hours, they were well on their way back to Vis.[193]

The 90-ton *Ennesta* and 50-ton *Dante* arrived in Komiza on the morning of the fifth, carrying an impressive haul of wheat, firewood, some 20mm cannons, and a "brand new 20mm Breda cannon fresh from the factory, with all spares and plenty of ammunition".[194] They also captured seven Italians and four Germans who, upon interrogation, revealed both schooners had departed Zara on route to Sibenik.[195] *Ennesta*'s skipper even shared with Fuller that the Germans were doing everything they could to entice schooner captains to carry cargo south. His cousin, "master of the *Svetj Nicola*, was thinking of coming down next evening!"[196] Fuller immediately relayed the information to Morgan-Giles, but, despite the golden opportunity, he decided to stay ashore for the evening. Exhaustion had worked its way through his whole body, causing aches in his back, stomach, and just about every major joint, making his extremities feel heavy and cumbersome. He didn't need a mirror to tell he looked haggard and worn. Ignoring his own health would do no good, so he intrusted the mission with Horlock. Plenty of paperwork had been piling up on his desk, and while he considered digging into it, once he laid on his bed he fell into a deep sleep. Even the sound of Churchill's bagpipes didn't wake him.

Horlock, along with Lt R. M. Cole in MGB *661*, went back to Murter Island and, as expected, intercepted *Svetj Nicola*. Their attack proved so fast that the Italians, taken totally by surprise, all threw their hands up in surrender before anyone set foot aboard their vessel.[197] Two German soldiers tried to escape, abandoning their arms and jumping over the side. However, they barely made it a few yards away from the schooner when *661* swooped around and cut them off. A good thing too – one of the soldiers carried recognition signals. Fuller congratulated both COs the next morning. He was proud of their accomplishment and ecstatic about the discovery. The schooner also yielded a large sum of wheat for their allies.

These successes didn't go unnoticed by the Partisans. Indeed, they "marvelled at the magic of the Dog Boat attacks."[198] Fuller even received personal thanks from Tito himself – the abundance of supplies and additional vessels were exceptional contributions. These were desperate fighters after all, in need of even the most basic things. Morgan-Giles recalled that when they first captured Vis, the Partisans found that there wasn't "much use" for their Italian prisoners, "and sent thousands of them home, minus their rifles and minus their trousers" [199] which they kept for themselves.

Having caught-up on some sleep, Fuller was back out on April 6 and 7, although he decided to give *651* a rest and joined Cole aboard *661*. *647*, which had been off the previous evening, also came along. Nightly, Dog Boats were striking enemy vessels like sharks in a feeding frenzy, and every CO wanted to dethrone Fuller and his record. But there could only be one Pirate King in these waters, and he was determined to remain on top.

CHAPTER 17

———◇◇◉◇◇———

Eighty-Five Pound Sledge

For a third time Fuller took his flotilla to Murter Island, coming across the 400-ton schooner, *Libecchio*. As in his other attacks, Fuller followed the pattern he'd now established for all Dog Boats patrolling these waters: find an island, idle along the shoreline, and once an enemy vessel was spotted crossing the horizon, come up her stern and board. This time, he used his RT speaker to further intimidate the crew. As Morgan-Giles explained, "he went upside some of these schooners, going right up close to them out of the blue, and roaring at them with loud speakers 'you're surrounded, surrender, you haven't got a hope' [and] half these scratch Italian crews would hop over the side."[200] All of this greatly impressed Morgan-Giles, who noted "[Fuller] was a rasping, extraordinary Canadian – a fantastic leader, I must say."

Boarding the schooner, Fuller went below and discovered that *Libecchio* was transporting food, notably 120 tons of Danish butter.

"That was really some capture," Conquest would later state, clarifying that "we never gave that one to them, it was too big for the Partisans."[201] Tito's forces would receive the food but Fuller kept the butter – upon returning to port, he made arrangements to have kegs sent to "every Allied admiral and naval flag officer in the Mediterranean, with a note saying: 'Compliments of Tom Fuller.' No rank, no reference."[202]

By this time, everyone knew who Gramps was – his exploits had reached the ears of just about everyone in the Admiralty. In response to Fuller's piratical tactics, one admiral even noted: "The tactics involved date from the 18th century and earlier and are evidently as effective now as then… these forces have brought their boarding and cutting-out tactics to an exceptionally high standard. Some people have all the fun – and deserve it."[203]

Letters addressed to Fuller began arriving at Vis: "every admiral replied in writing, giving their thanks – and mentioning the butter."[204] For Fuller, it was a prudent move – having already been reprimanded and nearly court-martialed, the butter gifts served as a bit of insurance. As Fuller would later explain: "It takes an admiral to sign a court-martial warrant… It was illegal for those admirals to accept that butter, and when they acknowledged those shipments in their letters I had a sort of blackmail on each of them." From that point on, he figured he was untouchable.

April of 1944 quickly became a woeful month for Axis operations in the Adriatic, chiefly due to the black-bearded Canadian pirate that seemingly struck every day. Three nights after taking *Libecchio*, he led *661* and *647* back north to his favourite hunting grounds. Murter Island was a key junction for supplies coming from the north, and he intended to exploit it.

It was another evening of decent weather. They were close to shore, waiting for signs of an enemy vessel. Fuller went to the galley to warm up his drink and popped in to see Ivanovik and the commandos. The faces were becoming familiar and the nods and smiles from the men told him that they were growing accustomed to their nightly routine.

"They respect you," Ivanovik noted privately, after Fuller left the main mess. "They all refer to you as Signor Commandante."

"As they do the other SOs," Fuller replied flatly. "Just like you and the Juggarizas that tend to my quarters."

Invanovik shook his head. "It's in the way they say it," he stressed, "and the fact that they still call you that when you're not around."

Before Fuller could respond he heard a voice from above. It was Cole, speaking from the wheelhouse. "Sir, our lookouts have spotted something."

Back on the bridge, Fuller observed not one, but three schooners off the horizon. More so, they were escorted by what seemed like an I-boat and two motorboats. "Looks like they're finally starting to realize they need to protect their boats," he mused. Lowering his binoculars, he rubbed his chin with the back of his hand, considering their options. Turning to Cole, he asked "did you inform *647*?"

"Aye sir."

"Okay, here's what we're going to do – engage the escorts and we'll sink one of schooners."

"You want to sink one?" Cole questioned.

"We can only bring back two, but we'll do so after we board them all and see what they're carrying."

Moments later, both vessels sped-up on the supply ships. This time the commandos huddled more amidships, while the gunners took aim.

"Starboard attack angle!" Fuller commanded and Cole immediately relayed the order. *661*'s guns opened, dotted lines of red falling onto the I-boat while *647* engaged one of the motorboats. Rounds punched through the enemy's wooden hulls, both launching into evasive movements in attempt to shake-off their attackers.

"Stay on him," Fuller stressed.

661 turned with the I-boat, staying directly aft of the vessel – her blind spot. Gunners continued scoring hits and as they whizzed past the lead supply ship, the rear guns sent a few rounds over the schooner, forcing the crew to take cover. Meanwhile, *647* pressed on the motorboats, twisting and turning while its guns slowly chipped away at their prey.

The I-boat tried to fight back, hurling shots wildly into the night, but nowhere near Fuller's ship. *661*'s gunfire, on the other hand, was deadly accurate, piercing the enemy's engines and setting her fuel tanks aflame. Men leapt over the sides as the MGB bore down, tearing through the disabled vessel and ultimately sinking her. *661* then rounded the burning wreck and once again passed the schooner, spraying more rounds into her side as she made her way to the motorboats. *647* scored several hits on one of the vessels, but Fuller spotted the other one coming up behind Mountstephens.

"Screw it, ram it!" he ordered. Perhaps a hasty decision, but Fuller knew his hull was reinforced and could survive the attack. Or at least, that's what he hoped.

While the rear motorboat closed on *647*, they didn't see *661* coming amidships.

"Brace yourselves boys!" Fuller yelled, securing handholds. He eyed the approaching vessel and ordered "cut the engines!"

They stopped a full second before *661*'s bow slammed into the side of the motorboat, caving in the hull and splitting planks. Loud cracking sounds rang out as their wake caught up and splashed into both vessels. Even with his handholds, Fuller's body slammed right against the bridge controls, although his German lifejacket absorbed a decent amount of the impact. The motorboat bounced away and spun, its engines and systems now inoperable. Water flowed through her wound, causing the vessel to list and eventually sink. Fuller had sunk his second boat without even firing a shot.

There wasn't time to celebrate though. "Get a damage report and get us back to that schooner," he commanded. "Prepare to board."

A minute later *661*'s engines roared to life, pushing the vessel towards the same schooner they'd shot at earlier. In short order, the two MGBs came alongside their respective objectives and sent boarding parties to capture them. The remaining motorboat came back but a few choice shots from *647*, as well as the sight of his sinking allies, encouraged its surrender. An officer and some of Mountstephens' crew went aboard and took control of the vessel while Fuller and half of his boarding party proceeded to the third schooner. Once all were captured, Fuller went aboard each vessel and surveyed their manifests. After choosing the best ships to bring back to Vis, he boarded the third vessel, carrying in his hands an eight-and-a-half-pound sledgehammer.

"Damn shame we can't take them all back," he told Ivanovik, who was supervising the Partisans moving what supplies they could off the doomed ship. The Yugoslav men caught sight of Fuller with his hammer resting over his shoulder, and proceeded to smile and laugh, none of which Fuller noticed.

"Right, that's good enough," he said. "I'll be right back."

Heading below, Fuller used the hammer to break the schooner's bilge valves, allowing water to seep in. Hurrying back up to the main deck, he rushed everyone off the ship and back onto the MGB. As he followed, he stole one last look back at the ship, before finally stepping aboard *661*. And in so doing, he'd stood for a moment in the moonlight, the black-bearded pirate with a sledgehammer resting on his shoulder. His crew, the commandos, and Partisans all saw it and cheered as he came aboard.

While he didn't realize it at the time, something special had just happened – the birth of a naval legend.

"We'll wait until she goes under and then head back," he told Cole before heading off to stow away the hammer. Later that morning, they arrived in Komiza harbour with an impressive haul of three boats and even more supplies.[205]

The winning streak continued. After some minor repairs to *661* – despite the collision, the damage was minimal – Fuller again set out with Cole on the evening of the fourteenth to fifteenth. This time he took along MGB *646*, under the command of Lt B.L. Knight-Lacklen. He hadn't yet assessed the man in battle – this venture would see how he acted under pressure.

Encounters with the enemy had been steadily growing in both frequency and scope. At first, solitary schooners were the norm, but now supply ships were traveling in convoys under protection of small warships. While things were becoming increasingly hazardous for the 61st, it also meant greater spoils.

Later that evening, while heading north the two-ship flotilla discovered a 100-ton tug towing a 400-ton tanker in open water. Even though they were guarded by a 250-ton F-lighter, Fuller gave the order to attack. *661* and *646* strafed the tanker and tug, each heading in opposite directions. They turned about, crisscrossing each other's wake, and again opened fire on the larger vessels. In so doing, they managed to cause enough damage for both the tug and tanker to start taking on water. As they sunk, *661* and *646* turned on the F-lighter. While they lacked the firepower to sink the escort, capturing it was still a possibility. Before converging, Fuller sent orders to Knight-Lacklen – they would each take a side and simultaneously board the vessel. Compared to taking a schooner, which at best carried four soldiers, this vessel was well armed. Still, Fuller's plan took them by surprise and both boarding parties were able to leap aboard and subdue the crew of thirty-five Germans. By the time they secured the warship and headed back to Vis, the tanker and tug were gone.

Fuller added two more kills and a significant addition to the Partisan's growing fleet. His record remained unmatched – in April alone he'd managed to capture eight schooners, one F-Lighter, one motorboat, and sink four vessels. Additionally, he held the record for the quickest boarding, capture, and towing of an enemy schooner – twelve minutes – one that would remain unbroken. The Partisans began to welcome him home with a scratch-made brass band and even composed a song in his honour: Old Uncle Tom Fuller with his Eighty-Five-Pound Sledge.

Throughout the region, stories of his exploits spread and, like all rumours, quickly took on a life of their own. Germans spoke of a pirate roaming the waters, a menacing figure who sprung from the shadows. At times he brandished a hammer the size of a person, a black-bearded giant who leapt aboard unsuspecting ships, swinging his weapon with enough force to break a vessel's main mast. His men, naturally bloodthirsty brigands, followed in his wake, killing all prisoners. As for the Partisans, 'Signor Commandante' became a quasi-folk hero, a socialist champion whose weapon became a symbolic image of the working-class revolutionary.

In either case, two important details were purposely omitted – this pirate in the Adriatic was, in fact, a naval officer, and his gruff accent wasn't an old English trope, but Canadian. Even soldiers stationed on the Italian mainland shared tales of Fuller's daring captures, single-handedly subduing the enemy with his colossal eighty-five-pound hammer.

"It was an 8.5-pound sledge," Fuller would insist, "but in the message somebody forgot to put the period in." Decades later, he still found himself dismissing the notion that he used the tool as a weapon during boarding operations. He gave up trying to squash these absurd stories – it might have been easier putting out a bush fire with a cheap water pistol.

Larger ships now were being encountered in the Adriatic and Fuller requested that ladders be supplied to each boat to assist commandos in boarding. "Sometimes the high freeboard of these craft made it almost goddamn impossible to board them," he complained. "It was the devil's own choice to get up on them."

By the end of the month, the loss of so many vessels and supplies forced the enemy to halt most of its sea-based operations. Bickering between the Wehrmacht and Kriegsmarine regarding Vis mounted, including what to do about logistical disruptions caused by RN coastal vessels. While both recognized that the "… continual interference with German coastal shipping" posed a significant problem, some argued that it "could not be stopped by the seizure of Vis, since the airport in Foggia and the ports on the southern coast of Italy are at the disposal of the British very close by."[206]

The 61st continued conducting patrols, although they didn't come across many lone supply ships. Schooners were now replaced with bolstered convoys: "the escorts had been strengthened and the goods were being carried far more often in F-Lighters, many of them with reinforced armament of 88mm, 40-mm and 20mm guns."[207] Additionally, the run of good weather also passed. Towards the end of April, turbulent conditions forced coastal vessels to focus on assisting Partisan raids. On the twenty-first, Partisan forces struck at Mljet, taking an entire German garrison, and the following evening, 756 Germans were defeated at Korcula.[208]

Fuller joined MTB *89* on the night of April 25 to 26 for a fruitless patrol, and then switched to *661* the next day. The following two evenings were both let downs. A few times they spotted what appeared to be enemy vessels, only to discover they were both civilian. The first yielded forty nervous sailors who kept repeating "Ni anti Tudeski, Ni anti Tudeski, fishermany, fishermany!", which Ivanovik explained meant 'No German, No German, fisherman, fisherman', while the second was transporting women away from the mainland.

The combination of slow activity, as well as successive nightly operations, left Fuller both physically and mentally fatigued. Upon his return to Vis, Morgan-Giles could see that the SO was looking haggard and granted him some leave in Italy on the condition that he first see the physician aboard the Italian seaplane carrier *Giuseppe Miraglia*, which served as the main tender for coastal forces operating in the region. From April 30 to May 5, he was assessed before being released to a "rest camp" – a place that allowed service members some respite from the stresses of combat. After a week's holiday, he returned to Vis on May 14, feeling refreshed and ready to continue the hunt for enemy ships.

While away, *645* and *667* did find themselves in a few scrapes. On May 1 to 2, both ships were on a patrol to the north-east, south of the coastal town of Split, when they were spotted by enemy gunners along the shores of Brac. *645* rounded the island and ended up on the south-east, where two enemy ships were spotted and engaged. After sinking them, both *645* and *667* were met by an I-boat. The enemy opened fire, and while the two coastal vessels were ultimately triumphant, *645*'s port side had been shot up and two of her guns were damaged.[209] Then, on the thirteenth, a repaired *645*, along with *647* and *649* assisted the Partisans on a raid of the island of Solta, situated a mere half nautical mile to the west of Brac.

Fuller took *661* out with *667*, commanded by Lt Charles J. Jerram, on the night of the eighteenth to nineteenth. Based on some information relayed by Morgan-Giles, he led his flotilla south, back to Peljesac, and entered the channel that separated the northern shore of Korcula Island from the southern shores of the Peljesac Peninsula. At 2330 hours both Dog Boats arrived at the south-western tip of the peninsula, situating themselves "about ten feet from the shore, in a slight indentation."[210] It was a calm night, and although the new moon significantly reduced visibility, it also meant the enemy might use it as cover to move much delayed supplies to surrounding islands. Anything passing through the channel from Cape Loviste from the west would have to cross their line of sight. All they had to do was sit tight.

Just over thirty minutes passed when they finally spotted a large 700-ton coaster heading for Korcula, escorted by two I-boats and an R-boat. They were nearly in range of the island's shore batteries – if he was going to attack, he'd have to do it now. A signal was sent to Jerram in *667* – attack. Engines roared to life and both boats increased to 10 knots on an interception course. Fuller kept his plan simple, take care of the escorts before moving on the slow-moving coaster.[211] Bows were angled so that their respective viewscreen sights were fixed on their chosen targets. The black bumps on the horizon grew larger, but Fuller held off on increasing speed, hoping to remain hidden. However, "owing to the lack of shadow from the poor background [they] were unable to close the convoy to any short range unobserved."[212] As such, at exactly 0052 hours, while still six to seven hundred yards away, "the enemy opened fire with a multiplicity of 20mm".[213] Shapes scattered – the convoy was going to disperse and try to escape.

Fuller would have none of it.

"Throttle-up and engage," he ordered. "Don't let them slip."

Both *661* and *667* sped up, all guns blasting once in range. Thanks to Fuller's ingenious gunnery system, rounds immediately hit both R and I-boats. Enemy tracers came baring down as both red and green streaks of burning phosphorus crisscrossed in the night. Fuller ordered *661* to focus on the R-boat which, despite the dark, stood out from "her heavy amount of fire".[214] In a few seconds, both vessels passed each other, each scoring hits, but the R-boat was using incendiary ammunition, which, despite *661*'s efforts to evade, caught the port turret. Suddenly, a fire "of considerable brilliance"[215] erupted on the boat, providing the enemy guns with an easy target. It "attracted all the enemy's fire like flies to a honeypot,"[216] Fuller recalled. He ordered the boat to disengage so that they could assess the damage and bring the fire under control.

A shape suddenly appeared in the darkness behind them, but having been distracted by the fire, none on deck could positively identify it. There was an equal chance it was *667* or the enemy in pursuit. Fuller ordered that his boat make a "display signal to make certain that the craft we were attacking was not *667*, who might have turned into our radius"[217] and they received the proper response. He'd later discover that as they'd been trading fire with the R-boat, *667* attacked both I-boats, as well as the coaster. An impressive showing by Jerram.

As they retreated north, out from below staggered the boat's MM. He seemed slightly asphyxiated and darkened by soot.

"There's a serious fire in the engine room, sir" he reported. "It's out of control."

"What about your crew?" Fuller asked. "Are they still below?"

"All engine-room personnel are on deck," he confirmed before collapsing into the SO's arms. He lowered the man to the deck while Cole attempted to activate the methyl-bromide extinguishers, but at their present speed of 14 knots, they couldn't effectively extinguish the flames. And with the enemy possibly on their heels, they couldn't risk slowing down. So, he ordered the crew to grab the standard extinguishers and get the fire under control.

Fuller took over for Cole and noted the R-boat near them. He immediately ordered the remaining guns to open on it. "Range was then decreased to some fifty yards" he would later report, "and it was my pleasure to witness the finest display of gunnery under heavy fire."[218] For a minute and a half, *661* continuously pounded the enemy with her pom-poms, splattering her from stem to stern. All the while, the Germans fired back with such ferocity that Fuller would later note in his action report: "The tenacity and fanatical ability of the German gunners to stand up under this punishment was something to be marvelled at."[219] In the end, though, Fuller and his boat's determination prevailed – the R-boat's guns fell silent, and the vessel succumbed to her wounds.

667 regrouped with the damaged *661* – she'd gone out and finished off one of the I-boats before again taking a run at the coaster, "delivering considerable heavy fire into the larger coaster, and glows of fire within it were seen through the scuttles."[220] Fuller intended to send *667* a message to that affect, but the damage to *661* knocked over both his generators and the bridge lacked a working visual-signalling lamp.

A few sailors came up on the bridge, bearing dreadful news – their efforts to bring the fire under control had failed. All fire-extinguishers were now spent. Fuller's report revealed the direness of the situation: "the fire in the engine-room of *661* was then well out of hand… The heat was becoming terrific and almost forcing the personnel off the bridge."[221] Making matters worse, the cox'n reported that vessel's steering jammed – they were stuck on their present course doing 14 knots, which meant they couldn't even draw water in buckets to throw on the fire below. There was no getting around it – their chances of saving the boat were growing slim.

Fuller turned to Cole and instructed him to remove the five wounded men to the foredeck (unfortunately the sixth had succumbed to his wounds) and bring any confidential books to the upper deck.

"If you have any personal knick-knacks you want to salvage from your cabin" he added, "now's the time."[222]

A signalman used the vessel's only serviceable flashlight to send 'Cs' – the signal to close – on *667*. Fuller wasn't ready to give up on saving *661*, but if his plan didn't work, his crew would need to evacuate to the other vessel. Meanwhile, *661*'s Leading Telegraphist L. Pegler was continuing to single-handedly "fight the fire with the dribs and drabs from extinguishers and half-used bromides which appeared to be a most futile and hopeless effort."[223] *661* came alongside *667* at speed, which Reynolds acknowledged as a "difficult manoeuvre"[224] in his book. Then, under Fuller's directions, lines were passed over to the other boat and both vessels were secured together. He then sent Jerram a signal to begin reducing his throttle. As *667* slowed, the lines connecting to *661* strained, pulling against the vessel's run away engines. The damaged MGB reluctantly began to slow, "a feat which was a perfect display of seamanship"[225] Fuller noted. *667*'s wash deck hose was passed over to *661*, along with their fire-extinguishers, which allowed Pegler and some of the crew to push the fire back into the engine space.

As a precaution, the wounded were transferred immediately to *667*. Men on both boats stood at the ready with hatchets to cut the lines, Fuller keenly aware of "the possibility of *661* blowing up".[226] Thankfully, by 0130 hours, the fire was finally extinguished, and after an additional thirty minutes of venting smoke from the engine room, MM J. A. Lacey from *667* came aboard and manually shutdown *661*'s engines.

Exhaustion showed on the faces of every sailor, so Fuller ordered "Up Spirits" and rum was distributed to all hands. They'd certainly earned it this evening. Both vessels remained linked all the way back to Vis, "miraculously [proceeding] rather gingerly"[227] home.

Overall, Fuller counted the evening a success. Moreso, the courage shown by those who fought the fire wasn't overlooked – he submitted a memo to Morgan-Giles recommending several crew members for honours. In the end, DSMs were awarded to Pegler and L/MM A.R. Hayter, while SLt R.S. Smith, who was piloting the vessel during the fire, was awarded a DSC.[228]

CHAPTER 18

———◇◇◉◇◇———

An Old Seadog's Swansong

The nature of combat in the Adriatic had changed. Fuller reflected on their most recent engagement and recognized a key issue – spotting and keeping track of smaller escort vessels. Unlike combat in the English Channel, these fights weren't happening in open water. There, one could keep track of ships against the horizon, but not so in the Adriatic. Against the backdrop of mountainous islands, R and I-boats practically vanished to the naked eye. Tracers alone were insufficient to track a vessel conducting evasive patterns. He needed to find a way around this.

Fuller's solution was characteristically practical – ensure the enemy was inshore. His reason was simple: "when they fire at you and when you fire back at them, all your overs would set fire to the brush ashore." Immediately, the flames would "put them in silhouette." As long as the helm kept their vessel on the seaside of the battle, the outline of the enemy would be easily seen.

He also developed a better way to hide his boats. The "shorelines were [...] forty-feet deep [and] mountains right down to the sea"[229], enabling Fuller to bring his vessels right up against the rock. Then, using bamboo poles and wires, their camouflage nets would be propped above the vessel and angled to make them blend seamlessly with the shore.[230]

Whether from the sky or even parallel at a short distance, one couldn't differentiate the MGBs and MTBs from the land.

Between patrols, the 61st aided the commandos on various raids, all part of the SOE's Maclean mission* but by the end of the month, an urgent request came to Mad Jack Churchill at Vis. On May 25, the German's launched Operation Rösselsprungsent, a joint airborne and land-based assault on Tito's HQ at Drvar. The goal – to capture or kill the Yugoslav leader and destroy his supreme command. However, the marshal and his men were able to make a last-minute escape into the forest.[231] With the enemy in pursuit, the British hastily created Operation Flounced, which pulled resources into the Adriatic and away from the mainland in the hopes of drawing the Germans off Tito's trail. The commander of Force 133 reached out to Mad Jack on Vis and requested that he launch an immediate attack on Brac. As his own No. 2 unit was presently undergoing parachute training, Churchill charged LCol R.W.B. Simonds, CO of the 43rd RM, with the mission.

On May 31, the 43rd RM Commandos, along with of a few troops of 40th RM Commando, imbedded with US Army Rangers, along with 1,500 Partisans, proceeded aboard coastal vessels to assault the Nazis' largest offshore holding in the Adriatic. Mad Jack noted that Brac was "a fairly strong position" and that the enemy had positioned themselves on three hills. As such, "we took over a bigger force than usual."[232] Fuller's flotilla assisted in the operation – in fact, Mad Jack joined Fuller aboard his boat. In typical fashion, the LCol wore combats with his basket-hilted sword and bag pipes.

On June 3, Mad Jack planned an attack by the 43rd, with the 40th as a reserve. The British would focus on hill 422, while the Partisans would engage hills 542 and 48. Additionally, the latter would dispatch a smaller force to engage "the German artillery OP post, which overlooked the

---

* Also known as 'MACMIS', it was a British operation, organized and led by Brigadier Fitzroy Maclean, the mission's namesake.

sea around the island."[233] They would proceed on schedule, the starting point set for 2100 hours that evening.[234]

Mad Jack dispatched Capt Roger Wakefield around 1430 hours to deliver a detailed attack plan to LCol James Calvert Manners, CO of the 40th. However, he would learn after 2000 hours that the unit had not received the orders and were unprepared for battle. Meanwhile, the 43rd had launched their attack and by the time the 40th, now led by Mad Jack, made their way to the hill, fires were already visible on parts of the fortification. He hoped that Simond had managed to take it already. Carefully treading over a series of trip-wire activated landmines (the four troops proceed in single file as if marching because if they stepped directly on a wire, it wouldn't pull the pin from the explosive)[235] they closed on the hilltop, and in the process overran three smaller German dugouts, each with about three men. Eventually, they made it to the top of the hill, sustaining many casualties. Mad Jack had expected to meet up with the 43rd, but they weren't there.[236]

Men were dispatched to search for them (the hilltop was a large, mostly flat, dome so it was possible they were still out of sight) when they began taking fire from opposing hills. Wakefield and Manners were both hit, and Mad Jack rushed to help them as bullets flew overhead. He took care of Manner's wound and then moved to Wakefield. A marine, who'd come to assist, took a shot in the head and fell over Wakefield. Mad Jack quickly moved the body and then gave the injured officer some morphine.[237]

Between the casualties incurred on the way up, as well as those from the recent counter fire atop the hill, he "quickly found himself isolated with only a handful of defenders around him."[238] Soon, only six men were left alive, half of them wounded.

"I was distressed," recalled Mad Jack, "... everyone was armed with revolvers except myself, who had an American carbine."[239] Soon the men were out of ammunition, save for the LCol who was down to his last magazine. Rolling onto his back, Mad Jack prepped his bagpipes and started playing "Will Ye No Come Back Again?", hoping the music would confuse and demoralize the Germans. He would later state that "At the time I deduced that our position was becoming somewhat untenable", which Fuller believed was easily the greatest understatement of the entire war. A grenade landed near Mad Jack and the blast knocked him unconscious. His pipes fell silent and he was eventually taken prisoner.[240]

Overall, fifty-one commandos were killed and seventy-six wounded. The Partisans sustained around sixty casualties. When Fuller and the others heard that their friend, along with members of No. 2 commando, were missing, they immediately set out on a rescue mission. Believing Mad Jack was likely a POW, and that the enemy would immediately send him to the mainland, the 61st went north to intercept shipping between Brac and Split in the hopes of catching him mid-transit. Unfortunately, while the Germans did move him that night, they chose a less conventional route.

The loss of Mad Jack resonated up the chain and little to nothing was spared to liberate him from enemy hands. Fuller's flotilla was joined by "four fleet destroyers to support our movement through the narrow waters and lay down a covering barrage to allow us to get in [and] to have the opportunity to intercept the shipping that night."[241] Even his captors held this officer in high regard, sending his bagpipes and sword to the museum in Vienna for safekeeping.

On June 7, a few days after the events of Operation Flounced, Marshal Tito came to Vis.[242] Since April, Fuller received some letters and gifts from the resistance leader in appreciation of his successes in the Adriatic. On one occasion, a full barrel of a select Proshak wine awaited him in his quarters. Another time, a letter arrived after his engagement in the waters between Korcula Island and the Peljesac Peninsula. In it, Tito wrote:

"We wish to congratulate yourself, your officers, your sub-officers, and your sailors of your flotilla for their actions in the last ten days. The sinking and capturing of twenty-four armed vessels and enemy

transports in our National Sea has brought us closer together, and has developed greater friendship and brotherhood between us. SFSN."

The closing, "Smrt fassesmo svata narudu", was a typical Partisan greeting meaning "Death to fascism, Life to liberty."

Now, he would at last meet the man in person.

Often, after a successful operation, lavish feasts were held in town hall. Naturally, the Partisans invited their allies, reserving places of honour for those who'd distinguished themselves. Fuller found himself given this seat on several occasions, including one dinner with Tito in attendance. To his surprise, the marshal requested that the Pirate of the Adriatic be seated beside him. Over the evening, the two developed a rapport over dishes of "pork and beans and lobster, octopus garnished with nuts and olives, and a red-fleshed fish baked whole in its skin."[243] The head of the latter was considered a "great delicacy" and, as a mark of respect, it was presented to Fuller at the banquet. He took one look at it and lost his appetite but knew rejecting the meal would be taken as a great offence. So, he kept a smile plastered onto his face, thanked his host, and picked away at the dish.

Alcohol featured prominently at these dinners. While Tito himself abstained from drinking, those in attendance would take part in a multitude of toasts. These were typically made with Rakija and were ritualistic in nature, requiring all to stand, raise their glass, roar a thunderous "Ziveli!" (to life!), and then down the entire drink in one gulp.[244] Every glass would be immediately refilled, and as the evening drew on, men would fall unconscious from excessive consumption of brandy and wine. Here, Fuller observed another custom. A sentry would draw his bayonet and use it to remove the bolts from the room's only door. Soldiers would then place the unconscious man onto the door and parade him outside while a string quartet played a dirge.[245]

During their conversation, Fuller learned that Tito enjoyed chess. The marshal was considered an excellent player, so Gramps later arranged for twelve men to play him. Tables were arranged in a circle to allow Tito to move freely from one player to the next, and in this way "[he] played them all simultaneously, and won every game."[246]

Tito's strategic thinking extended beyond the battlefield and chessboard. Fuller noticed that if people assumed he didn't speak English, the marshal would play along. As Fuller recalled: "One night, on my boat, he [Tito] was briefed by a British intelligence officer and the whole conversation was being laboriously translated by an interpreter. When the officer had finished the briefing, he left. And Tito turned to me and said: 'Rub a dub dub, three men in a tub,' grinned, and walked away."[247] Decades later, Fuller would find himself standing beside Tito during a reception in Ottawa in 1971. At some point, Fuller turned to Governor-General Roland Michener and asked, "does the marshal still pretend he doesn't speak English?" Tito glanced at his old friend and flashed a knowing smile.[248]

When Tito passed away nine years later, the Canadian government sent a delegation under then Governor-General Ed Schreyer, which also included Fuller.[249]

Between June 16 and 26, he stayed ashore on Vis before heading over to *Miraglia* on the twenty-seventh, followed by another stint at a rest camp. Those closest to Fuller were growing concerned about his health. The years of warfare, including an unusually high number of skirmishes, were taking a toll and even the Pirate of the Adriatic wasn't immune to the effects of combat fatigue. Irregular schedules, high-stress, and acute exposure to various combat-related stressors, were making it harder and harder for him to get any sleep. Symptoms of insomnia emerged, which contributed to a growing number of anxiety attacks. Fuller simply tried to ignore it and pretended everything was fine, but people like Morgan-Giles took notice.*

---

* References for this are a report from a medical board of inquiry dated Nov 16, 1945, as well as comments made by Morgan-Giles.

On the July 1, his first S.206 as SO of the 61st was compiled by none other than his old nemesis, Cdr Welman. After *St. Christopher*, he took on various roles in the Mediterranean, served as XO of the coastal forces base in Algiers and then staff to the C-in-C. He listed Fuller's general conduct as 'satisfactory' and of 'temperate habit', while rating him as follows:

Professional Ability:	7
Personal Qualities:	5
Leadership:	6
Intellectual Ability:	5
Administrative Ability:	5

Interestingly, penciled-in beside his scores were updated numbers:

Professional Ability:	8
Personal Qualities:	6
Leadership:	7
Intellectual Ability:	6
Administrative Ability:	6

When the report came across Capt John Felgate Stevens, who served as Captain Coastal Forces Mediterranean in Malta, he not only bumped Fuller's score but added his own comments. On August 18, he noted that "I would add +1 to the assessment in Sect. II" of the report. Fuller's ability in ship handling was listed as 'good', and 'fit for more important sea command'. Despite any personal reservations, Welman's overall assessment was surprisingly praising of the Canadian:

> *"A first-rate Coastal Force Gunboat Officer who has established a reputation in action and can always be relied upon to do his best. A sociable and agreeable personality, but of somewhat dogmatic point of view, which is liable to detract from his otherwise good qualities of leadership. Of average intelligence in arts and interested in sport*

generally, particularly motor racing, in which he has previously taken part."

Stevens also added his own comment, writing: "Lt. [sic] Fuller has shown himself to be a born leader of small craft in close action with the enemy. He thinks out his tactics beforehand yet is resourceful in emergency." The report lastly indicated that Fuller be considered for promotion in 'ordinary course'. Fuller would later see document in his file and comment "It was the only time that I ever saw a correction factor of plus four by the Senior Officer." While Welman's view of Fuller might have softened, Fuller didn't take kindly to his scoring. "Welman and I had fought like hell," he explained, "and he'd given me such a low mark that the Commander in the Mediterranean ruled a plus four error and had changed it."

Before heading back out on a patrol, Fuller reluctantly took yet another trip to Italy on July 13 for a two-day stint at a rest camp. His anxiety attacks were growing more frequent and pronounced, but the short holiday helped a bit. He returned to Vis on the seventeenth, and while far from being in perfect health, he was allowed to resume his duties. On the nineteenth he was back out patrolling.

July had been quiet. The flotilla's first encounter occurred on the night of July 17 to 18. MTBs *649* and *670*, along with MGB *659*, discovered a convoy in the Mljet Channel and, after a short fight, managed to score two kills in addition to damaging a ferry.[250] Fuller found things similarly dull – the Adriatic was uncharacteristically void of shipping traffic and they came upon nothing the first few nights. Shore based intel also offered no solutions. It was almost like the war had ended and nobody remembered to tell them about it.

On the evening of July 25 to 26, Fuller led three vessels to the far northern shores of Peljesac: MTB *651*(Ennis), MTBs *667*(Jerram), and *670*, now commanded by Lt Eric Hewitt. Again, the SO chose to travel with Ennis, and the flotilla left harbour and into the familiar warmth of a mid-summer's evening. From Komiza, they headed east, and as darkness fell, the heavens revealed a clear sky replete with stars, planets, and the all too familiar band of the Milky Way. Without any breeze, the mirrored waters reflected the cosmos, making it appear as if they were three boats travelling through space. If it had been another time, one where they weren't hunting for enemy vessels, the boats might have stopped to fully appreciate the beauty of the moment, but tranquility was seldom afforded in times of conflict.

Around 2309 hours, they reached the north-eastern shores of Peljesac and began the customary crawl along the coastline until they located a suitable spot to put their boats into neutral and scour the horizon for signs of movement. Conditions were optimal this evening – compared to other nights, things were decently illuminated by moonlight, although the steep shoreline and mountains dominating much of the peninsula obscured many areas with large shadows. Fuller ordered his flotilla to settle into a tiny cove, a mere twenty yards from the shore, which allowed them to stay out of sight. With any luck, an unsuspecting enemy convoy would pass and break the rut in his record.

Time dragged. The first hour yielded nothing but a few shooting stars and the barely perceptible movement of the constellations. Fuller took a few sips of his special drink – his second of the evening – despite the vessel's lack of motion. At some point during the last couple of months, he began relying on the beverage to sooth more his nerves than his stomach, but now the shot of alcohol was having less and less of an impact. He glanced at his cup, momentarily tempted to pound it back and fix another, but repressed the urge. Nothing went unnoticed on a ship, especially one as small as an MTB. Everyone took note of the person in charge and if they noticed him drinking more, it might raise some concern. For their sake, he needed to maintain the persona of the pirate his men had come to worship, and that the enemy feared.

Finally, at 0013 hours, one of the sailors reported an object, about a mile away and towards the north-west. The news invigorated Fuller, and his instincts came alive. Orders followed – a signal was sent, engines roared, and in moments all three boats were moving to attack. As always, the plan was straightforward – pounce on the vessel, surround it, and then capture the prize. There was, however, one problem, which only became evident as they neared their target.

It wasn't only one ship.

Obscured by the backdrop of mountains, the 400-ton flak schooner *Vega* was nearly invisible, especially since a recent conversion had removed her mast and bowsprit. To make matters worse, the ship's higher freeboard made it impossible to see an additional escort of five E-boats and two I-boats, which were all travelling on the seaward side of *Vega*.[251] The 61st was both outgunned and outnumbered, although, for what it was worth, still had the element of surprise. A decision needed to be made – break off or engage – but every member of the flotilla already knew what the SO would do. There was really only one option for the pirate.

At 0024 hours, Fuller ordered *670* to attack the flak schooner as Hewitt was closest to it. *Vega*, alerted by the sound of approaching engines, opened fire into the night and the SO signaled *670* to fire a starshell to illuminate the target. However, rather than launch one, Hewitt released three into the sky, which turned out to be a good thing, because one of them managed to land on *Vega*'s deck – directly into an unshielded bucket of petrol. A violent explosion of liquid fire erupted across the upper deck, setting the schooner "ablaze her entire length".[252] *Vega*'s guns immediately fell silent as sailors sought cover and scrambled for extinguishers. But spraying the accelerant only served to spread the flames to other areas, and in less than a minute the entire vessel became a raging inferno. Fuller watched as men, overwhelmed by the heat, started to abandoning ship.

The battle was far from over though. Shore batteries along the eastern tip of Hvar lobbied a dozen 105mm rounds towards them. The rounds all missed and, as Fuller observed, did more to "[inconvenience] the hundreds of Germans swimming".

While Hewitt's starshell had been a lucky break, the burning timbers had an added benefit – a torch in the night. Tongues of flickering orange now danced across the I-boats, making them easy to see. *651* raced up to the escort's rear and unleashed a devastating torrent of bullets that punched through I-boats *302* and *309*. It was a stellar example of naval gunnery – in a single pass, both vessels lost the use of their engines. Fuller watched with immense satisfaction as the I-boats, adrift and without power, came to a halt, neither having managed to fire a single shot.

Nudging Ennis with his elbow, the SO told him to stop "in the immediate vicinity"[253] and regroup with the others. He wanted to ensure that neither *667* or *670* mistakenly sunk the disabled I-boats, which he intended to take back as prizes. Both crews were now jumping over the side, sailors hoping to evade capture by swimming ashore. Fuller tasked *667* with boarding both vessels, as well recovering anyone in the water. As for *670*, Hewitt had moved on one of the E-boats, also "perfectly silhouetted"[254] by the inflamed schooner. His guns made short work of the unsuspecting vessel, which immediately started to sink. Turning about, the MTB came back to wreck and rescued the survivors.

A lookout aboard *651* spotted an object moving in the distance and alerted the bridge. It appeared to be a smaller boat – possibly the original vessel they'd spotted – making a run for the coastline.

"Nice try," Fuller thought.

The MTB gave chase and quickly caught up to the fleeing vessel. Too small to defend itself, the two-occupant craft surrendered without a fight and both men were brought aboard *651* as prisoners.

Four E-boats remained at large. They had all distanced themselves from *Vega* and sought cover in the dark, but after regrouping decided to retreat rather than engage the MTBs. Catching them wouldn't be possible – the Germans vessels were too fast and already had a head start – but Fuller knew a way to lure them back. Both his and Hewitt's

MTBs proceeded "due south to the coasts" where they "turned east and streamed 28 knots a hundred yards from the shore."[255] Meanwhile, Jerram positioned his MTB between the burning schooner and the fleeing E-boats, allowing himself to be "beautifully silhouetted by the fire".[256] The plan was simple: the Germans, upon seeing *667*, stationary and alone, would turn back for the easy pickings, unaware that *651* and *670* were positioning to flank.

As predicted, the enemy took the bait. In formation they changed course, unaware that in so doing they allowed both *651* and *670* to swoop in behind. Now *Vega*'s light provided the Dog Boats with clear targets, but the E-boats moved quicker than Fuller anticipated and launched torpedoes before they could intercept them. As *667* secured the last of "some fifty prisoners" and readied tow lines, a lookout alerted Jerram to the approaching threat. He immediately repositioned himself behind the I-boats, using the captured vessels as a shield. Just then, three white streaks, "one passing astern and two directly under *667*"[257] shot by, narrowly missing the MTB. The E-boats turned around to face their pursuers, this time launching four torpedoes. *651* and *670* maintained course and speed, allowing the warheads to pass between them, and then opened fire on the enemy. At 150 yards, *651*'s guns "repeatedly hit" the "fourth in line" E-boat, while *670*'s pom-pom's tore through the "third-in-line" causing a "loud explosion".[258] However, the remaining two enemy vessels responded in kind, sending a hail of green tracers at Fuller's MTB. Several rounds caught the hull, shaking the craft with deafening blows. Then, the boat shuddered from her stern and lost propulsion. The SO glanced at Ennis, who's ear was already pressed against the voice pipe connected to the engine room. *651*'s Packards had sustained a direct hit – they were now without power and unable to move or use their gun turrets.[259]

It was 0115 hours and the Pirate of the Adriatic was a sitting duck.

Raising his binoculars, Fuller found the two E-boats in the distance and watched as they broke off, one heading left while the other to the right. He predicted that they would circle around and finish them off – its exactly what he would do in their position. Looking back at Ennis, he gave the man a knowing nod.

This was it.

The end.

Continuing their respective turns, the enemy didn't straighten to bare down on the Dog Boat. Instead, they proceeded around until they were facing each other, bow to bow. Before Fuller could voice his confusion, the two vessels closed and "very obligingly turned on each other and carried out a spirited gun action as we lay in a grandstand seat."[260] History was repeating itself – just like the convoy of trawlers Fuller had attacked in the English Channel, both Germans mistook their ally for the MTB and proceeded to gun each other down. All around, men "cheered as they watched the bits and pieces fly from both E-boats", each managing to disable the other.

"I'll be damned," he whispered.

The sound of *670*'s engines drew his attention to Hewitt's boat. In short order, a line was secured to *651*, after which all three Dog Boats proceeded home. As they passed *Vega* – careful to stay to the landside – they observed Hvar's guns continue to assault the burning ship. At that moment, some ammunition exploded aboard the wreck, sending "a lone two-star signal cartridge, which evidently was the correct one, as the shore batteries ceased and did not reopen."[261]

They returned to Vis with "no fewer than sixty-five prisoners"[262] and a score of enemy vessels destroyed, damaged, or captured. Victorious as they were, their success still came at a cost.* *651* would be written-off – yet another to Fuller's already sizeable tally – and *667's* navigator, SLt John Dean, had either slipped or was struck by enemy flak during the

---

* Fuller reported that at least two E-boats had been sunk in the engagement, but, as Reynolds reveals, "German lists of the Mediterranean E-boat flotillas, giving the 'fate' of every boat, have no record of boats lost on this night, so possibly they were damaged rather than sunk." (156)

boarding operation. Whatever the cause, he fell between the I-boats and vanished. Fuller delayed their departure by twenty minutes to search for him, but sadly failed to find any trace of the officer. Eventually, the RN would list him as K.I.A.[263]

As for the SO, the battle would be his last. Symptoms of his combat fatigue became more pronounced after the engagement, but all attempts made by Morgan-Giles to persuade the Canadian to step back were, predictably, resisted. Fuller would remain at Vis until August 20, conducting the odd, uneventful patrol, but agreeing to remain mostly ashore. By the end of the month, Capt Stevens arrived on the island and staged an intervention.

"I'm relieving you as SO of the 61st," he said, adding "whatever job you want, just tell me, and I'll put in a request for you."

"No," Fuller replied, rejecting the olive branch. "I want to stay put. After all, Peter Evenson [sic] has been in this longer than I have."

Stevens shook his head. "No, I put Peter ashore six months ago in Alex."

Fuller didn't respond, and Stevens took the opportunity to continue. "Look, you have the distinction of having served longer than any man in attack warfare in the Royal Navy, and you're ten years older than anybody in the job." It wasn't an exaggeration. All told, Fuller had been in 135 actions at sea: 105 firefights, and 30* hazardous actions. Sg Lt J. A. Virtue RCNVR, would note in a medical review that the Canadian had served a total of five years, two months, and twenty-six days during the war. He also recorded that Fuller had shrapnel removed from his right foot and leg in August, and while listed as operationally fit (physically), he suffered from an "anxiety state". Elaborating, Virtue explained that "after operational duties he was sent ashore for one month at Yugoslavia [before] suffering from operational fatigue – had insomnia and crying spells."

---

* Fuller explained that he didn't fire a single round in these actions, but that didn't mean he wasn't in peril. Certainly, the bombing of his boat counted among these.

Decades later, Morgan-Giles reflected on this, saying "Tom Fuller – a much written up man – a fantastic leader, I must say." Pausing, he lifted his chin and sucked in his lower lip before adding, "Tom Fuller got invalided home, he'd been at it quite a long time."[264]

Realizing there was no way to sway Stevens' decision, the Canadian finally relented, and asked to finish his service back home. They shook hands and with that, the Pirate of the Adriatic retired his sledge.

CHAPTER 19

◇◇◉◇◇

Fair Winds...

News that the SO of the 61st was going home spread across the island. Preparations for Fuller's departure commenced immediately – as far as the Partisans were concerned, nothing short of a large banquet would suffice for "Signor Commandante". BGen Thomas (Tom) Bell Lindsay Churchill, Mad Jack's younger brother and the ranking officer on the island, elected to host the farewell celebration. He'd been stationed at Vis back when Fuller arrived with his flotilla but had been recalled to England for "consultations", returning on the twelfth of June.[265]

The whole island seemed to resonate with energy during those last days in August. While those under his command were less than enthused to see him go, the genuine admiration of all those who'd served with the old pirate, coupled with the excitement over what promised to be one hell of a send-off party, softened the blow, even for Fuller. It provided a convenient distraction – he was still unwell and coming to terms with being removed from his position. He respected Stevens and knew, in his heart, that he'd made the correct decision. Furthermore, he could trust the Capt, along with Morgan-Giles, to remain discreet about the matter. It would take decades before the public developed an understanding and appreciation of things such as post-traumatic-stress-disorder (PTSD)*, and Fuller wanted to avoid the stigma associated with mental health related issues. Even though few could boast a service record as exceptional as his, being the Pirate of the Adriatic pressured him to live up to the moniker he'd been prescribed.

The Italian vessel *Larina*, now crewed by the Partisans and berthed in Komiza harbour, served as the venue for Fuller's sendoff. He would later recall that the evening of August 19 was a splendid event, including "a cocktail party on board, and dinner, and it was extremely well carried out." Throughout the party, a "Jug band" provided music for the guests, which included every CO, their officers, as well as senior army officers.** Throughout the dinner, men came up to convey their sentiments and thank him for his service and mentorship. Even those he'd been hard on expressed gratitude: "Some officers who hated your guts because they figured you'd been pretty rough on them, said, 'You know, I never understood when you bawled me out, and you kept me on board for four days and you said, 'Goddamn well learn what an attack angle is, and don't get astern again on a convoy.' Now I agree that that was what I needed.'"

Food and drink flowed freely, and as the man of the hour, Fuller's cup never emptied. Naturally, he soon became quite inebriated: "Of course they had seven different kinds of wine and liquor and I was pretty well boiled." After the dinner, a throng of drunk men decided to pile onto a tender to head back ashore. Fuller explained: "They had a little bumboat as a tender, with a little diesel engine, completely housed, so everybody got on top of the roof of the goddamn thing. I thought, "My God, how did we ever get into this? We've got to try to keep this thing

---

* The American Psychiatric Association would only add PTSD to the Diagnostic and Statistical Manual of Mental Disorders (DSM) in 1980, nearly forty years after the Second World War.
** During his interview, Fuller grimly noted that "most of the Colonels were dead then—at Brac Mountain we lost them all."

from capsizing, and we were always moving around on top to try to keep the equilibrium."

The next morning, Fuller boarded an MTB with his kit and a raging hangover. "It sailed at six o'clock in the morning," he explained, "and when I got aboard, I have never been so drunk in my life." Stevens joined him for the journey to Brindisi, Italy.

On September 5, Fuller was awarded his second bar to his DSC "For good service in coastal force in the Mediterranean". He had now been awarded three DSCs during his naval career, which put him in a very rare group. According to the *London Gazette*, there were 4,524 DSCs awarded during the Second World War, with 434 receiving a bar, and only 44 a second bar (and one who would be awarded a third!). Of that number, 199 DSCs were presented to Canadians, with thirty-four first bars and five second bars.

Fuller moved to HMS *Byrsa*, a shore establishment in Naples, on the twenty-seventh of September and stayed until the twenty-eighth, before moving to HMS *Fabius*, a RN base in Taranto, at which he stayed until September 30. A S.206 evaluated his latter performance as SO of the 61st from March 1 to September 14, 1944 (despite the previous one having covered the periods from March 1 to July 1, 1944), signed off again by Cdr Welman. Fuller's general conduct was, as always, listed as 'satisfactory' and of 'temperate habit'. His scores were as follows:

Professional Ability:	7
Personal Qualities:	5
Leadership:	7
Intellectual Ability:	5
Administrative Ability:	5

His ability in ship handling was listed as 'good' but most striking were Welman's comments: "A very courageous officer, who has proved a fine Coastal Forces Flotilla leader, and is well respected by his officers and men." While surprisingly gracious, especially considering that there was little love lost between the two, Welman did find something to critique, noting his "… somewhat narrow outlook, which makes him dogmatic and rather difficult to deal with." The observation is interesting – while Fuller demonstrated a penchant for innovation and openness to rethinking ways of doing things, questioning orders, straying from procedure, and ultimately bending or breaking guidelines were all hallmarks of his command. There were those who admired his ingenuity and there were others who detested his refusal to tow-the-line. As demonstrated throughout his wartime service, the only rules Fuller rigidly followed were his own. Welman ended the report by noting that he was "fit and keen on games and sport" and Stevens, who ultimately approved the form on November 6, added "Forwarded concurring generally; an officer with a splendid record in action against the enemy."

Before heading back to Canada, Fuller "flew over to Ischia", which was the island directly west of Procida and known for its hot springs. During a brief layover, he recalled "on getting to the harbour, great big yellow letters reaching from the sill of one window to the other down the side of the building, that said, EVERY WOMAN ON THIS ISLAND HAS VENEREAL DISEASE." His accommodation was the lavish, former residence of the German ambassador, but after a day, he was "turfed out" so that it could be given to some VIPs, who turned out to be none other than Winston Churchill and King George VI. Both had just finished inspecting troops on the mainland and were heading to the island for a brief vacation. While Fuller was less than enthused to relinquish his berth, he would witness something memorable:

> *Churchill, with a great big straw hat, towel over his arm, naked as the day he was born, went down the path to the highway, stopped the traffic this way, stopped the traffic that way, and walked across. Not the towel around him, just over his arm. He went down and plunged into the harbour and then he dried himself off with the towel and*

walked up. Stopped the traffic this way, stopped the traffic that way, with George saying, "Churchill, put some clothes on!"

By November 21, Fuller was once again back in Canada at HMCS *Stadacona*. A MiD was awarded to him on December 5 "For Services in Action in Coastal Craft in the Mediterranean", which, in addition to his three DSCs, certainly made him a uniquely decorated officer. Years later, as part of a collection of veteran experiences in war, Dave Brown would note Fuller glancing at his medals and observing "we made a few trips to Buckingham Palace."[266]

Fuller soon became an Acting Cdr, although he felt he technically skipped a rank upon receiving the promotion. His bump to Lt Cdr was listed as "Temporary" and only "whilst holding appointment at sea". As he was now ashore, technically he should have reverted to Lt but he'd been made a Cdr without ever holding a substantive Lt Cdr rank. However, Fuller's service file reveals that he was actually made a substantive Lt Cdr in the RCNVR on New Year's Day, 1945, although that bit didn't appear to have been communicated to him.

Over the next nine months, Fuller assumed roles at various shore establishments, specifically *Burrard* and *Naden*. Capt Givenchy, CO of *Naden*, noted that Fuller had performed "in all respects to my entire satisfaction, a keen valuable officer."[267] Another evaluation specified that Fuller "has handled *Naden* well under very difficult circumstances; i.e. 4000 ratings of a transitionary nature and practically no officers other than those waiting demobilization. Has proved loyal, efficient, and hardworking."[268]

In November 1945, he returned home and assumed command of Ottawa's naval reserve unit, HMCS *Carleton*. It was now that he recalled details he'd ascertained after rescuing shipwrecked Germans submariners – in particular the sailor who noted that his aunt lived in the city on Flora Street. Fuller visited the address and knocked on the door. A woman answered and once her identity was confirmed, he passed along news that her nephew was alive and safe as a POW.

"My nephew?" she questioned.

"Yes, from the German Navy," Fuller confirmed. To his surprise, she frowned and shook her head, replying, "You can't trick me like that – I have no nephew in the German Navy." He shared his name and description, but the woman still shook her head, insisting, "I don't know of any such person at all."

Fuller wasn't convinced the woman was telling the truth. Upon returning home, he picked up the phone and called the RCMP. The next day, a few investigators paid the woman a visit, and after some conversation, she reluctantly admitted that she was indeed the aunt to the POW.

Another incident occurred just after the end of the war. He'd been invited to a ball at Government House and took particular note of a Maj in highland uniform. Something about his dress appeared off – the colour of his rank insignia didn't match the kilt of his regiment. He also wore paratrooper wings with an MC, and while everything else appeared in order, Fuller still felt he was "a very peculiar character" and decided to question him.

"I was wondering what outfit you are with," he asked, explaining "I noticed the black pip and yet you're not wearing a Black Watch kilt, nor the Inniskilling, which I thought were the only ones to wear them."

The man waved a hand through the air and replied, "oh, I was in an outfit that nobody ever knows about in Canada."

Fuller raised an eyebrow, "Yeah, but what?"

"Well, I was in the Special Air Service," the man revealed.

Growing more suspicious, Fuller prodded further and asked "what force, the 313, 266, or 399?"

The man studied Fuller before responding "313."

"Well, you'd know Andy Lassen and David Sutherland and George Jellicoe and all those people?"

"Yes," he confirmed, before turning to look behind him and saying, "I'm afraid I'm being called in the next room."

Fuller kept his eyes fixed on the man as he left. Something still didn't feel right about him. He called James Pratt* at Naval Intelligence and explained what transpired.

"This might be all bunkum," he admitted, "but there's this fellow, and there's something fishy about him because these were all characters that I mentioned, and when you run into someone who knows them, you don't just walk away from him."

"I'll look into it," Pratt promised and the very next day, he called Fuller back with an update.

"You haven't got any more of those hunches, have you?" he asked.

"Oh?"

"First of all, he's an Imperial Officer on loan to the Canadian Army; he's a captain, not a major. He had claimed his Gazette hadn't caught up with him, and so he was wearing a crown and they paid him as a major."

"I knew something was up about him," Fuller stated.

"That's not all," Pratt said, "He was never awarded an MC, nor is he entitled to paratrooper's wings. I also discovered that an officer on the base had sold him a car and he never paid for it. He owes money to about ten other people around the place."

"Where is he now?" Fuller asked.

"He's on his way to England under close arrest."

Despite being in Canada, Fuller still wound up getting in trouble – he was arrested on VJ day under the authority of RAdm Victor Brodeur who was CO of the Pacific Coast, . "It was the only time I was ever placed under open arrest," Fuller explained. "All I did was to send two hundred ratings and five trucks down [to the Brewer's Warehouse] because some guy by the name of Yardley, who ran the Liquor Control Board, wouldn't give us any booze." He went on to say:

---

* Fuller only stated he spoke to "Pratt in Naval Intelligence". James Pratt, who would head naval intelligence in 1950 and retire a Commodore, appears the most likely candidate.

So I sent another officer down and I said, "Get two hundred of the biggest, best and burliest tattooed ratings you can get, and get trucks and things and go down there and get twenty five tons of beer, and bring it back here. Sign my name for it. If they won't give it to you, just tell them to look outside." He had them all lined up and swinging web belting outside, and Yardley bloody well gave them the beer.

Once gone, the man reached out to Brodeur, who in turn called Fuller from Vancouver. Sounding less than pleased, the man questioned him: "I understand you broke into the Brewer's Warehouse and stole twenty-five tons of beer?"

"No sir," Fuller replied. "I didn't steal it, I signed for it. Well, I had somebody else sign for it, but I gave the order."

"Well, consider yourself under open arrest," Brodeur snapped. "You will report to me by 0800 in the morning by the first aircraft!"

His time at *Naden* was recorded in an S.206, noting him as "keen, hard-working, and enthusiastic". Overall, he was viewed as "a very valuable commanding officer and accepts increased responsibility with keenness."[269] After being demobilized on January 1, 1946, he returned to the service as CO of *Carleton* two years later. Another S.206, conducted on July 7, 1948, noted that while Fuller was "opinionated", he was also "loyal and devoted to the service." Additionally, he also appeared to do "a good job inspiring sailing."

Starting February 7, 1949, Fuller spent a month in HMS *Jamaica* traveling along the western shores of South American. As always, a few stories emerged after his venture. The first had to do with uniforms: when he came aboard, officers were wearing No.13 dress, an informal tropical uniform consisting of a white shirt, matching shorts, white socks and shoes, along with a white cap. For dinner, officers in the wardroom wore their Red Sea Rig, a less formal black-tie dress that did without the jacket, honours, and insignia, instead wearing a red cummerbund and matching bowtie. On one evening ashore, the Chilean Navy threw a cocktail party at the O'Higgins Hotel in the city of Viña del Mar. Full mess kit was to be worn, and for the first time, Fuller appeared before the other officers with his decorations and medals. "As I say, on that ship everybody treated me with a great deal of courtesy, but when I walked in there with miniatures on, the whole attitude of the officers' mess just changed BANG! like that," he explained.

The second anecdote regarded his steward. When he entered his cabin he noted a bald RM Cpl attending to his room, which struck him as odd. The man turned and, upon seeing Fuller, flashed an ear-to-ear grin that made the Canadian wonder if there was something wrong with his gear.

"What's the matter, marine?" he asked, and gesturing around the neat cabin, added "you seem to enjoy it."

"Sir, don't you remember me?"

Fuller's eyes narrowed as he studied the man's face.

"I asked for this appointment with you," the marine explained. He then pointed to his scalp and said, "It was on your ship I lost all my hair."

It turned out, he'd been with the RM commandos at Vis and relayed that "he had a pretty rough night of it one night in my ship."

Years later, the same marine called Fuller out of the blue. He was, at that time, a guard at the Kingston Penitentiary and asked if Fuller would come visit him. As he was in Ottawa, and only couple hours away, Fuller decided to accept the offer. When he arrived, he presented the old pirate with a leather wallet, upon which was carved the outline of his old MTB.

"I want to ask a favour of you," he said. "A fellow tried to knife me and another prisoner came to my rescue and jumped him."

Fuller, who'd been admiring the gift, looked him in the eyes.

"He got pretty badly cut up," the man continued, "but he's up for a pardon for coming to my help. I'd have been a goner if he hadn't. They are going to give him a parole and I'm out looking for a job for him. Have you got a job you can give him?"

By this time, Fuller had returned to his construction business and was doing quite well for himself. He thought for a moment, and then answered, "all we can give him is a job as a truck driver or something like that."

The old Cpl smiled. "That's fine as long as he's got something to go to when he gets out." In the end, the man managed to acquire another job, and Fuller appreciated the wallet, one of several gifts of his service and time as the Pirate of the Adriatic.

Upon his return to Ottawa, tensions with his superiors began to mount. His proximity to NSHQ meant dealing with a fair bit of politics, and while he enjoyed his command, especially the relations he forged with his subordinates, Fuller's assertiveness, and habit of calling things the way he saw it began to rub the higherups the wrong way. They overlooked his temperamental nature at first, mostly in deference to his impressive war service, but gradually their tolerance faded. The comments on success evaluations are revealing. In 1950 he was described as "an unorthodox officer, [with a] dominating personality and unshakable opinions." Still, the observation concluded that he "has shown more interest in his division in the past year [and] is a natural and colourful leader." Then, in 1951, it was reported "[Fuller] could be an excellent CO if he devoted the time" and that he was "a strong personality, stubborn, and inclined to be critical of H.Q." While still noting his loyalty, it was stressed that he had the "ability if he cared to apply it." Despite these misgivings, Fuller still found himself promoted to Capt in the RCNR on New Year's Day, 1951.

From all accounts, Fuller appeared ready to move on. In a letter to the Naval Secretary at NSHQ, Fuller suggested "Cdr R.B. White OBE RCN(R) as [his] successor" and that he intended to "turn over to my successor on the 25th of January, 1951, which is the nearest drill night to my actual retirement date."[270] He also stressed that "I do not wish to avail myself of the Naval General Order which I understand will be promulgated shortly, that would enable me to continue in Command until the end of the Training Year."[271] Clearly, he didn't want to delay relinquishing command. While butting heads certainly contributed to the decision, it may have been more influenced by the needs of his civilian life, especially his booming business.

His request was granted and Fuller swallowed the anchor on the twenty-fifth of January. He also applied to receive the newly created Canadian Forces Decoration, a medal the government struck in 1949 to recognize twelve years of "good service" in the Canadian Armed Forces. His prior service with the army would make him eligible for the honour and so he requested a copy of his service record with the 3rd division's signals regiment. Unfortunately, Army HQ in Ottawa could produce no records – the Area Records Officer for Eastern Ontario, Capt E Dickson, wrote on January 29, 1951, that "it is regretted no documents can be found" and indicated that "paylists covering this period in question are not now held by this Headquarters."[272] In his response, Dickson noted "NGO 20.00/29, paragraph (25)" and underlined the directive in red: "It will be the responsibility of the applicant to obtain the necessary proof when service in units of the Canadian Army Reserve Force is being claimed." Without documentation to prove his prior service, Fuller was unfortunately considered ineligible to receive the honour.

His energies turned to his company, which grew into a multi-million-dollar operation. While the trauma of his wartime experience remained, his business gave him something new to focus on which, in turn, provided some remedy. Decorated USN SEAL veteran, author, and entrepreneur, John Gretton "Jocko" Willink Jr, has argued the necessity of veterans "finding a new mission" to help cope with the transition from combat to civilian life. As he explains, "while you're in the military, of course, you have this mission, you're focused, you know what your job is – you have this long term strategic goal of what you're trying to accomplish and if you leave the military without finding a new mission, that can be problematic and that's were I think sometimes guys get tripped up and they end up going down a bad direction." Like Willink, Fuller found a new mission – his business venture helped him heal from the wounds left by the Second World War. And applying the same focus that he used in Coastal Forces, it's little surprise that he became a construction powerhouse...

... this was the Pirate of the Adriatic after all.

In 1954, the PMC of *Carleton*'s wardroom sent Fuller a gift on behalf of the officers and Capt White, stressing "We would rather you didn't feel it a reciprocal gift evolving from your very generous donation to start out wardroom's 'mug line'" but a "reminder of the comradeship which we feel as shipmates with you and we hope, too, that the use and sight of it will suggest that you visit us soon and often."[273] That same year, he married Jeanne Fuller and started a family, situating their new home directly across the Britannia Yacht Club, where he would enjoy much of his free time. He converted a tugboat into the famed brigantine, *Black Jack*, which, in 2004, was named Ottawa's "signature tall ship". Then, in 1982, he designed and built yet another, much larger brigantine, *Fair Jeanne*, and traveled around the globe a total of six and half times with his wife, which included going back to the Adriatic.

On May 9, 1994, at the age of eighty-five, Capt Thomas G. Fuller DSC**, MiD, died. He was given a military funeral with full honours and was laid to rest in Beechwood Cemetery. In November 2023, Ottawa Mayor Mark Sutcliffe honoured Fuller's military legacy by announcing the naming of a new street in the neighbourhood of Queensview, Ottawa, "Captain Fuller Way."

EPILOGUE

A Hero's Rest

"We need two boatswains to pipe for a former Commanding Officer," announced a senior rating.

AB Dean Boettger, along with LS Mike Grinstead, a senior killick in the deck department, volunteered on the spot. It was the fall of 1984 and Boettger, a naval reservist who'd joined HMCS *Carleton* a year earlier, had only just returned from a stint on the east coast. There, he'd tasted life at sea, and returned to Ottawa with "plenty of salty dips to tell." Before leaving Halifax, he ventured down to the Canex and bought himself "a real 'pusser' belt buckle", which, unlike the plain brass version issued by ship's stores, was adorned with the gold leaves, crown, and anchor of the navy.

"Who are we piping for?" Grinstead enquired.

"Captain Tom Fuller," the man replied.

The name sounded familiar to Boettger. Later, he made his way to the flats outside the cox'ns office, where photos of former COs hung against the bulkhead. "I found his picture and stared at it for some time," Boettger explained. "The other COs posed for their formal portrait, stoic and unemotional [but] Tom Fuller's photo was caught on the go, his eyes intense his smile broad." He noted the numerous ribbons on his chest, and for a moment regretted his decision. This wasn't just any officer – this man was a decorated war hero and senior officer. Looking once more at the picture, Boettger noted the grin and thought "how bad could he be with such a big smile?"

That Saturday, both sailors arrived at the Britannia Yacht Club, dressed in their best S1's – mirrored boots, sharp creases, and boatswain calls tucked into their tunic's pocket with the chain draped over their shoulders in two, silver loops. They were instructed to head to Fuller's vessel, which lay alongside.

"This guy owns this?" Boettger thought upon seeing the ship. He then noticed "an old gentleman with a beard regard[ing] us" as they approached. Grinstead, the senior of the two, spoke. "Permission to come aboard, sir," he asked. The old man gave a curt nod, and in a gruff voice replied "Granted."

Boettger followed the LS and noticed the man eyeing them. Despite the years, his face was still recognizable – it was Fuller.

The young AB felt a lump building in throat, "I felt as though Captain Fuller was sizing me up – I felt the intensity of his stare. How could I not?" A torrent of thoughts flooded his mind. "What had I faced in my short life when compared to his? He saw combat, and a lot of it."

Just then the old man smiled. "So, who's going to climb the mast?" he asked.

Boettger paused – did he hear that correctly? Something in Fuller's eyes made him realize he was being dead serious. He traded glances with Grinstead and instantly "knew from the look he gave me that it wasn't going to be Mike."

"Aye sir," he finally replied, and without another word, and in full dress, Boettger started "up the shrouds of the foremast" and ascended "until I reached the top of the main yard." He then draped his torso over the wooden spar, so that his waist acted as a balancing point, with his hands outstretched and grasping the horizontal timber for extra support. He was easily about thirty feet in the air, looking down upon the tiny frames of Fuller and Grinstead. The men regarded the young AB "with some amusement" before Fuller gave a nod of approval and waved him back down.

After returning to the main deck, Boettger noticed that something had changed in the old salt's disposition. It was hard to describe but Fuller now looked at him differently.

"It seemed to me that I had passed his test," Boettger would later explain.

Black Jack sailed out into Britannia Bay, where the two sailors piped for him and the assembled guests. After the short ceremony, Fuller brought them down below and poured them both a drink, whereupon they mingled with the other guests who "made us feel very welcome." Fuller spoke to each of them, and Boettger recalled feeling both energized and inspired by him (and still more than a bit intimidated).

Later that evening, he returned home and proceeded to his room to change, making a thorough inspection of the "wear and tear on my uniform caused by my brief stint as a Jolly Tar." To his dismay, he discovered that his new belt buckle was damaged – it was missing the anchor that had been welded to the centre of the badge, obviously a casualty of his trek up the mast. A momentary pang of disappointment was soon replaced by gratitude for the unique adventure he'd just had. It now held special meaning for him, and so he "replaced the damaged belt buckle with a plain brass one and put the damaged one away in my keepsake drawer."

The following year, around the same time, another request came for two boatswains to pipe for Fuller. Boettger was first to volunteer again, and while he wasn't asked to climb the mast this time, "in hindsight I wouldn't have minded very much." Again, *Black Jack* slipped from the club and into the bay. Drawing out their boatswain calls, the "side" was piped in honour of Fuller before he invited all the guests below for "Up Spirits", which Boettger gladly participated in. As before, everyone was warm and welcoming.

"I felt very fortunate to share in their company," he reflected, "even for just a short time.

It would be the last time he would ever see Fuller.

A decade passed. Boettger, now a PO2 working at NDHQ on the Canadian Patrol Frigate program, noticed a tasking seeking sailors to volunteer for a ceremony.

"What kind of ceremony?" he asked, his interest peaked.

"A funeral," he was told, "for a Second World War veteran named Captain Tom Fuller."

The news hit Boettger in the gut, and he remained silent for a moment. Noticing the change in his demeanour, the other man asked, "Hey, are you alright?"

Boettger nodded. "I want to volunteer for the ceremony," he said.

"You knew him?"

"I was fortunate to have met him a couple of times," he replied.

"Okay," his boss finally confirmed, "I'll put your name forward."

A few days later, Boettger along with a small division of other volunteers, gathered to rehearse the ceremony. He was selected to be the insignia bearer, the person who would follow the casket carrying Fuller's medals on a pillow. The importance of the role wasn't lost on him and he felt especially grateful to be intrusted with the care and presentation of a naval war hero's honours, the formal recognition of his valour and service. On the day itself, he recalled the decorations and medals being placed on the cushion, the silver cross suspended from a navy blue and white ribbon, adorned with two silver bars to denote Fuller's subsequent awards. Further down, past an impressive four campaign stars, as well as the defence medal, and Canadian volunteer service medal, a bronze oak leaf was centred on the 1939-1945 war medal – an MiD. A surge of patriotism welled inside him, and Boettger wondered at what exactly Fuller must have done to be honoured so many times.

Entering the church, his eyes recognized the late captain's widow, holding the hand of a young girl. The child took note of what was on the cushion and turned to Mrs. Fuller to ask "Grandma, why is that man holding Grandpa's medals?" Boettger smiled at her, and thought "don't worry, his medals couldn't be in safer hands."

It wouldn't be until much later in life that he'd come to truly appreciate "just how outstanding an individual Captain Fuller was." Every now and then, Boettger catches himself thinking about the Capt. "I take a great deal of solace meeting him," Bottger explains, "and raising a glass of rum in his company."

As for that broken belt buckle, it has become a cherished heirloom, a reminder of the time he met one of Canada's greatest war heroes – the Pirate of the Adriatic.

About The Author

Sean E. Livingston is a naval historian, author, reserve officer, and teacher. His first book, "Oakville's Flower: The History of HMCS *Oakville*" (2014), documents the story of a Second World War Canadian Corvette named after the Town of Oakville. In 2016, he helped to create a memorial to HMCS *Oakville* in Tannery Park, and in 2022, an exhibit at Queen Ellizabeth Park Community and Cultural Centre. In 2024, his work became a permanent display at Oakville Town Hall. He is also the co-founder of the Canadian Naval Tribute Project, a memorial that recognizes the historical contributions of unsung naval heroes in Canada. Sean is featured in "Service in the Cause of Humanity" (2024), a book documenting the 1,394 people around the world who, since 1874, have received the Life Saving Medal of the Order of St. John. He was inducted as a life member in the Gallantry Medalist League and is the recipient of numerous awards for his historical contributions to Canadian history.

DOUBLE‡DAGGER
— www.doubledagger.ca —

Double Dagger Books is Canada's only military-focused publisher. Conflict and warfare have shaped human history since before we began to record it. The earliest stories that we know of, passed on as oral tradition, speak of war, and more importantly, the essential elements of the human condition that are revealed under its pressure.

We are dedicated to publishing material that, while rooted in conflict, transcend the idea of "war" as merely a genre. Fiction, non-fiction, and stuff that defies categorization, we want to read it all.

Because if you want peace, study war.

Sources

Published Books

Andrew Browne Cunningham, *The Cunningham Papers: Selections from the Private and Official Correspondence of Admiral of the Fleet Viscount Cunningham of Hyndhope*, Farnham, UK: Ashgate Publishing Ltd, 2006

Brown, Dave, *Faces of War: A Collection*, Burnstown, Ontario: General Store Publishing House, 1998

Cooper, Bryan, *The Battle of the Torpedo Boats*, New York, USA: Stein and Day, 1979

Dickens, Peter, *Night Action: MTB Flotilla at War*, United Kingdom: Seaforth, 2008.

Drury, Tony, *A History of HMS King Alfred*, Royal Navy Research Archive, 2005

Duffy, James P, *Hitler's Secret Pirate Fleet: The Deadliest Ships of World War II*. Westport, Conn: Praeger, 2001

Groner, Erich, *German Warships 1815-1945*. Volume 1: Major Surface Warships. Annapolis, Maryland: Naval Institute Press, 1990

Hichens, Lt. Cdr. Robert, DSO, DSC, *We Fought Them in Gunboats*, HMS Beehive Edition, Essex, UK: Golden Duck Ltd, 2023

Holman, Gordon, *The Little Ships*, London, UK: Hodder & Stoughton, 1944

Insolvibile, Isabella, *Kos 1943-1948. La Strage, La Storia*, Napoli, Italy: Edizioni Scientifche Italiane, 2010

Jones, Geoffrey P., *The month of the lost U-boats*, United Kingdom, London, Book Club Associates and William Kimber, 1977

Konstam, Angus, *British Motor Torpedo Boat 1939–45*, United Kingdom: Bloomsbury USA, 2003.

Lavery, Brian, *In Which They Served: The Royal Navy Officer Experience in the Second World War*, London, England: Conway Maritime Press, 2008

Lavery, Brian *The Royal Navy Officer's Pocket-Book 1944*, London, UK: Bloomsbury Publishing, Osprey Reproduction, 2018

Law, Anthony C., RCN, *White Plumes Astern: The Short, Daring Life of Canada's MTB Flotilla*, Halifax, Nova Scotia: Nimbus Publishing Ltd, 1989

Nolan, Brian and Brian Jeffrey Street, *Champagne Navy: Canada's Small Boat Raiders of the Second World War*, Toronto, Ontario: Random House, 1991

Paker, John. *Commandos: The Inside Story of Britain's Most Elite Fighting Force* London, UK: Headline Publishing, 2000

Peakman, Julie, *Hitler's Island War: The Men who Fought for Leros*, London, UK: Bloomsbury Publishing, Kindle Edition, 2020

Phibbs, Brendan, *The Other Side of Time: A Combat Surgeon in World War II*. London, UK: Robert Hale Ltd, 1989

Pope, Dudley, *Flag 4: The Battle of Coastal Forces in the Mediterranean 1939-1945*, London, UK: Chatham Publishing, 1998

Reynolds, L.C. OBE, DSC, *Dog Boats at War: A History of the Operations of the Royal Navy D Class Fairmile Motor Torpedo Boats and Motor Gun Boats 1939-1945*, Stroud, Gloucestershire: The History Press, 2009

Reynolds, L. C., *Dog Boat 658: The Small Boat War in the Mediterranean*, London, UK: William Kimber, 1955

Richards, Brooks, *Secret Flotillas - Vol 2 Clandestine Sea Opertaions in the Mediterranean, North Africa and the Adriatic 1940-1944*, London, UK: Whitehall History Publishing, 2005

Rohwer, Jürgen, *Chronology of the war at sea, 1939-1945 : the naval history of World War Two*, Annapolis, Maryland: Naval Institute Press, 2005

Scott, Peter, *The Battle of the Narrow Seas: The History of Light Coastal Forces in the Channel and North Sea 1939-1945*. Barnsle y, UK: Seaforth Publishing, Pen & Sword Books Ltd, 1945

Stewart, Ninian, *The Royal Navy and the Palestine Patrol* Cambridge, England: Routledge, 2013

W.A.B. Douglas, Roger Sarty, Michael Whitby, Robert H. Caldwell, William Johnston, and William G.P. Rawling, *No Higher Purpose: The Official Operational History of the Royal Canadian Navy, 1939-1945*, Volume II, Part 1, St. Catharines, Ontario: Vanwell Publishing, 2002

W.A.B. Douglas, Roger Sarty, Michael Whitby, Robert H. Caldwell, William Johnston, and William G.P. Rawling, *A Blue Water Navy: The Official Operational History of the Royal Canadian Navy in the Second World War, 1943-1945*, Volume II, Part 2, St. Catharines, Ontario: Vanwell Publishing, 2007

Williamson, Gordon, *E-Boat vs MTB: The English Channel 1941-45*. Oxford, UK: Osprey Publishing, 2011

Wilson, Alistair and Jospeh F. Callo, *Who's Who in Naval History: From 1550 to Present*, Abingdon, UK: Routledge, 2004

Unpublished Works

Boettger, Dean, "My Story of Captain Tom Fuller", 2020

Articles, Interviews, Newspapers, Periodicals, and Weblogs

Bollettino d'archivio USMM – La partecipazione della marina alla Guerra di Liberazione

Brown, Dave, "Har! War Hero Thomas Fuller Built Business Empire", Ottawa Citizen, May 11, 1994

Byard, Michael Ian, "BRITISH POWER BOAT Co. Page 4, Motor Gun Boats Pre and Second World War, 1936-1945", https://www.yalumba.co.uk/Framesets/British%20Power%20Boat%20Co%20-%20Page%204,%20MGBs.html

Canadian War Museum, Democracy at War: Canadian Newspapers and the Second World War, "By the Way" Hamilton Spectator, August 20, 1942

Churchill, John Malcolm Thorpe Fleming. Oral History Reel 2. Imperial War Museum, March 5, 1986, 28:30

Collins, Whilt, "George S. Patton: Guns That Made Him Great", Guns & Ammo Magazine, August 1971 Issue

Conquest, David. Interview SLt David Conquest, Cpt. Trevor Robotham, May, 18, 2000, 90:00

Daily Telegraph Obituary Major-General Tom Churchill. Feb 1990

Fuehrer Conferences on Matters Dealing with the German Navy, 1939-1945 "Minutes of the Conference of the Commander in Chief, Navy and the Fuehrer at Headquarters Berghof on 12 and 13 April 1944"

Fuller, Thomas. Fuller, Cdr. Tom – Interview. Navy News, July, 31, 1945, 16:03

Fuller, Thomas. Interview with Captain (N) Mack Lynch, 1981, original transcript, DND Directorate of History Collection, Ottawa, Canada.

Holden-Brown, Derrick. Interview Sir Derrick Holden-Brown, Lt RNVR. Capt Trevor Robotham, February 22, 1999, 1:10:00

Instructions for Coastal Forces on Plotting; tactics; day torpedo attacks; use of hydrophones; smoke floats; decoy flares, April 1943

Kirkpatrick, James Ralph Hilborn Service Information, www.unithistories.com/officers/RCNVR_officers2.html

Kirkpatrick, James Ralph Hilborn, Waterloo Hall of Fame, https://regionofwaterloomuseums.ca/en/visit/list-of-hall-of-fame-inductees.aspx#James-R-H-Kirkpatrick-1916-1997

Klinger, William, and Denis Kuljiš, 'A Rendezvous with Stalin: Moscow 1944', Tito's Secret Empire: How the Maharaja of the Balkans Fooled the World,

2021; online edn, Oxford Academic, 23 Sept. 2021, https://doi.org/10.1093/oso/9780197572429.003.0026

London Gazette, July 14, 1942-October 8, 1948

London Telegraph, "Obituary Commander Christopher Dreyer", July 25, 2003, https://www.telegraph.co.uk/news/obituaries/1437033/Commander-Christopher-Dreyer.html

Lynch, Mack, *Salty Dips: When We Were Young and in Our Prime*, Volume 1, Ottawa, Ontario: Naval Officer's Association of Canada, 1985.

Lynch, Mack, *Salty Dips: Did We Say All?*, Volume 3, Ottawa, Ontario: Naval Officer's Association of Canada, 1988

Mason, LCdr Geoffrey B, "World War 2 at Sea: Royal Navy Minelaying Operation", 2006, http://www.naval-history.net/xGM-Ops-Minelaying2.htm

Morgan-Giles, Morgan. Interview Rear-Admiral Sir Morgan Giles. Capt Trevor Robotham, July 28, 1997, 1:49:29

Picton, Jonn. "How Pirate Tom Helped Tito Beat the Nazis" The Sunday Star, Toronto, Sunday October 19, 1980

Pocok, Michael W. (2007), Maritimequest.com

"Savannah (CL-42) iv", Naval History and Heritage Command, June 4, 2015. Archived from the original on 3 March 2016. https://www.history.navy.mil/research/histories/ship-histories/danfs/s/savannah-iv.html

Sencicle, Lorraine The Dover Historian – Lord Warden Hotel, doverhistorian.com/2013/10/02/lord-warden-hotel-house/

Service Record, *Fuller, Thomas George, Captain (N), RCNVR*, Documenting Periods 1940-1951, O.G.P.R.C. 02-50106, Library and Archives Canada

Slessor, Kenneth, "H.M.S. King Alfred Australian Naval Men", Townsville Daily Bulletin, Brisbane, Tuesday December 10, 1940

Smith, Robert Barr. "The Real Story of "Mad Jack" Churchill—a Rare Breed of Warrior" World War II History Warfare, Volume 4, Issue 4, July 2005

Ta' Xbiex: Parroċċa San Ġwann Tas-Salib, "Allied Coastal Forces in Malta during World War II." Parroċċa San Ġwann tas-salib – Festa, 2007

Treason Act 1351, United Kingdom, http://www.legislation.gov.uk/aep/Edw3Stat5/25/2/section/II

Trento in Cina, www.trentoincina.it

Uboat.net, uboat.net/allies/warships/ship/13617.html

Welman, Eric Arthur Pole Service Information, www.unithistories.com/officers/RN_officersW3.html

Yonson, Doug. "Fuller Hoists Sales" The Citizen, Ottawa, Tuesday February 21, 1984

Image Gallery

COMMANDER THOMAS FULLER DSC RCN(R)
22 JANUARY 1948 TO 24 JANUARY 1951

Fuller's CO Picture, HMCS *Carleton*, 1948

Thomas Fuller, Prominent Canadian Architect (1823-1898)

CO's Naval Division Conference, Naval HQ, 1949. Fuller is seated in
the front row, second from the left

MGB *13*

MTB *651*, March 1944

MTB 655 at sea

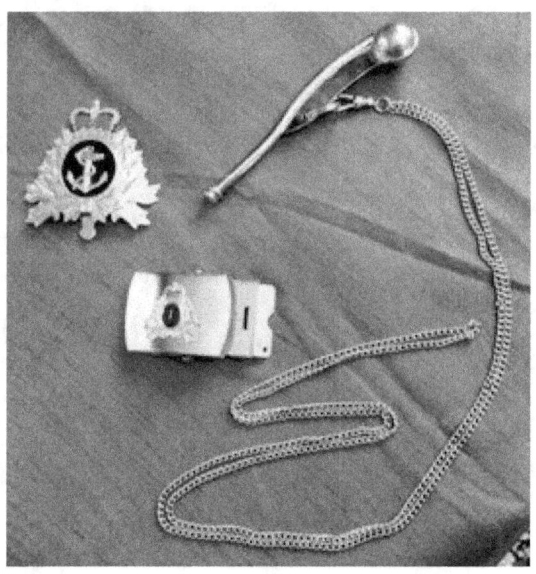

Dean Boettger's Belt. The anchor broke off the buckle when
Fuller ordered him up the mast.

All maps created by the author

Endnotes

1   Most of Fuller's dialogue and conversations presented in these chapters are taken from his 1985 interview with Capt (N) Mack Lynch, published in the Naval Officer's Association of Canada's (now the Naval Association of Canada) first volume of "Salty Dips: When We were Young and in Our Prime", 117-175. I'm using Lynch's original, unpublished transcript of his interview, along with accompanying notes.

2   Service Record, *Fuller, Thomas George, Captain (N), RCNVR*, Documenting Periods 1940-1951, O.G.P.R.C. 02-50106, Library and Archives Canada.

3   Service Record, *Fuller, Thomas George, Captain (N), RCNVR*, ibid

4   W.A.B. Douglas, Roger Sarty, Michael Whitby (with Robert H. Caldwell, William Johnston, and William G.P. Rawling,) *No Higher Purpose: The Official Operational History of the Royal Canadian Navy, 1939-1945, Volume II, Part 1*, St. Catharines, Ontario: Vanwell Publishing 32.

5   Service Record, *Fuller, Thomas George, Captain (N), RCNVR*, ibid

6   Ibid

7   Ibid

8   Ibid

9   Fuller's actual appointment, via letter from the Minister of National Defence, took effect September 9th

10 Service Record, *Fuller, Thomas George, Captain (N), RCNVR*, ibid and Fuller Construction Company Website

11 Brown, Dave, *Faces of War: A Collection*, Burnstown, Ontario, General Store Publishing House, 119

12 Service Record, *Fuller, Thomas George, Captain (N), RCNVR*, O.G.P.R.C. 02-50106, LAC

13 Yonson, Doug. "Fuller Hoists Sales" The Citizen, Ottawa, Tuesday February 21, 1984 p. 41

14 Brown, ibid, 119

15 Service Record, *Fuller, Thomas George, Captain (N), RCNVR*, ibid

16 He also mentions the company "Goggin and Ripley Inc [sic]" located in New York, although the connection is unclear.

17 Service Record, *Fuller, Thomas George, Captain (N), RCNVR*, ibid

18 Brown, ibid, 119

19 Ibid, 119

20 Ibid

21 Picton, Jonn. "How Pirate Tom Helped Tito Beat the Nazis" The Sunday Star, Toronto, Sunday, October 19, 1980

22 Drury, Tony "*A History of HMS King Alfred*", Royal Navy Research Archive, 2005 & Lavery, Brian, *In Which They Served: The Royal Navy Officer Experience in the Second World War*, London, England: Conway Maritime Press, 150-151, & Reynolds, L.C. OBE, DSC, *Dog Boats at War: A History of the Operations of the Royal Navy D Class Fairmile Motor Torpedo Boats and Motor Gun Boats 1939-1945*, Stroud, Gloucestershire: The History Press, 11

23 Lavery, Brian *The Royal Navy Officer's Pocket-Book 1944*, Bloomsbury Publishing, Osprey Reproduction. Pelly's comments are taken from a quote at the outset of the book.

24 Ibid

25 Slessor, Kenneth, "H.M.S. King Alfred Australian Naval Men", Townsville Daily Bulletin, Brisbane, Tuesday December 10, 1940, 4. *King Alfred* would in fact suffer bombing raids for most of the war. The nearby city of Brighton was bombed 56 times from July 1940 to February 1944.

26 Ibid, 4

27 Floradora was an Edwardian musical comedy that opened in London in 1899. Spreading to North America, it became one of Broadway's first hits. In the play there were a group of six singing and dancing women who were called 'the English ladies', but would later come to be known as Floradora Girls. This Josey had portrayed one on stage about thirty to forty years prior to meeting Fuller. As he would later explain, "The Kit Kat Club became my hangout in England, and when I'd go for a refit in Southwick, I'd move into the Club."

28 Welman served with distinction in the First World War, first in destroyers before moving to HMS *Arrogant* (base flagship for Dover Patrols) where he joined Costal Forces. In 1917, while in command of Costal Motor Boats (CMBs) operating along the Belgian Coast, he received his first DSC and two DSOs conducting blocking operations against Zeebrugge and Ostend. His citations for both of the latter awards read: "During the action the units of the coastal motor-boat flotilla under his command were handled in a masterly manner, rendering the greatest service in screening and rescue work. He, himself, was in a coastal motorboat, and always in the most exposed positions across the harbour entrance covering 'Vindictive', 'Iris II', and 'Daffodil' by smoke screen"; and "The part played by the Coastal Motor Boats during the operation was all-important. Lieut. Welman organised and led them in a coastal motor boat in a most spirited manner. He encountered an enemy torpedo boat near the entrance of Ostend, which switched on searchlights and opened fire. He at once closed with her, and engaged her with Lewis guns to such good effect that she withdrew and left the channel clear for the approach of the blockships." He also received the Legion of Honour at

the end of the war, and his second DSC on July 26, 1940, for "preventing of war materials falling into enemy hands." Source: www.unithistories.com/officers/RN_officersW3.html

29 Instructions for Coastal Forces on Plotting; tactics; day torpedo attacks; use of hydrophones; smoke floats; decoy flares (April 1943), 2

30 Reynolds, ibid, 9

31 Ibid, 10

32 Ibid 12

33 Ibid

34 Ibid 12-13

35 Ibid 13. Again, depending on the class, the numbers varied.

36 Ibid, 5. Reynolds describes the typical Farimile D as "2-pdr pom-pom on the focs'le and the twin 0.5-in mountings on each side of the bridge, with twin Vickers . 303 machine-guns in the bridge wings. The MTBs had their two 21-in torpedoes, and a twin Oerlikon aft, while the MGBs mounted their twin Oerlikon on the coach roof and had a hand-operated Hotchkiss 6-pdr aft [...] Later, some of the MGBs in the Mediterranean replaced the twin 0.5-in turrets with single Oerlikons; a power-operated semi-automatic 6-pdr replaced the pom-pom and the manual 6-pdr, and there were many local adaptations and experiments."

37 www.unithistories.com/officers/RCNVR_officers2.html and Waterloo Region Hall of Fame

38 It is unclear what training they were doing at *St. Christopher*; Kirkpatrick seems to have already completed his initial Coastal Forces training just prior to Fuller, while Villiers seems to have done so afterwards. It could be that the former was doing some additional training while Villiers' training may have been interrupted (or he was not yet formally moving into Coastal Forces training).

39 Possibly the wife of Chieftain of Clan MacDonald or a respected woman who had been awarded the title by the local population, who unofficially referred to her as 'Lady Donald'. Likely, she was a noble, considering her status, wealth, and influence.

40 Nolan, Brian and Brian Jeffrey Street, *Champagne Navy: Canada's Small Boat Raiders of the Second World War*, Toronto, Ontario: Random House, 1991, 41

41 Ibid

42 Sencicle, Lorraine The Dover Historian – Lord Warden Hotel, doverhistorian.com/2013/10/02/lord-warden-hotel-house/

43 According to Fuller.

44 Fuller even took note of the gun's number, which was fifty-eight. However, he had the gun for only two months before he received orders to have it removed: "the order came straight from Admiralty" he recalled, "which had suddenly discovered I had an Oerlikon. It was to be removed forthwith, and sent to HMS *Carlisle*, an anti-aircraft cruiser in the Mediterranean." Although he was disappointed to lose the gun, Fuller realized that it was necessary. There wasn't an abundance of weapons lying about and every gun had to be accounted for. Fuller himself explained "It just shows you the situation at the time – how scarce armament was.". *49* was

instead outfitted with a forty-millimetre Rolls Royce gun, also known as a "goose gun", which Fuller stated was a "fine weapon, but the only trouble was it was so rigged that you had to bring it to horizon to get the goddamn shell into it, and it was only a single load."

45   Fuller's explanation is less clear, stating that "So we took the plugs of the engine that was U/S on that side and were driving with the forward engine through the other one, still turning it, to get back home." Gordon Laco responded to this, stating: "if the short shaft between the yoked engines fractured; it would be the engine astern not forward which could be put back into service. The forward engine had the after engine between it and the propeller shaft." Laco further explains that "In basic principal, yoked engines are not at all a problem except that trouble with the after one would put the forward one out of action too. Many successful vessels still use yoked engines. I expect the trouble with this boat's engine yoking was that the alignment was not good. That would cause the shaft to be likely to fracture due to metal fatigue. The description of vibration, thumping then the break would indicate a fractured shaft due to poor alignment. The trouble with yoked engines is not that they are yoked... that is quite a normal way to boost power (in fact most Sherman tanks during the war had yoked engines) The problem in a wooden vessel is that they are more vulnerable to misalignment."

46   uboat.net/allies/warships/ship/13617.html

47   These were confidential reports on an officer, which was reduced to a single page after 1925 and, from 1931 onwards, used numerical grading when assessing various attributes. Fuller's was completed by Cdr James Sanders RN, the occasion for the report being listed at "A.F.O. [Admiralty Fleet Order] 102/41" for the period of April 4 to May 16, 1941, which summarized the overall impression he left as CO of 49 at Wasp. Admiralty Fleet Order 102/41 states "… that the Admiralty should be aware of the names of all officers of the Reserves who are considered outstanding and suitable for higher rank even though they are not qualified under this Order and recommendations of such officers should continue to be forwarded to the Admiral Commanding Reserves." It also goes onto note that "The recommendations should be supported by Forms S.206" which was what Fuller's appraisal was completed on. Although these reports were meant to be confidential, some COs allowed their officers to view them, or they (the COs) read portions of the reports aloud to their officers. Fuller only saw his S.206s once back from the war.

48   There wasn't much that the officer making the report could say in this section – he had choice between 'satisfactory' and 'unsatisfactory' and could only indicate 'yes' or 'no' for the officer in question being of 'temperate habit'.

49   Service Record, *Fuller, Thomas George, Captain (N), RCNVR*, ibid

50   Ibid

51   Ibid

52   Ibid

53   Picton, Ibid. This was likely the cause of his unsatisfactory diet, as noted by the medical officer.

54 Ibid

55 Ibid

56 It had been founded in 1927 when Hubert Scott-Paine purchased the Hythe Shipyard and, after updating and renaming the facility, built the 26-foot hydroplane racing boat *Miss England*. After the original plant burnt down, the new building steadily increased work for the Admiralty, and when the war broke out, the company focused heavily on building MTBs, MGBs, and MLs.

57 Despite being referred to as 'Betty' by Fuller, when interviewed years later, she expressed her distaste for the nickname, which was the result of a mistake by the North American Press. Unfortunately, the moniker stuck, and she would constantly need to correct people who called her by it; she preferred being called 'Joe'.

58 Service Record, *Fuller, Thomas George, Captain (N), RCNVR*, ibid.

59 According to Fuller's service record, it seems he reported to *Wasp* in MGB *11*, but then took command of *13*.

60 Konstam, Angus, *British Motor Torpedo Boat 1939–45*, United Kingdom: Bloomsbury USA, 2003, 8. In March 1941 President Roosevelt had signed the Lend-Lease Act, "whereby the United States agreed to supply Britain with war materials, including warships, weaponry and funds."

61 Dickens, Peter, *Night Action: MTB Flotilla at War*, United Kingdom: Seaforth, 2008, 5 Dickens, Night Action, 5

62 Ibid, 5

63 While waiting in his boat, Fuller explained that, as a captain, you'd stay near "… your WT [Wireless Telegraphy] while you were sitting in the Ferry Dock in Dover, and they would come up and give you a Flag Johnny." Skippers would receive orders and "it would read something like '124, 26.4' and the time of origin. The time of origin was not the time of origin of the signal but the time of origin of the plot, and Dungeness Lighthouse was the point of bearing." The lighthouse was situated southwest of Dover and served as the starting point for MTB/MGB skippers to plan their routes to intercept their targets. As Fuller explained, "You would take a true bearing on that, and run off your distance, and that was the position of the convoy."

64 Signed on the 19th by Cdr Sanders. This time the occasion for the report was listed as 'Suppression of Commanding Officer H.M.S. *WASP*'

65 Fuller's scores were as follows:

Professional Ability:	6
Personal Qualities:	6
Leadership:	5
Intellectual Ability:	6
Administrative Ability:	5

66 Service Record, *Fuller, Thomas George, Captain (N), RCNVR*, Ibid. George Dick 'Dicky' Kendall Richards DSO, DSC, had joined the RN in 1935 and by 1940 he was already a full Lt and had ample experience commanding MGBs. If there was an officer who was qualified to asses Fuller, it was certainly Richards.

67 Nolan & Street, ibid, 5

68 Ibid 5-6

69 Ibid 17

70 Williamson, Gordon, *E-Boat vs MTB: The English Channel 1941-45*. Oxford, UK: Osprey Publishing, 2011, 52.

71 Duffy, James P, *Hitler's Secret Pirate Fleet: The Deadliest Ships of World War II*. Westport, Conn: Praeger, 2001, 185-186.

72 Pocok, Michael W. (2007) Maritimequest.com

73 Scott, Peter, *The Battle of the Narrow Seas: The History of Light Coastal Forces in the Channel and North Sea 1939-1945*. Barnsley, UK: Seaforth Publishing, Pen & Sword Books Ltd, 1945, 64

74 Duffy, ibid, 185

75 Ibid, 185

76 Ibid, 185

77 Duffy, ibid, 185

78 Ibid, 185 & Williamson, ibid, 52

79 Williamson, ibid, 52 & Scott, ibid, 64

80 Scott, ibid, 64

81 Groner, Erich, *German Warships 1815-1945*. Volume 1: Major Surface Warships. Annapolis, Maryland: Naval Institute Press, 1990, 193

82 Scott, ibid, 64

83 Ibid, 64

84 Ibid 64 – Scott notes that the MGBs didn't manage to reach MTB *219* but his account was based off fragmented information and wasn't able to account for German reports, which later publications would draw from. Still, much of this event unfortunately remains unknown due to the loss of MTB *220*.

85 Fuller would explain that, depending on where they ended-up patrolling, "If we couldn't get back to Dover we'd go in to Ramsgate"

86 Scott, ibid, 64

87 The London Gazette, July 14, 1942

88 Service Record, *Fuller, Thomas George, Captain (N), RCNVR*, ibid

89 Hamilton Spectator "By the Way" August 20 1942.

90 Brown, Dave. "Har! War Hero Thomas Fuller Built Business Empire", Ottawa Citizen, May 11, 1994

91 Mason, LCdr Geoffrey B, "World War 2 at Sea: Royal Navy Minelaying Operation", 2006, http://www.naval-history.net/xGM-Ops-Minelaying2.htm: In fact, analysis after the war would show that the offensive minelaying done by Coastal Forces was responsible for "53% of the total enemy casualties". It proved a key part in taking the fight to the enemy and keeping local waters safe. Throughout the war Coastal Forces would conduct a total of 1,257 mine laying operations, laying an impressive 7,014 mines which would sink 73 ships, 38 of which were warships. By virtue of their proximity, speed, and stealth, coastal vessels were well suited for this type of operation. Rather than lay mines and wait for the enemy to come to them, MTB/MGB/MLs would bring the mines to the enemy.

92 Nolan & Street, ibid, 12

93 Byard, Michael Ian, "BRITISH POWER BOAT Co. Page 4, Motor Gun Boats Pre and Second World War, 1936-1945", https://www.yalumba.co.uk/Framesets/British%20Power%20Boat%20Co%20-%20Page%204,%20MGBs.html. It is likely that MGB *13*'s engines were also upgraded to Packards by the time Fuller took command.

94 Nolan & Street, ibid,12

95 Ibid 12 - From Spark's vantage point, situated within the radio/radar cabin, the telegraphist's experience of the fight was different from those topside. In many respects, he appeared cut-off from the action, although the sounds and quick movement of *13* likely didn't leave much to his imagination. He might have smirked at his CO's snappy dispatch.

96 Noland & Street, ibid, 13

97 Ibid 13

98 Ibid 12

99 Morgan-Giles, Morgan. Interview Rear-Admiral Sir Morgan Giles. Capt Trevor Robotham, July 28, 1997, 1:49:29

100 Reynolds, ibid, 4. The look of the boat is where the nickname 'Dog Boat' derives. Reynolds notes that "one CO joining his boat… was heard to mutter, 'Is that the boat or the box it was delivered in?'

101 Holden-Brown, Derrick. Interview Sir Derrick Holden-Brown, Lt RNVR. Capt Trevor Robotham, February 22, 1999, 1:10:00

102 Ibid.

103 Reynolds, ibid, 47-48

104 Ibid, 45

105 Ibid, 48

106 Ibid, 47

107 An interesting anecdote regarding Maitland when he arrived in Gibraltar. Attending to his damaged boat, he was more than a little disappointed to see "that during the engagement with the U-boat his rum locker had been hit, resulting in the loss of four jars." (Nolan & Street p. 80) He summoned his CPO to get the rum replaced and locker fixed, but when he asked for the shipwright, the chief cautioned him "Oh no, Sir […] We'd better not get the shipwright." When Maitland demanded why, the Chief replied "Let's leave it the way it is. When we're in action, we'll get hit in that rum locker every time." (Noland & Street p. 80). Maitland caught-on immediately: "The rum was sealed and, if damaged, the jars had to be produced with the seal intact before more could be issued. Henceforth they would 'decant' their rum ration and point to the holed lockers as 'proof' of the circumstances in which the official ration was lost." (Nolan & Street) It was certainly, as Nolan and Street surmised, "a delightful scam – worthy of Fuller" adding that "Maitland's boat never did run out of rum as a result." (Nolan & Street p. 80)

108 Reynolds, ibid, 48

109 Ibid, 50 – The Sinking of *U639* and *U439* on 4 May 1943 in Atlantic after attack on Coastal Forces convoy, as sourced by Jones, Geoffrey P., *The month of the lost*

U-boats, United Kingdom, London, Book Club Associates and William Kimber, 1977, and Reynold's own experience/previous works

110 Ibid, 48

111 *Treason Act 1351*, United Kingdom, http://www.legislation.gov.uk/aep/Edw3Stat5/25/2/section/II

112 Reynolds, ibid, 48

113 Fuller provided no further information about Jock during his interview – the German's fate, or how long he was aboard Fuller's boat, remains unknown.

114 Ta' Xbiex: Parroċċa San Ġwann Tas-Salib. (2007). "Allied Coastal Forces in Malta during World War II." Parroċċa San Ġwann tas-salib - Festa 2007, 7

115 Service Record, *Fuller, Thomas George, Captain (N), RCNVR*, ibid

116 Ashby went on to say "under the terms of AFO 4240/42". Admiralty Fleet Order 4240/42 was "… to enable the Admiralty to fill all appointments which require Lieutenant-Commander's rank by the officers most suited to hold these appointments"

117 Pope, Dudley. Flag 4: The Battle of Coastal Forces in the Mediterranean 1939-1945, Chatham Publishing, 1998, 112

118 Ibid, 113

119 Ibid

120 Ibid

121 Uboat.net. U561 would lose 42 sailors – only 5 would survive Dryer's attack.

122 Pope, ibid, 113

123 London Telegraph, "Obituary Commander Christopher Dreyer", July 25, 2003. The CO of U561 was Oberleutnant Henning and U375 Kapitanleutnant Konenkamp. They had been patrolling since July 10th. Konenkamp had warned U-boat Command in Italy that he'd been attacked and that U561 was lost. Henning actually survived the attack and managed to swim ashore at Messina while another rating was able to swim to Reggio.

124 Pope, ibid, 115

125 Reynolds, ibid, 63 and Pope, ibid, 116

126 Pope, Ibid, 116

127 Ibid

128 Ibid

129 Phibbs, Brendan, *The Other Side of Time: A Combat Surgeon in World War II*. London, UK: Robert Hale Ltd, 1989. A Medical Doctor and Second World War Veteran, Phibbs observed that Truscott was "… so tough he could chew up a ham like Patton without bothering to pick his teeth"

130 "Savannah (CL-42) iv". Naval History and Heritage Command. 4 June 2015.

131 Ibid. 197 sailors were lost in the explosion.

132 Vathy is a town and a former municipality on the island of Samos, North Aegean, Greece. It is north of Bodrum, Turkey, and the Island of Leros, both which will feature later in the narrative. Fuller's file also indicated that he was "operationally in command of V. 10" , which might indicate he was in charge of some American personnel operating in the area.

133 The London Gazette [Supplement]. 8 October 1948. p. 5373. He'd been in the RN during the First World War, where he participated in the Battle of Jutland, and had stayed in the navy during the inter-war years. He was part of Cunningham's staff at the outset of the war, before being appointed C in C South Atlantic in 1941. By February 1943, he was made the Flag Officer commanding Force H (North African Operations), and then subsequently the Allied invasions of Sicily and Italy.

134 Andrew Browne Cunningham, *The Cunningham Papers: Selections from the Private and Official Correspondence of Admiral of the Fleet Viscount Cunningham of Hyndhope*, Farnham, UK: Ashgate Publishing Ltd, 2006, 69. By December, the title would be changed to Flag Officer, Levant and East Mediterranean and, by 1944, it would once again become part of a single Mediterranean command. (Stewart, Ninian (2013). The Royal Navy and the Palestine Patrol. Cambridge, England: Routledge. 27)

135 It's written in Salty Dips as 'Castelorison'. Fuller recalled the island well, describing it for Lynch as "A little volcanic island about three miles off the coast of Turkey, south of Rhodes, and it's absolutely due north, about three hundred miles, from Great Pass Beacon buoy at the entrance to Alex Harbour."

136 Campbell himself states that Fuller was the Flotilla Leader, although when he was moved to *2106* it is unclear if he was skippering the boat or directing the flotilla from the boat until a new one could be made available to him.

137 Insolvibile, Isabella, *Kos 1943-1948. La Strage, La Storia*, Napoli, Italy: Edizioni Scientifche Italiane, 2010]

138 Bollettino d'archivio USMM – La partecipazione della marina alla Guerra di Liberazione.

139 Ibid

140 Pope, ibid, 181-182

141 Lynch, Mack, *Salty Dips: Did We Say All?*, Volume 3, Ottawa, Ontario: Naval Officer's Association of Canada, 1988, 142

142 Peakman, Julie, *Hitler's Island War: The Men who Fought for Leros*, London, UK: Bloomsbury Publishing, Kindle Edition, 2020.

143 Peakman, ibid

144 Ibid

145 Bollettino et. al., ibid

146 Ibid

147 Trento in Cina, www.trentoincina.it/dbminori2.php?short_name=MAS%20555

148 Peakman, Ibid

149 Ibid

150 Ibid

151 Based on an image of Müller on Leros

152 During Fuller's interview he consistently refers to his pistol as a 'revolver' but then said that Müller unloaded 'the clip'. For the purpose of the narrative, I decided to go with the former.

153 The outcome of the Germans aboard the boat is uncertain; Fuller never explained if they were left ashore, made to swim back, brought back to Turkey, or terminated.

It seems unlikely that they would have killed them as, if they were caught, it would certainly forfeit their lives.

154 Nicholas, Jellicoe C. (2021) *George Jellicoe: SAS and SBS Commander.*Yorkshire: Pen & Sword Books, 146

155 Fuller's Service File shows the promotion as of April 1, 1944, but he would have received it before then.

156 Conquest, David. "Interview SLt David Conquest" Cpt. Trevor Robotham, May, 18, 2000, 90:00

157 Ibid

158 Ibid

159 Ibid

160 Morgan-Giles, Ibid

161 Ibid

162 Ibid

163 Ibid

164 Wilson, Alistair and Jospeh F. Callo, *Who's Who in Naval History: From 1550 to Present*, Abingdon, UK: Routledge, 2004, 114.

165 Ibid & Picton, ibid

166 Ibid

167 Ibid

168 Reynold, ibid, 134

169 Fuller, Thomas. Fuller, Cdr. Tom – Interview. Navy News, July, 31, 1945, 16:03. Fuller was asked by the interviewer what age Churchill was when he met him on Vis, which he estimated to be around forty years old.

170 Ibid

171 Morgan-Giles, Ibid

172 Ibid

173 Reynolds, L. C., *Dog Boat 658: The Small Boat War in the Mediterranean*, London, UK: William Kimber, 1955

174 Pope, ibid, 207

175 Ibid

176 Ibid, 209

177 Nolan & Street, ibid, 176

178 Reynolds, *Dog Boats at War*, ibid, 152

179 Ibid

180 Picton, ibid

181 Nolan & Street, Ibid, 177

182 Conquest, ibid

183 Picton, ibid

184 Nolan & Street, ibid, 177

185 Ibid

186 Ibid

187 Reynolds, ibid, 152

188 Morgan-Giles, Ibid

189 Nolan & Street, ibid, 177

190 Ibid

191 Service Record, *Fuller, Thomas George, Captain (N), RCNVR*, ibid

192 Reynolds, ibid, 152

193 Ibid

194 Ibid, 152-153

195 Ibid 153

196 Ibid

197 Ibid

198 Ibid

199 Morgan-Giles, ibid

200 Ibid

201 Conquest, ibid

202 Picton, ibid

203 Nolan & Street, ibid, 178

204 Picton, ibid

205 Pope, ibid, 210 & Reynolds, ibid, 153

206 Fuehrer Conferences on Matters Dealing with the German Navy, 1939-1945 "Minutes of the Conference of the Commander in Chief, Navy and the Fuehrer at Headquarters Berghof on 12 and 13 April 1944" 40-41

207 Reynolds, ibid, 153

208 Ibid, 154

209 Ibid

210 Pope, ibid, 213

211 Ibid

212 Ibid

213 Ibid

214 Ibid

215 Ibid

216 Ibid, 214

217 Ibid

218 Ibid

219 Ibid

220 Ibid

221 Ibid

222 Ibid

223 Ibid, 215

224 Reynolds, ibid, 155

225 Pope, ibid, 215

226 Ibid, 215

227 Reynolds, ibid, 155

228 Ibid, 155

229 Nolan & Street, ibid, 181

230 Ibid, 122

231 Churchill, John Malcolm Thorpe Fleming "Oral History Reel 2" Imperial War Museum, March 5, 1986, 28:30
232 Ibid
233 Ibid
234 Ibid
235 Ibid
236 Ibid
237 Ibid
238 Smith, Robert Barr. "The Real Story of "Mad Jack" Churchill—a Rare Breed of Warrior" World War II History Warfare, Volume 4, Issue 4, July 2005, 10-17
239 Ibid
240 Paker, John. *Commandos: The Inside Story of Britain's Most Elite Fighting Force* London, UK: Headline Publishing, 2000, 150-152
241 Fuller, ibid
242 Klinger, William, and Denis Kuljiš, 'A Rendezvous with Stalin: Moscow 1944', Tito's Secret Empire: How the Maharaja of the Balkans Fooled the World, 2021; online edn, Oxford Academic, 23 Sept. 2021, https://doi.org/10.1093/oso/9780197572429.003.0026
243 Ibid 178-179
244 Ibid 179
245 Ibid
246 Picton, Ibid
247 Ibid
248 Ibid
249 Picton, Ibid
250 Pope, ibid, 220
251 Ibid, 220 & Reynold, ibid, 156
252 Ibid, 220
253 Ibid
254 Ibid 221
255 Ibid
256 Ibid
257 Ibid
258 Ibid
259 Reynolds, ibid, 156
260 Pope, ibid, 221
261 Ibid, 222
262 Reynolds, Ibid, 157
263 Pope, ibid, 222
264 Morgan-Giles, ibid
265 Daily Telegraph Obituary Major-General Tom Churchill. Feb 1990
266 Brown, ibid, 120
267 Service Record, *Fuller, Thomas George, Captain (N), RCNVR*, ibid
268 Ibid

269 Ibid
270 Ibid
271 Ibid
272 Ibid
273 Ibid

Index

Page numbers in italics followed by *n* refer to footnotes.

HM Ships
    Abdiel 186n
    Abercrombie 52
    Chitral 31-32, *32*n
    Coverley 140, 148
    Echo 200, 210
    Fury 211-212, *212*n
    Jamaica 281
    Letitia 32n
    London 212
    Onslow 147-148
    Patroclus 48
    Shannon 107n
    Warspite 186n

Kriegsmarine
    I-boat *302* 269
    I-boat *309* 269
    Iltis 83
    Seeadler 83
    Stier 75-76, 80-83, 85, *85*n, 87, 100
    U*99* 48
    U*375* 158-159, 309
    U*437* 148
    U*439* 140, 144, 308
    U*534* 148
    U*561* 158, 309
    U*639* 140, 144, 308

Merchant/Passenger Ships
    Duchess of Richmond 23-24
    Vallaran 117

Regia Marina
    3rd MAS Flotilla 190
    Euro 190
    Giuseppe Miraglia 254, 264
    Larina 275
    MA/SB *555* 197
    MA/SB *559* 197

Schooners
    Dante 1, 245
    Ennesta 1, 245

General Index

Campbell, Lt Ross 182, *182*n, 183, 192, 309

Campbell and Shepherd Ltd 19

Campioni, Admiral Inigo *209*n

Canada (also Canadian) 5, 13, 23, 25, 33, 35-36, 43, 49, 55-57, 73, *74*n, 99, 108, 110, 115, 118, 121-124, 127, 129, 144, 151, 167-168, 171, 178, 182, 199, 206, 209, 215, 221-222, 227, 230-231, 239, 247-248, 253, 264-265, 272-273, 277-280, 282, 290

Canadian Armed Forces 284

Canadian Army 6, 18, 30, 48, 58, 284

Canadian Army Reserve Force 284

Canadian Forces Decoration (CD) 284

Canadian Heating Plant 19

Canadian International Paper Company 19

Cap Blanc Nez 62

Cape Allessio 162

Cape Finisterre 142

Cape Loviste 255

captain (appointment/position) 32, 35, 66, 142, 148-149, 211

Captain Coastal Forces Mediterranean 155, 170, 265

Captain Fuller Way 285

Calabrian Coast 159

Canex 286

Cardiff 117

Carpathos 180 (map)

Carstairs, Marion Barbara "Joe" 69-70

Casteloriso (aka Kastellorizo) 180 (map), 181, 188, 310

Castle Hill 198

Catania 156 (map), 170

Charing Cross 198

Chateau Laurier 5

Chilean Navy 281

Churchill, LCol John Malcolm Thorpe Fleming (Jack) "Mad Jack" "Fighting Jack" 226, *226*n, 227, 229, 246, 260-262, 274

Churchill, BGen Thomas (Tom) Bell Lindsay 274

Churchill, Winston 28, 212, 277-278

circling (tactic) 44-45

citizen sailors 74

clove oil 150, *150*n

CNS Form 2324 (see Officer Qualification Questionnaire)

Coastal Forces 34-35, 37, 40, 57, 65, 68, 71-72, 85-88, 91-92, 100, 118, 129, 145-146, 152, 156, 170, 181, 217, 219, 221, 234-235, 254, 265, 276, 285, 304, 307

coastal vessel 2, 40, 46-48, 238

cocaine *150*n 151

Cole, Lt. R.M. *225*n, 246, 249, 251, 256-257

Collins, Whilt *173*n

Comacchio 214

commandant 24

Commander-in-Chief (C-in-C) 24, 157-158, 166-168, 179, 191, 265

commanding officer (CO) 32-33, 36-38, 40, 43, 45, 49-50, 52, 55, 58, 64-65, 67, 71-73, 86, 88-89, 98-100, 108, 111-112, 119, 135, 138, 145, 150-153, 155-157, 173, 198, 200, 220, 224, 238, 241, 244, 246, 260-261, 275, 278, 280-281, 283, 286

commandos 2-3, 40, 47, 190, 195, 220, 238-239, 242-245, 248-249, 251, 253, 260, 262, 282

Commonwealth 117, 229

Confederation Building 17, 19

Conquest, SLt David 220, 236, 238, 242, 245, 247

construction 6

convoy(s) 23, 31, 33, 47, 82, 96-99, 133, 136, 147, 211, 234-235, 251, 253, 271

cook 46

cordite *212*n

Coril, Air-Vice Marshal George Mitchell 6

Cornish, Lt Eric Alfred Edward 81, 83

Corpach 36

Corsica 147 (map)

corvette 55, 102

Cos (aka Kos) 180 (map), 181, 189-190, 212

Cossette, Capt J.O. 10, 12, 14

court-martial 224, 248

Cowichan Bay 74

coxswain (cox'n) 46, 79, 82, 88, 91, 93, 97, 107, 109-110, 125, 140, 160, 163, 184, 186, 194, 196, 257, 286

Crete 180 (map)

cruiser 75-76, 80-83, 129, 179, 212, 304

Cunningham, Admiral Andrew Browne 157, *157*n, 159, 167-169, 186, *186*n, 223, 310

Cyprus 181

Dalmatian 218

Damasta 189

Dane (also Danish) 215, 247

Davidson, Lt R "Bob" 235

Dean, SLt John 271

defaulters 52

depression (the Great Depression) 6, 21

depth charge 46, 101, 149, 159

destroyer 33, 48, 66, 71, 102, 122, 124, 129, 147-149, 190, 195-196, 200, 211-212, 233, 262, 303

DeWolf, Vice-Admiral Harry 66-67

Dickens, Capt Peter 100

Dickson, Capt E 284

Distinguished Service Cross (DSC), 2, 37, 85-86, *99*n, 100, 122, *182*n, 243, 258, 276, 278, 285, 304

Distinguished Service Medal (DSM) 85, 258,

Distinguished Service Order (DSO) 37, 100, 226, 303

dit (also dip) 28, 86, 286

Dodecanese 180, 180 (map), 188-189, 191, 211

Dog Boat (see Fairmile D) 45-46, 122, 128-129, 158, 235, 246-247, 255, 270-271, 308

Dornier Do 217 179

Dorset 67

Dover 56-57, 59, 61 (map), 63, 65, 69-70, 73, 76, 86, 98, 102, 115, 118, 128-129, 303, 306-307

Dover College 57

Dover Strait 75, 81

Dreyer, Lt Christopher 157-159, *158*n, *159*n, 158-159, 162-164

Drvar 260

Dunkirk *158*n, 190

E-boats (also see Schnellboot, or S-Boot) 48, 59, 62-63, 87, 92, 96, 103, 113-114, 118, 130, 139-140, 159-162, 233-234, 268-271, *271*n

Egypt 180

England 14, 16, 57, 108, 115, 117-118, 135, 144, 149, 274, 280, 303

English Channel 26, 57, 61 (map), 75, 89, 113, 217, 259, 271

English longbow 226, *226*n

Ennis, Lt L. 225, *225*n, 266, 269-271

Europe 57

Executive Officer (XO) 45, 70, 75, 77-78, 88, 91, 103, 125, 132-134, 138, 140, 171, 201, 265

Fair Jeanne 285

Fairmile B *44*n

Fairmile D 45, 47, 122, 128

Farrow, John Villiers *15*n

Fascism (Fascist) 16, 23, 263

Franklin D. Roosevelt (FDR) 212

First World War (see also The Great War)18, 24, *24*n,

flag four, 81

flak trawler 92, 95-98, 101, 103, 118, 196, 271

Flora Street 144, 278

Foggia 213, 253

Folkstone 100

Force 133 260

Forder 150-151

Forster, SLt Mark Arnold 83-84

gunnery (gunners) 28, 44, 77, 82-83, 85, 92, 97-98, 107, 122, 122n, 125, 127, 130, 136, 138, 140, 143, 151, 171, 196, 249, 256-257, 269

Gurna 197

Haifa 213, 224

Halifax 14-16, 117, 286

harmonizing *108*n

Harry Four 135

Hayter, A.R. 258

Headquarters (HQ) 57, 155, 172, 194, 197-200, 208, *208*n, 283-284

Heavy Cruiser 75

Light Cruiser 179

Hell-Fire Corner (see also Dover) 61, 115

Hewitt, Lt Eric 266, 268, 269, 271

Hewitt, Vice Admiral H. Kent 177-179, 223

Highlands 35

Highland Hotel 37-40, 43

Hill 48 260

Hill 422 260

Hill 542 260

Hitler, Adolf 22

Holden-Brown, Lt Derrick 130

Holocaust of Kedros *189*n

Horlock, Lt Ken M. *128*n, 224-225, 235-242, 244-246

Horns of Jericho 182

Houghton, Capt Frank Llewellyn 115-117

Hove 24, 28, 35, 61 (map)

Hughes, Lt Peter *128*n, 224

Hunter, Gp Capt J. E. 9-10

hurdy-gurdy 29

Hurricane 79, 85

Hvar 219 (map), 228, 234-235, 268, 271

Hyslop, Lt P. 235

I-boat 235, 249, 254-257, 259, 268-270, 272

in-routine 36

Indian Army Engineers 185

Inniskilling 279

intelligence 77, 241, 264, 280

Ionian Sea 147 (map), 162

Ireland 134, 144

Irish Sea 56, 65, 134

Ischia 277

Italy (also Italian) 3, 129, 155, 157, 161-163, *162*n, 170, *172*n, *186*n, 189-190, *190*n, 193, 195, 198-199, 205, 209, *209*n, 217, 220, 222, 227-229, 235, 239-240, 245-247, 253-254, 266, 275-276, 309

limey 33, 58, 142

Liquor Control Board 280

Lira 211, 214

Lisgar Collegiate Institute 17

Liverpool 16, 24, 28

Loading Numbers 136

Loch Eli 36

Loch Linnhe 35-36, 44, 65

London 56-57, 109, 113, 115, 224

London Gazette 276, 280

loon, red-throated 38

Lord Tennyson 177

Lord Warden Hotel 57-59

Luftwaffe 129, 190, 193

Lynch, Capt Mak 232

MacBrayne 51

Macedonia 213

machine-gun 45

Maclean, Fitzroy 221, *260*n

Maclean mission 260

Maitland, John Douglas 73-74, 99, 133, 138-139, 308

Malta 129, 147 (map), 154-155, 164, 172, 217, 265

Manners, LCol James Calvert 261

Marinefahrprahm (aka Naval Ferry Barge, MFP, or F-lighters) 190, 196, 234, 252-253

Marsala 156

Marsamxett 155, 166

Marizuta 186

Mascherpa, Capt Luigi 190

Masson *128*n

McGrigor, RAdm Rhoderick 221

McDougall, Dr. A.H. 17-18

ME 109s 78-79

Mediterranean (Med) 74, 129, 133-135, 147 (map), 149, 156 (map), 167-169, 180, 191, 212-213, 217, 224, 247, 265, *271*n, 276, 278, 304, 310

merchant raider 80-82

merchant ship 76, 242

mess 25, 28, 49, 112

Messina (see also Straight of Messina) 156 (map), 162

Mention in Dispatches (MiD) 85, 224, 278, 285, 289

Michener, Roland 264

Milford Haven 130-131, 133

Military Cross (MC) 214, 226, 279-280

Military Police (MP) 56, 145, 216, 223-224

militia (see also Canadian Army) 18, 26

Milky Way 267

mines (also water mines) 35, 89, 91, 104-105, 229, 231, 261

minesweeper 76, 80, 190

Mljet 219 (map), 235, 254, 266

Miss Dalrymple 56, 116-117

Morgan-Giles, LCdr (later RAdm) Sir Morgan, 100, 221-222, 228-229, 233, 240-241, 243, 246-247, 254-255, 258, 264n, 272-274

morphine 261

mortar launcher 205, 241, 245

Motor Anti-Submarine Boat (MA/SB or MAS-boats) 58, 95, 162-164, 190-191, 193, 197

Motor Gun Boat (MGB) 1, 36, 44-46, 57 specifications, crew compliment, duties 45-48, 63, 67, 70-71, 73, 75-76, 78, 81, 83, 93-97, 101-104, 108, 112-113, 118, 124-126, 136, 151, 192, 196, 219, 225, 243, 249-251, 258, 260, 266

Motor Launch (ML) 44-45, 55, 133, 136-138, 192, 213, 225

Motor Mechanic (MM) 46, 111, 185, 256, 258

Motor Torpedo Boat (MTB) 1, 33, 36, 45-47, 57-58, 75-76, 78-79, 81-83, 100, 118, 125, 128-134, 136-138, 140-143, 148-152, 155-158, 158n, 160-164, 172, 174-179, 181-183, 185-186, 190, 192, 196-197, 220, 222, 238-239, 260, 266-267, 269-271, 276, 282

Mount Appetici 198

Mount Hum 218

Mount Maraviglia 198, 208

Mountstephens, Lt M. 235, 241-244, 250

Müller, Generalleutnant Friedrich-Wilhelm 189, 189n, 190-191, 193, 195-196, 198-199, 205-207, 310

Murter Island 1, 219 (map), 244, 246-248

Mussolini 170

NAAFI 151

napier engines 95

Naples 276

Narrow Seas (see also English Channel) 62, 70, 99, 115

Nash turret 71

Nation (person) 214-217

Naval Service Headquarters (NSHQ) 13-14, 86, 118, 283

navigation officer 32, 45, 219-220

Nazi 1 5, 8, 22, 26, 183, 217, 219, 221, 240, 260

Nelles, Rear-Admiral Percy 14

New Brunswick 48

New Entry Training Course 26

New Zealand 129

nissen hut 36

No. 2 Commando Unit 226, 260, 262

No-Man's Land 57

Pelly, Capt John 24-25, 28, 33-35, 37
Pembroke 130
Phipps, Lt Alan 207, *207*n
physical training (PT) 37, 42
pilot (aka third officer) 45, 62, 79, 91
Piraeus 189
pirate 1, 4, 43, 88, 98, 217, 237, 239, 241, 246, 248, 252-253, 263, 267-268, 273-275, 283, 285, 290
plot(ting) 32, 44, 57, 62
pom-pom 46, 78, 220, 257, 270
Poland 22
Poole 67, 101
Portland 61 (map)
Portolago (Lakki) 191-192, 195, 199, 208, 209
Portsmouth 28, 61 (map)
post-traumatic-stress-disorder (PTSD) 275, *275*n
Pratt, James 280, *280*n
President Mess Committee (PMC) 285
Preston Street 29
priest 21
Prime Minister, Bennett *15*n, King *15*n, Laurier *15*n, Meighen *15*n
Prisoners of War (POW) 143-145, 147, 206-207, 211, 228, 262, 278-279
Procida 277
Prophylactics 105
prostitute 50, 52
Prznjak 241
PT boat *223*n
qualified officer (QO) 170
quarrymen 20
quaterdeck 119
Quebec 19
Queen Street 10
Queensview 285
R mines 102-104
radar 75, 80, 223, *223*n
radar operator 46
Radio Telephony (RT) 84, 90, 247
Rakija 227, 263
Ramsgate 61 (map), 70, 85, 106
rating 24, 178
Royal Canadian Mounted Police (RCMP) 279
recruitment 5-8
Red Castle 181
Red Ensign 5

scripps engines 58, 63

Second Sea Lord 56, 116-117

Second World War 44n, 285, 289

Senior Officer (SO) 46, 66, 71, 73, 83, 88, 90-93, 95, 97, 97n, 101, 104, 138, 143, 155-157, 159-162, 170, 217, 221-223, 235, 237, 242, 245, 248, 256, 266, 268-270, 272, 274, 276

sextant (also bubble sextant) 32, 32n,

shore establishment 24, 35, 57, 155, 180

Sibenik 219 (map), 245

Sicily (or Sicilian) 129, 147 (map), 154, 156, 156 (map), 157, 160, 166, 170, 309

Siebel Ferries 233

Sieckenius, MGen 172

signal(s) 44, 57

signalman 46

Simonds, LCol R.W.B. 260-261

skipper (also see captain) 45, 88, 98, 101, 110, 181

Smith, Lt G. R. 157, 159

Smith, SLt R. S. 258

Solta 219 (map), 255

Spain 142

Spanish Coast 134

Special Air Service (SAS) 279

Special Boat Service (SBS) 190, 195, 214

Split 219 (map), 254, 262

SRD-2 208

St. Nazaire 225

Stahlhelm 205

steamer 196

Stevens, Capt John Felgate 265-266, 272-274, 276-277

steward 211

Straight of Messina (see also 'The Narrows')129, 156 (map), 157, 170

Strait Street (aka "The Gut") 166

Strong, Lt L.V. 157

Stuka Dive Bomber 182-183, 193

Sturgeon, Lt J.B. 157, 235

Solta 219 (map)

South African Naval Force 224

South America 281

South Downs 119

South Street 166

sparks (also see telegraphist) 46, 97, 163, 171, 184-185, 194, 200

sperrbrecher 76

spies/spy 47

Spitfire

Tunis 191
Tunisia 129
Turkey (also Turkish) 179, 188, 211, 309-310
twin point fives 85, 106-108, *108*n
Tyrrhenian Sea 156 (map), 174
Ubitsu 229, *229*n, 230
U-boat 23, 33, 58, 101, 139-141, 143, 147-149, 158-159, 176, 178-179
Union Jack 5
United States (see also America/American) 71, 151
United States Navy (USN) 223
USN SEAL 284
"Up Spirits" 258, 288
Ursula suit 89
US Air Force 176
US Army Rangers 229, 260
US Fifth Army 172
US Seventh Army 172
US Navy Base Operations Division 172
Valletta 166
Vancouver 281
veteran 24, 28, 37, *203*n, 278, 284, 289, 309
Viannos 189
Vickers (machine gun turret) 46
Victoria Cross (VC) 214
Vienna 262
Villiers, Alan 48-52, 304
Viña del Mar 282
Virtue, Sg Lt J. A. 272
Vis 218-221, 225-229, 233-235, 237, 244, 246, 248, 251, 253-254, 258, 260, 262,
    264, 266, 271-272, 274, 282
Volturno River 170
Wakefield, Capt Roger 261
Wales 117, 130, 134, 139
War of 1812 *107*n
wardroom 100, 149, 281, 285
warship 1, 11, 31, 33, 35, 47, 191, 194, 240, 251-252, 306
*Waverly Hotel 37*n
wavy navy *15*n
Wehrmacht 234, 253
Welman, Cdr Arthur Eric Pole 37-43, 49, 51-56, 65, 116, 265-266, 276-277, 303
Weymouth 61 (map), 122, 124-125
Whale Island 122, *122*n, 123, 125
wheelhouse 62, 83, 107, 133, 153, 160-161, 171, 183, 186, 249
White, Cdr (later Capt) R.B. 283, 285